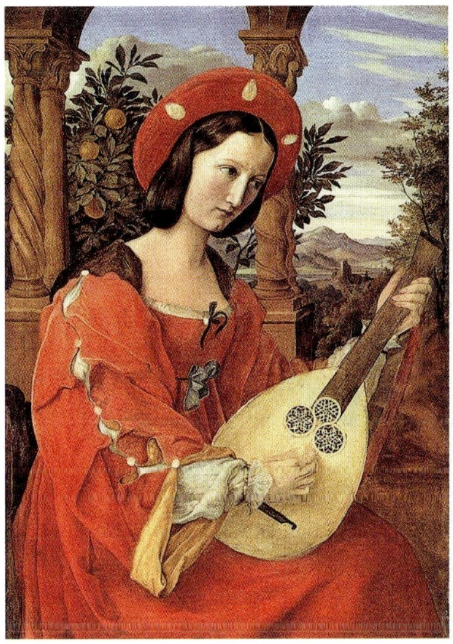

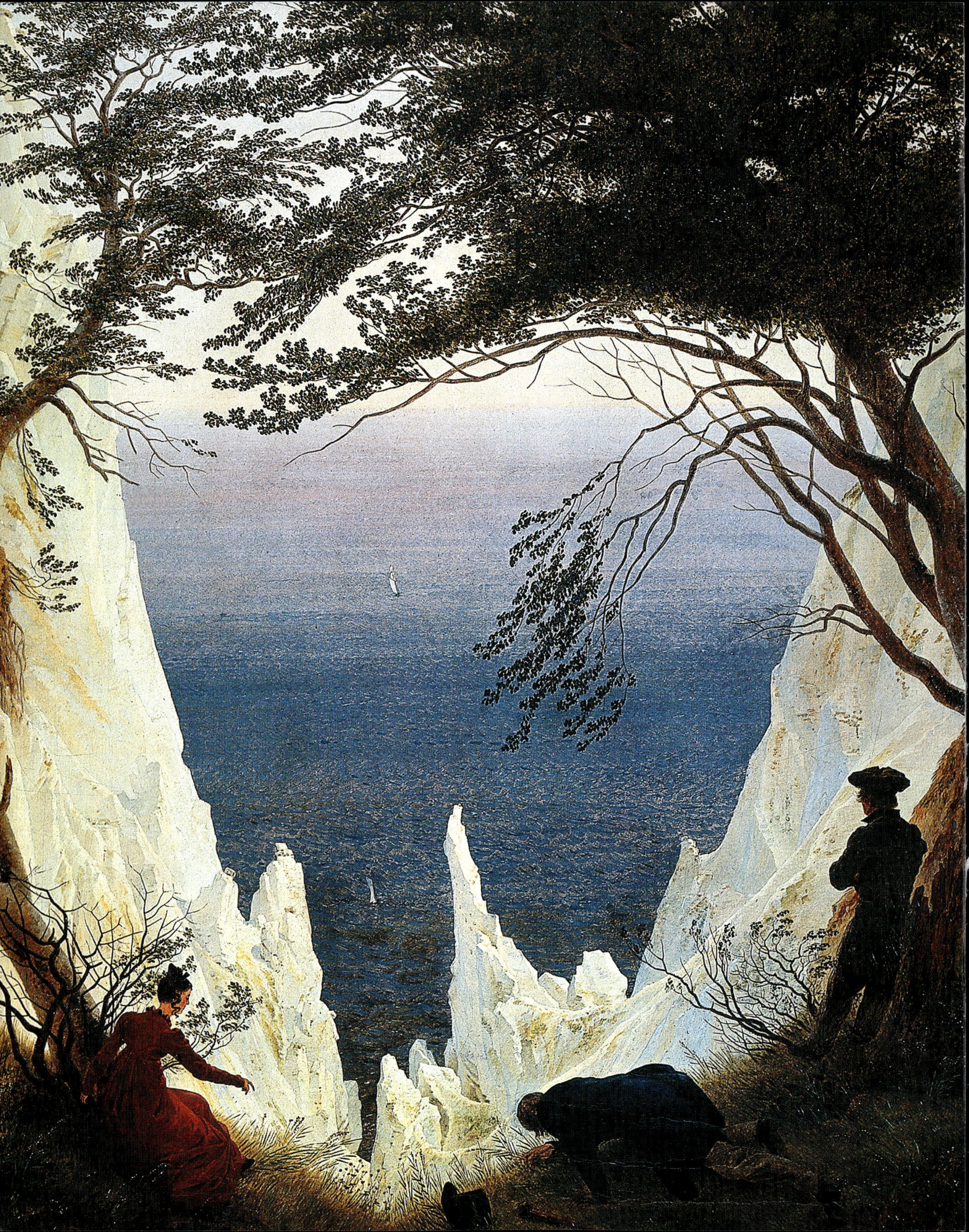

Romanticism

NORBERT WOLF
INGO F. WALTHER (ED.)

TASCHEN
HONG KONG KÖLN LONDON LOS ANGELES MADRID PARIS TOKYO

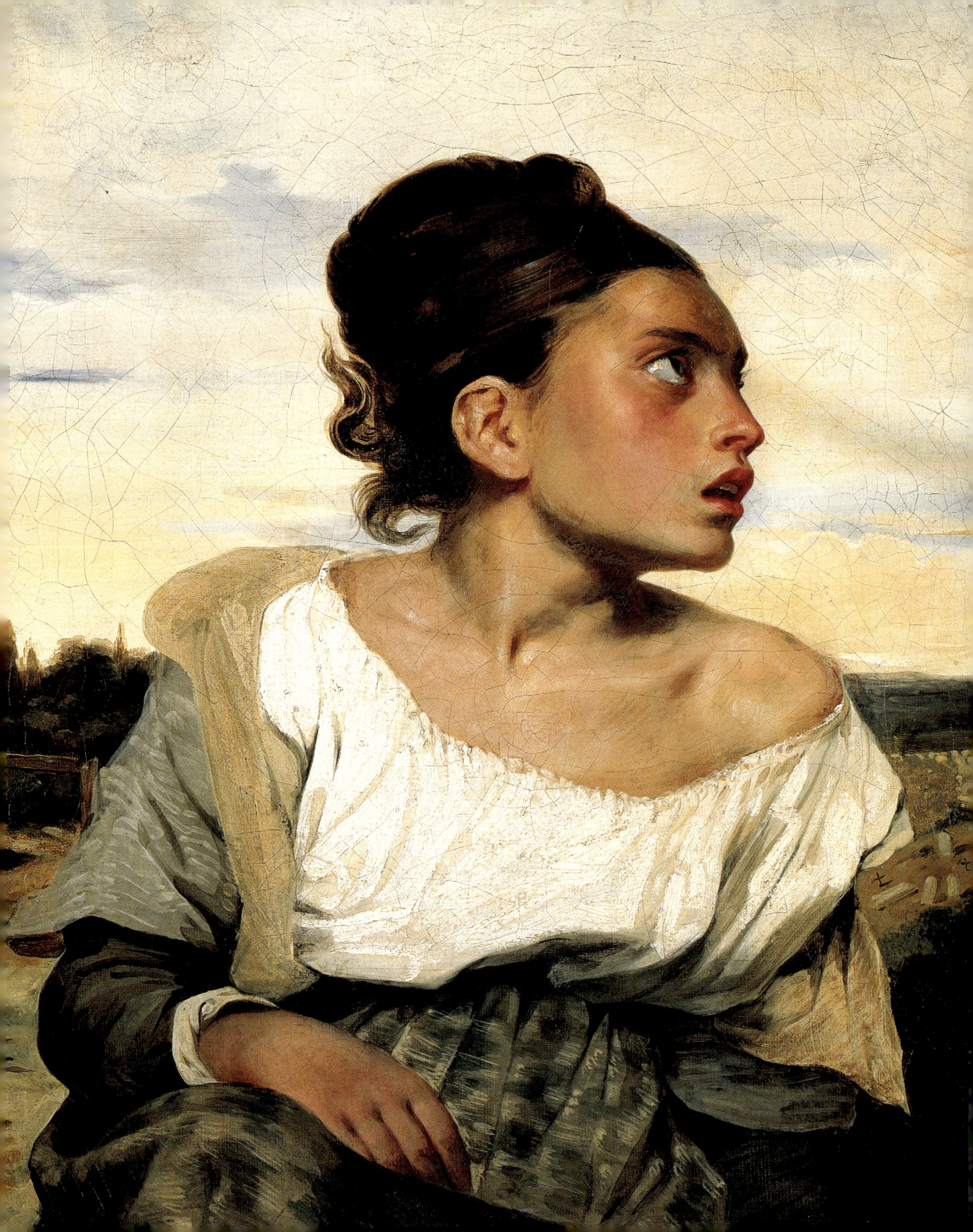

Contents

ideals in Nineteenth-century Painting

Around the year 1800, philosophers, writers, and artists in Germany began to propagate a new vision of the world they described as "romantic." The term covered a range of ideas: that nature was informed with the divine spirit and that the individual human imagination could immerse itself in the universal fabric; but also that the creative mind, being profoundly solitary, would yearn for harmony between man and nature.

Romantic ideals developed largely in opposition to a neoclassicism that had become entrenched in the traditions of Greco-Roman antiquity, and advocated an open-ended and progressive – that is, a modern – view of the age. Yet, Romantic artists also turned back to the late medieval and Renaissance periods, for themes from the Judeo-Christian heritage, because only with its aid, they believed, could the utopia of a politically and intellectually enlightened European future be achieved.

The openness and highly subjective character of such ideals suggest why the Romantic Movement could not, nor wished to, produce any normed artistic style, and why painting in the various European countries, and by extension in the United States, employed a great gamut of subjects and treatments, extending from tranquil contemplative scene to spectacularly staged event. It is precisely this diversity that lends Romantic art its fascination, a fascination from which many subsequent art movements of the nineteenth and twentieth centuries would not remain immune.

clarity and vagueness of the stylistic category

"Oh Dear Friend, I wish Romanticism had never been invented in the first place," sighed Fortunat, the hero of an 1834 novel by the romantic author Joseph von Eichendorff. That sigh has since been repeated many times over by modern historians of the era, in grappling with a term that so persistently eludes precise definition and yet, despite its irritating vagueness, has long since become indispensable.

In contemporary usage, the adjective "romantic" carries an enormous range of connotations, being applied to the scenic roads of Europe and the hotels that dot them, to "romantic love" in the movies and television soap operas, to sunsets behind palm trees and cozy garden nooks, apart from standing for certain aspects of literature, music, and visual art. When we say something is romantic, we think of sentiment and sentimentality, a poetic, nostalgic, or dreamy mood, but one that might also verge on the irrational, even the insane. The term invariably has an undertone of the imaginative and fantastic, and of a remoteness from reality paired with longing. As antonyms, we think of mundane, banal, pedantic.

Not even the scholarly disciplines concerned with Romanticism have been able to do more than arrive at an approximate definition, because the content and substance of the movement, by their very nature, invite controversial interpretations and speculations. The only point on which everyone seems to agree is that Romanticism was an intellectual and artistic transition that occurred at the turn of the eighteenth to the nineteenth century. Yet, problems arise as soon as we try to date its beginning and end. While in the field of music, most composers, from Beethoven to Richard Strauss, are considered Romantics,

---

1786 — Death of Frederick II, king of Prussia since 1740
1789 — Beginning of the French Revolution
1790 — Emmanuel Kant writes his *Critique of Judgment*
1790 — Mozart completes his opera *Cosi fan tutte*

"I did not paint it to be understood, but I wished to show what such a scene was like."

J. M. W. Turner

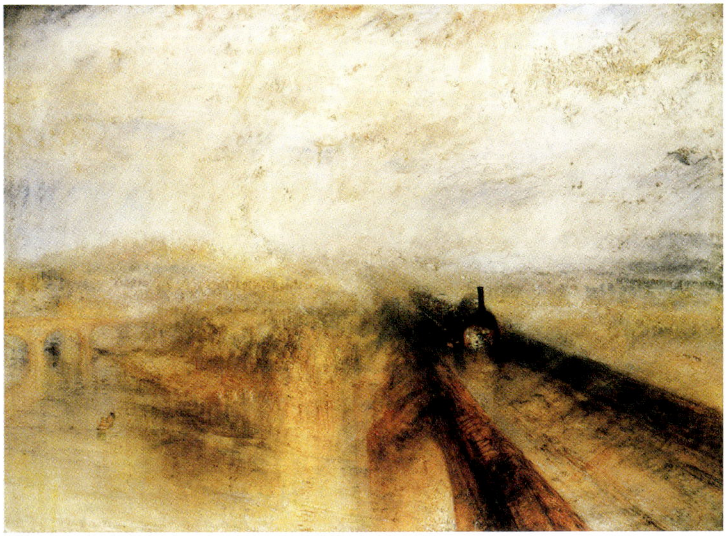

1

1. WILLIAM TURNER

Rain, Steam and Speed: The Great Western Railway
1844, Oil on canvas, 91 x 121,8 cm
London, The National Gallery

literary history concentrates on two or three decades around the year 1800. Art history either restricts itself to the period between about 1790 and 1840, or, on the other hand, extends the research field enormously, seeing the Romantic attitude at work in painting from the eighteenth to the twentieth century, which inevitably leads to an overlapping with other stylistic categories.

Then again, due to the tendency of Romantic art to the fantastic and irrational, it is often treated as a substream of Symbolism, which, after many fits and starts, blossomed into the Sturm und Drang of the late eighteenth century and bore its finest fruit in the latter half of the nineteenth. On the other hand, the sentimental and, as it were, cozy aspects of Romanticism make it difficult to distinguish from the style known in German as Biedermeier, which is usually dated from about 1815 to 1850. And, finally, since Romantic art includes not only an escape from reality but a fearless confrontation with it, such terms as "romantic naturalism" and "idealistic naturalism" have been coined in an attempt to bridge the gap. Basically all of these names reflect scholars' embarrassment in the face of a range of artistic expressions that, unlike earlier styles such as Renaissance and Baroque, resist being pressed into a hard and fast system.

The word "romance" itself goes back to the Old French word "romanz", which characterized the vernacular Romance dialects as opposed to church Latin. Soon, verse and prose narratives about chivalrous knights and their adventures came to be called "romances," which developed into the medieval "roman," a term still used in many European languages today to designate the novel.

In the seventeenth century, we find the word employed in two different senses. When the Englishman Thomas Baily used the adjective "romantick" for the first time, in 1650, it was to criticize the untruth of fictional writings. At the same period, "romantic" was applied in a positive sense to the landscape paintings of Claude Lorrain (1600–1682), Nicolas Poussin (1594–1665), and Salvator Rosa (1615–1673). So in parallel to the motley untamed inventiveness of the fictional world we have the "picturesqueness" of depictions of nature informed with emotion.

In the eighteenth century, when tales of horror set in the Gothic past came into fashion, the aspect of the eerie and spine-tingling phantasmagoria came into play. In France, the Shakespeare translators Letourneur and Émile de Girardin used the term "romantique" in 1776 to characterize the emotional qualities of a scene. And, in 1777, in his *Musings of a Lonely Vagabond*, the philosopher Jean Jacques Rousseau (1712–1778) firmly established the Romantic ideal in French thought.

For a long period, the concept remained synonymous with the content of popular novels, with medieval chivalry and adventures in remote times and lands. Novalis (Friedrich von Hardenberg, 1772–1801), who was the first to speak of "the Romantic," meant nothing other than a writer of novels. Novalis belonged to a young generation of German authors who, around 1800, gave the term an entirely new twist, and who himself provided what may be the best-known definition of Romanticism: "By giving the commonplace a high meaning, the ordinary a mysterious aspect, the known the dignity of the unknown, the finite an aura of infinity, I romanticize it."

Jean Paul (1763–1825), explaining why everything that fed only on longing and memory, everything remote, dead, unknown, had the charm of transfiguration, said that these things triggered the magic power of the imagination and helped it soar into infinity. And it was Novalis, again, who formulated a rule that was taken to heart by many

1792 — Civil marriage is introduced in France

1793 — Louis XVI and Marie Antoinette are guillotined in Paris

1793 — Jacques-Louis David paints *The Death of Marat*, an icon of French Revolution art

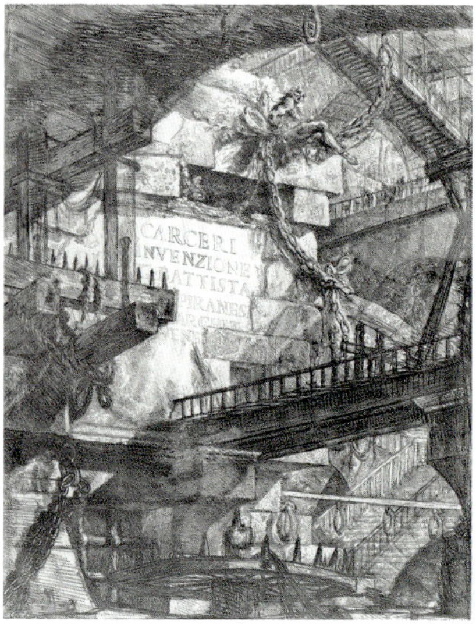

2

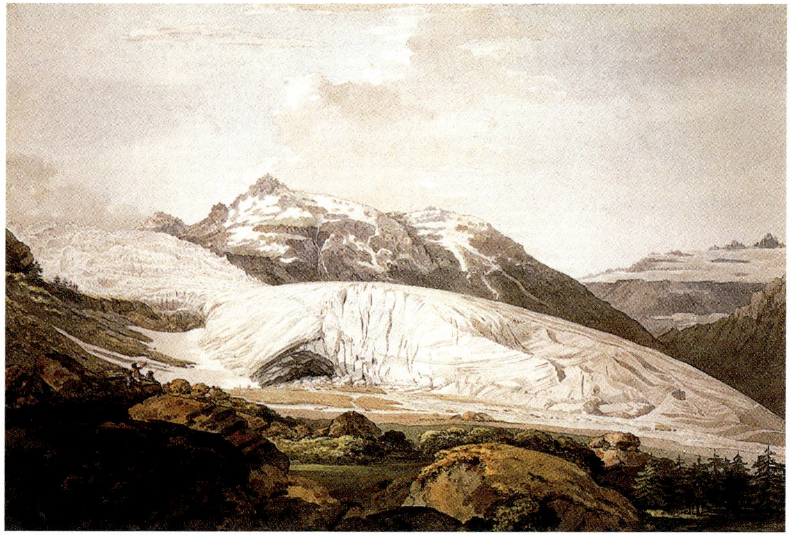

3

painters as well as writers: "Everything seen from a distance becomes poetry: distant mountains, distant people, distant events. Everything becomes romantic."

In reaction, the English painter Joshua Reynolds (1723–1792), in an academy lecture of 1778, attacked pictures that expressed nothing but vague ideas and ignored all rules of science and scholarship as established by the classical art of antiquity. This was a slap at precursor forms of Romanticism and an argument in favor of classical clarity, which, according to academic doctrine, was even capable of morally improving mankind. Ever since Reynolds, Romanticism has borne the onus of representing anti-classicism per se. Even its subjects, derived from the medieval world and European Christianity, were said to run counter to the repertoire of Greco-Roman art.

In 1820, Johann Wolfgang von Goethe (1749–1832) reported on "classicists and romanticists in Italy, violently battling one another." One could not simply jettison the classical education if one wished to be modern, Goethe concluded, yet neither could one belie the thought that stemmed from the Bible. For the great mass of people, he said, it was enough to attach the label "romantic" to "everything that is dark, absurd, confused, incomprehensible." Nor was all "patriotic and homegrown" art necessarily romantic, either.

It was Goethe, celebrated by the Germans as their quintessential classical writer, but elsewhere usually considered a Romantic, who supplied the prime example of that often-sought blend of classical theme with medievalist setting, of clarity with phantasmagoria. This was his *Faust*, the first French translation of which, published in 1827, not coincidentally fueled the fire of French Romanticism. Eugène Delacroix's (1798–1863) illustrations to this edition struck Goethe as being "devilishly good stuff."

The earliest, most cogent and comprehensive theories of Romantic art were developed in the German-speaking countries around the year 1800. This circumstance has led many commentators to state that the Germans invented the style, whose intellectual and aesthetic attitudes were supposedly particularly attuned to the "German character." One such author was the historian Gordon Craig. In his highly praised 1982 book, *The Germans*, Craig saw a certain melancholy wistfulness, an undefined longing, an alienation from reality, sentimentality, a tendency to introversion, an unpolitical attitude, an immersion of the self in "the mysterious forces of nature and God," and finally, a pervasive pessimism and obsession with death as symptoms that led to this potentially pathological alliance. Though much of this argument is correct, many aspects of it are placed in historically incorrect contexts.

There can be no doubt that Romanticism, though it had an enormous resonance in Germany, was a phenomenon that pervaded all of Europe during the late years of the eighteenth century and the transition period to an industrialized society in the nineteenth. It even occasionally overleapt the borders of Europe, for instance stimulating American painters of the late nineteenth century to develop a unique version of the style, above all in the field of landscape painting. As far as the unreal and eerie, the dark and evil ingredients of the Romantic mood are concerned, sufficient examples are found in English and French literature and art, where they were indeed often carried to extremes, giving rise to the concept of "black Romanticism."

An indicative example is the interpretation placed on the work of the Italian engraver Giovanni Battista Piranesi (1720–1778). Piranesi was an extravagant artist. His penchant for the fantastic culminated in the dungeon imagery of the Carceri (ill. p. 8), depicting

1794 — German philosopher Johann Gottlieb Fichte publishes *Foundation of the Science of Knowledge*

1795 — Friedrich Schiller writes *On Naive and Sentimental Poetry*

1795 — Joseph Haydn completes his twelve London symphonies

2. GIOVANNI BATTISTA PIRANESI

Carceri, Title page (second version)
1761, Etching, 54.6 x 41.8 cm
London, The British Architectural Library

3. WILLIAM PARS

The Rhône Glacier and the Source of the Rhône
c. 1770/71, Watercolor and India ink, 33 x 48.4 cm
London, The Trustees of the British Museum

4. CLAUDE-JOSEPH VERNET

A Seastorm
1752, Oil on canvas, 99 x 137 cm
Private collection

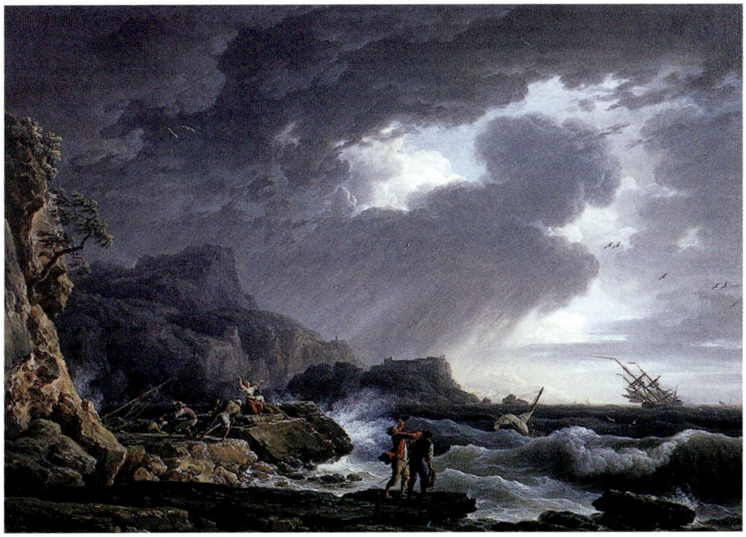

4

interiors that ran counter to all spatial logic, fitted with instruments of torture that called orgies of violence to mind. The demoniacal character of these prints inspired the English writer Thomas De Quincey (1785–1859) to his *Confessions of an English Opium Eater*, which, on its publication in 1821, caused a furore throughout Europe and had a profound influence on French Romanticism in particular. Alfred de Musset (1810–1857) translated the book in 1828, and stimulated later terror fantasies, including an "aesthetics of evil," among such writers as Charles Nodier (1780–1844), Victor Hugo (1802–1885), Théophile Gautier (1811–1872), and Charles Baudelaire (1821–1867).

Impulses from the Eighteenth century

The example of Piranesi in itself suggests the enormous influence exerted by eighteenth-century art on the emergence of Romanticism. Many of the ideas developed back then were revived at the turn of the nineteenth century, and incorporated into a new philosophical and artistic view of the world.

From the late seventeenth century until well into the following decades, for example, artists and intellectuals in France and elsewhere struggled with the question of the extent to which the dominant classical model should be retained. Advocates of "modernity" doubted the continuing validity of its norms. This reservation not only led to a reevaluation of Judeo-Christian culture, it subsequently raised the issue of what artistic standards could take the place of the classical codex. Instead of an aesthetics based on ineluctable values, there developed in England and France a doctrine of the beautiful based on individual taste and sensibility. The feeling and "sentiment" of the individual artist and viewer of art now became the key factor. Ultimately, this implied a turn to a psychological approach to art, which by the middle of the nineteenth century had begun to concentrate on its more sensational aspects.

Divergencies from the normal and mundane led writers and artists into the realm of the "romanesque," as the French philosopher Charles de Montesquieu (1689–1755) put it, the realm of the exciting, alarming, and the range of qualities that at the time were subsumed under the notion of "the interesting." Artistic spontaneity that ignored all borderlines, strokes of genius and creative intoxication, which spirited the artist into exotic, archaic, and barbaric realms, were praised as the new means of aesthetic experimentation.

In the book *A Philosophical Enquiry into the Origins of Our Ideas of the Sublime and Beautiful*, published in 1757, Edmund Burke (1729–1797) paved the road to an aesthetics of awesome and pleasurable terrors. After Burke's attempt to base the visual arts on a theory of human passions, the categories of the grand and sublime, the archaically rugged, the mental stimuli provoked by the bizarre, obscure, chaotic, even the shock effects that exposed the depths and abysses of the human soul, came increasingly to figure in European thinking as the motivating forces behind truly compelling works of art.

Around the time of Burke's treatise, the concept of the "picturesque" became a key term of the epoch. As in "romanesque" landscapes à la Claude Lorrain, Nicolas Poussin, and Salvator Rosa, the word connoted psychological moods triggered by certain themes, but also by certain modes of formal depiction. The year 1795 saw the publication of Uvedale Price's *Essays on the Picturesque*, followed around the turn of the century by several publications by Richard Payne

1795 — Introduction of the metric system in France

1796 — Bonaparte's invasion of Italy

1797 — Wilhelm Wackenroder and Ludwig Tieck: *Outpourings of an Art-loving Friar*

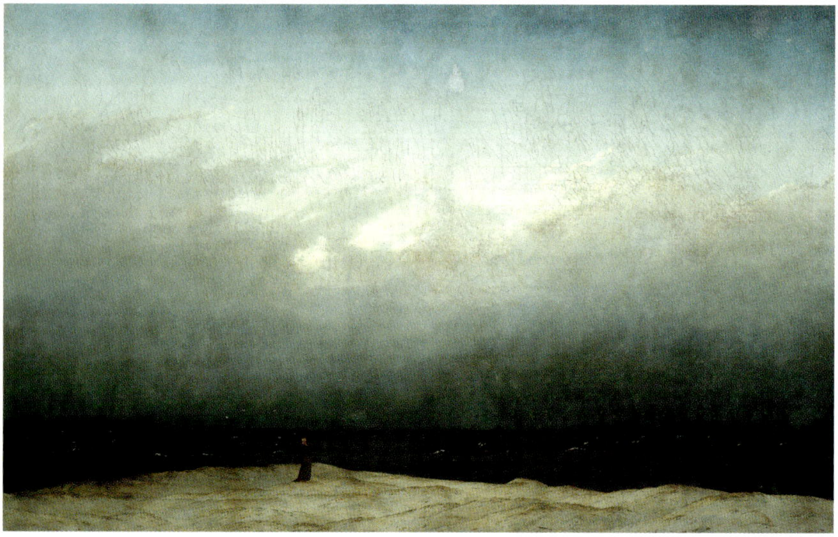

5

"I must surrender myself to what surrounds me, unite myself with the clouds and rocks, in order to be what I am. I need solitude in order to communicate with nature."

Caspar David Friedrich

Knight, who maintained that picturesqueness was based above all on values of light and color. This amounted to a theoretical anticipation of the dissolution of concrete subject matter into pure coloristic effects, which a short time later would be put into practice most superbly by William Turner (1775–1851) in watercolors and oils of a decidedly Romantic flavor.

As we can see, much of what moved Romantic artists around and after 1800 had already been prepared in theory years before. This also holds for artistic practice. A good example is the English Garden, which emerged around 1720 and whose apparently untamed, natural tree groupings burst the geometric constrictions of the French Baroque garden. From the start it had been looked upon as a reservoir of picturesque and atmospheric moods. It was no coincidence that the diverse views and vistas of the English Garden were often based on the romantic pictures of Claude Lorrain. After the appearance of Burke's treatise on the sublime, gardens were increasingly fitted out with artificial ruins, Gothic chapels, Chinese pagodas, and Moorish kiosks. Their layouts were suffused with the same sublime longing for distant places and times, a penchant for the exotic and medieval, and an aesthetics of decline and decay, which would come to characterize later Romantic painting.

Even more: The landscape gardener William Chambers (1726–1786) planned (though never executed) landscapes of "terror" and "melancholy" that would have fit seamlessly into pre- and early Romantic Gothic novels. He envisaged burned out and inundated ruins populated by half-starved wild animals, instruments of torture strewn about the grounds, subterranean dungeons from which the screams of the martyred could be heard, and artificial volcanoes spewing fiery red clouds of smoke. In gloomy caves, visitors to the park would come across wax corpses of famous kings and the most heinous criminals of all time, as eerie celestial music from water organs played in the background. Not only would the pedestrian be visually and acoustically assaulted but physically as well, by artificial earthquakes, electric shocks, mechanical rainshowers, and sudden explosions. A walk through the park was to be a theatrical spectacle, a spine-chilling experience.

The English Neo-Gothic style that arose in close conjunction with the gardens in the eighteenth century soon became a means of romantic self-expression on the part of its first contractors. Strawberry Hill, for instance, was based on the ideas of Horace Walpole (1717–1797), an aristocratic art collector who in addition, with *The Castle of Otranto* (1764), penned one of the earliest horror novels in literary history. The interior decoration of Walpole's house was derived from Gothic cathedrals and funerary chapels, an extravagant suffusion of the private sphere with the enigmatic sacred aura of the Middle Ages.

The medieval chivalrous romance had, as it were, found its concrete setting in preindustrial England. This was even more strikingly the case of Fonthill Abbey (built 1796–1807). Once again its builder, William Beckford (1759–1844), was the author of an "oriental" novel, *Vathek*, of 1786. Initially conceived as a church, painting gallery, and sepulcher, the huge complex of buildings in the Neo-Gothic style was soon converted into a residence. Those who lived there must have felt lost in the overwhelmingly dimensioned, cavernous rooms and staircases descending into abysmal depths.

Another eighteenth-century phenomenon that fits into the prehistory of Romanticism is the change in people's experience of distant and foreign places. This change initially took place with respect to that traditional land of European dreams, Italy. For about two centuries

1798 — Bonaparte's Egyptian campaign

1798 — The *Lyrical Ballads* of Samuel Taylor Coleridge and William Wordsworth mark the beginning of English Romanticism

5. CASPAR DAVID FRIEDRICH

The Monk by the Sea
1809/10, Oil on canvas, 110 x 171.5 cm
Berlin, Nationalgalerie, Staatliche Museen zu Berlin – Preussischer Kulturbesitz

6. GEORG FRIEDRICH KERSTING

Caspar David Friedrich in his Studio
1812, Oil on canvas, 51 x 40 cm
Berlin, Nationalgalerie, Staatliche Museen zu Berlin – Preussischer Kulturbesitz

7. JOHAN CHRISTIAN CLAUSEN DAHL

View of Pillnitz Castle from a Window
c. 1824, Oil on canvas, 70 x 45.5 cm
Essen, Museum Folkwang

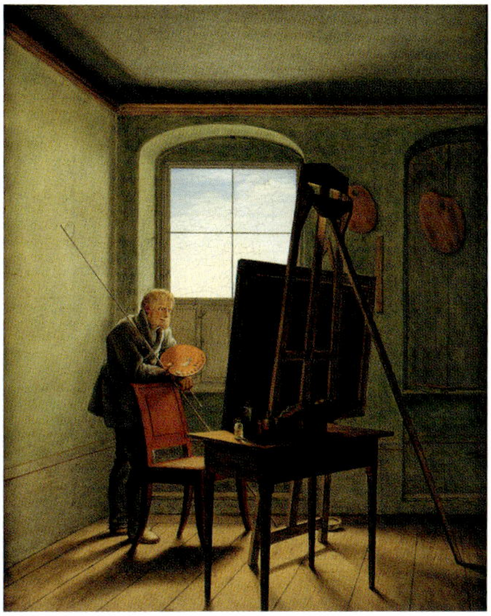

6

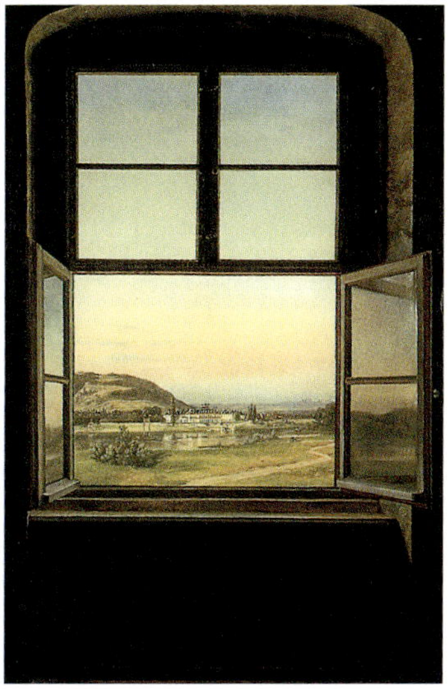

7

well-placed young men had been traveling to Italy to expand their knowledge of antique sites and Renaissance art. In addition to this educational interest, in the eighteenth century ever more travelers felt the desire to cultivate moods, feelings, and sensations, especially those inspired by the beauties of the Italian landscape.

At the same time, the English in particular took watercolorists along with them on their journey in order to record the atmosphere they so enjoyed. Ever since Burke and that magic word, the sublime, their interest had been increasingly attracted by areas seen on the way south that were especially picturesque or thrilling.

While the Swiss Alps, the quintessence of sublime landscape, had already been painted in the 1760s by William Pars (1742–1782; ill. p. 8), Lord Byron (1788–1824) subsequently raised the Rhine Valley and Venice to embodiments of Romantic scenery, and soon streams of tourists were following in his footsteps. For young intellectuals and artists, the poet Byron became a symbolic figure of Romantic melancholy. In addition, with his travels in Albania and Greece, where he fought in the War of Independence against the Turks, Byron embodied that striving for ever more distant and exotic climes, which, likewise, had its roots far back in the eighteenth century.

In Germany in the 1770s, Johann Gottfried Herder (1744–1803) attempted to make the Orient popular, an attempt continued by Friedrich Schlegel (1772–1829), who in 1800 declared that "the supremely romantic" must be sought "in the Orient" – which for him encompassed North Africa and all of Asia. Schlegel also waxed enthusiastic about the travel reports of Georg Forster (1754–1794), who had accompanied Captain Cook on a South Seas expedition in 1772–1775. In France, the heroes of the novels of Abbé Prevost (*Manon Lescaut*, 1797) and Bernardin de Saint-Pierre (*Paul et Virginie*, 1788), surfeited with civilization, experienced their adventures in the New World, as later did François René Chateaubriand's (1768–1848) "romantic" hero René (*René*, 1802), in French America.

Finally, mention must certainly be made of the new role that landscape painting had begun to play. Art theory in earlier eras had denigrated this genre, since it could not fulfill the classical demands that were met above all by history painting. In academic instruction, this judgement was largely to retain its validity far into the nineteenth century. Yet already in the eighteenth, when such thinkers as Henri Rousseau, Denis Diderot (1713–1784), and Friedrich Schiller (1759–1805) had lamented the alienation of man from nature, a fundamental change in attitude had begun to emerge. The subjectively felt moods of landscape, impossible to capture in rules, now came to be valued as qualities in their own right.

Burke had viewed landscape as the arena of the sublime and, accordingly, wild, untamed nature, the Scottish highlands or the Alpine ranges – dramatic scenery in general, as a setting for thrilling occurrences – increasingly attracted artists' attention. The French painter Claude-Joseph Vernet (1714–1789) depicted storms at sea and foundering ships (ill. p. 9); Philippe Jacques de Loutherbourg of Strasbourg (1740–1812) took up Vernet's themes before eventually, in England, applying their sensational effects principally to depictions of industrial landscapes (ill. p. 15). Portions of German and English Romanticism after 1800, and American Romanticism during the nineteenth century, then exalted the landscape to a favorite, and often enough symbolically charged subject.

1798 — August Wilhelm and Friedrich von Schlegel found the magazine *Athenäum*

1798 — Francisco de Goya completes his etching series *Los Caprichos*

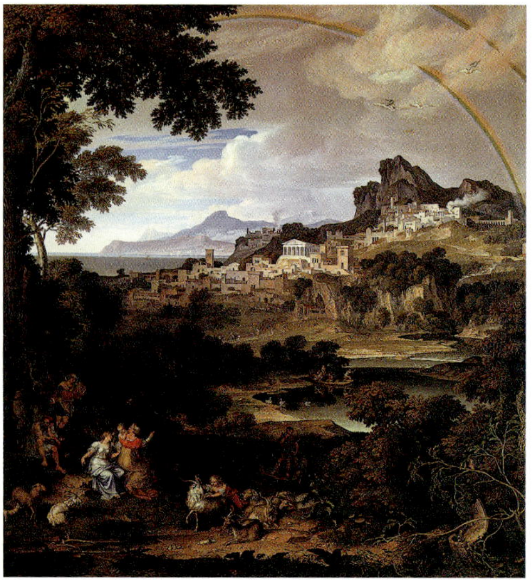

8

"There are different kinds of imitation. Some artists are driven by necessity, the lack of their own artistic talent. They believe that masterpieces kindle their own little flame and call this 'being inspired'."

Joseph Anton Koch

Principles of Romantic Painting

Change as a program – this phrase alone makes it understandable why, in Romantic art, there were literature, music, painting, and drawing, but no Romantic architecture or sculpture. It was Novalis who, in his *Heinrich von Ofterdingen* of 1802, created the erotic myth of the "blue flower," which soon burgeoned into a myth of longing and yearning for the faraway: The color blue as a symbol of the nocturnal, of tender, longing sensations. Painting might be called the medium of the unlimited; ever since Goethe's treatise on color, painters became preoccupied with the symbolic potentials of light and color, Philipp Otto Runge (1777–1810) and Turner foremost.

Lending color and light a dominant role enabled Romantic painters to abandon the rational scheme of perspective in favor of an indeterminate space, suitable for conveying universal ideas. Caspar David Friedrich (1774–1840) created the exemplary specimen in his *Monk by the Sea* (ill. p. 10), and Turner, again, took the principle to an extreme that almost recalls modern abstraction.

This explains why in many countries, especially England and Germany, landscape became the principal motif of Romantic painting. In the landscape, nature as the arena of higher powers was to be revealed. The infinite expanse of the ocean, the sublime Alpine realm, the panorama view to the far horizon, but also "Waldeseinsamkeit," or sylvan solitude – a key term of German Romanticism, coined in 1797 by Ludwig Tieck – could evoke the divine presence in elemental nature and make the observer feel it; yet they might equally express human isolation in the face of the limitless universe. Ultimately, the natural environment was not depicted for its own sake, but as a mirror of internal mental and emotional processes.

Carl Gustav Carus (1789–1869; ill. pp. 72, 73), significant painter and theoretician, saw the goal of landscape pictures in rendering states of mind transparent through corresponding moods in natural life. In this sense, Runge ranked landscape as the central subject of the art of the future. Yet some Romantic landscape artists concentrated on natural history and the processes of growth and decay. This explains the key role played by landscape cycles illustrating the times of day or seasons of the year, symbols of the natural cycle. It also explains the signs of the historical past so frequently seen in Romantic landscapes: Gothic cathedrals, monasteries and castles, ruins, cairns, populated by monks, eremites and knights; and in many cases, the evidence of geological study in the landscapes, which revealed the natural forces of formation and erosion – factors that could lead beyond Romanticism to a more objective and prosaic approach to landscape.

Another characteristic motif of Romantic painting was the framed view, a landscape seen from an interior through an open window or door. Carus introduced two of his *Nine Missives on Landscape Painting* of 1831 with a suggestive description of an interior, making reference to Goethe's *Faust* (II, Act 2): "Enclosed space suits the artificial best. The universe can hardly hold the natural rest." The tension between the landscape expanse outside and the intimacy of the enclosed room conforms perfectly with Novalis' dictum of evoking an "aura of the infinite" in the finite.

In Caspar David Friedrich's *Woman at a Window* of 1822 (Berlin, Gemäldegalerie), the dark interior has been interpreted as standing for the constricted, earthly world which receives its light only from the window, symbolizing the supernatural world. The opposite bank of the river below the window has been said to represent the

1798 — Casanova dies

1799 — Beginning of Alexander von Humboldt's exploration of Central and South America

1800 — Novalis writes *Hymns to the Night*

8. JOSEPH ANTON KOCH

Heroic Landscape with Rainbow
1815, Oil on canvas, 188 x 171.2 cm
Munich, Bayerische Staatsgemäldesammlungen, Neue Pinakothek

9. CARL ROTTMANN

Taormina and Mt. Etna
1828/29, Oil on canvas, 49 x 73 cm
Munich, Bayerische Staatsgemäldesammlungen, Neue Pinakothek

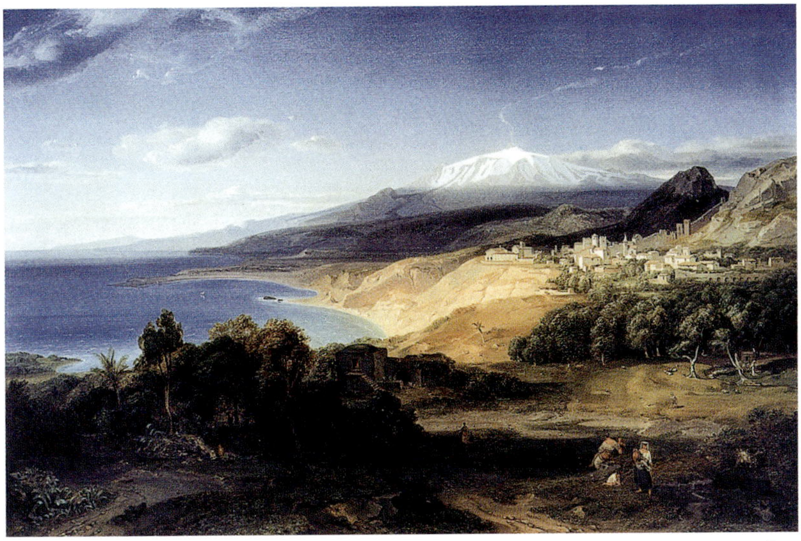

9

Beyond in the religious sense, while the ships' masts rising into the frame stand for a Christian recasting of the classical motif of the underground river across which Charon ferries dead souls.

Though weighty objections have been made to this strictly theological interpretation, the isolation of man from nature in the picture remains indisputable. The figure seen from the back, leaning against the window – the artist's wife – seems imprisoned in the small, sparsely furnished room and the linear gridwork of the composition. Only the middle pane of the window is open, underscoring by contrast the glazed upper aperture that separates the brilliant expanse of sky and landscape from the somber room.

In *Caspar David Friedrich in his Studio* (ill. p. 11), Georg Friedrich Kersting (1785–1847) shows the artist leaning on a chair, musing before his easel. The painted canvas is hidden from view. What goes through Friedrich's mind in the process of painting can only be surmised from his absent gaze. The single window of the bare room is entirely closed, the lower part shuttered; only at the top is a section of gray-blue sky visible. "A painter who sees no world within himself should desist painting," Friedrich once declared. Here a painter who recreated the world out of inward vision is shown at work in a darkened room, into which a tiny excerpt of the exterior world reflects what he struggles to evoke, the glory of a higher existence as a refuge for the troubled soul.

In the case of any movement in art which emblazons continual change on its banner, which sets out to explore unknown and uncharted territory, a common denominator from artist to artist and country to country will be difficult to find. This makes it all the more important to look at individual nations and painters, with an eye to discerning further characteristic traits of Romanticism.

German Painting

Romantic artists in Germany found little in eighteenth-century painting that inspired them or could be adapted to their purposes. In southern Germany and the Alpine provinces, the reign of Rococo and its brilliant final culmination in ecclesiastical art, lasted into the 1770s. In other regions, toward the end of the century, a French-influenced neoclassicism with a certain idyllic mood and atmosphere began to spread. An example is the work of Asmus Jacob Carstens (1754–1798), who waived color to produce compositions reminiscent of Michelangelo, the themes of which occasionally had a sentimental tendency. Yet it would be mistaken to call them Romantic, since there had always been streams within European neoclassicism that avoided all academic pedantry and infused the classical vocabulary with emotion.

For similar reasons it is likewise problematic to associate the "heroic" or "ideal" landscapes of the Tyrolean Joseph Anton Koch (1768–1839) with Romanticism. Problematic, but not impossible, for as the artist himself said, in good Romantic manner, "Let the creative soul take the separate part, the tiniest detail into itself and shape out of itself the whole, as if at one fell swoop, under a lightning flash of the idealizing imagination."

In *Heroic Landscape with Rainbow* (ill. p. 12), the 1815 version of which was acquired by the Munich Academy as an outstanding example of a genre usually scorned by such institutions, Koch showed that neoclassicism could seamlessly blend into Romanticism. The picture spirits the viewer into a distant, byegone realm populated by shepherds and shepherdesses. From the foreground, the eye is led by clear compositional lines over copses and lush river valleys to sunny plateaus and rugged mountains, over whose slopes spread classical

1800 — London and Tokyo are each home to over a million people; Paris has 550,000 inhabitants; New York approximately 60,000

1801 — August Wilhelm Schlegel translates Shakespearean plays into German

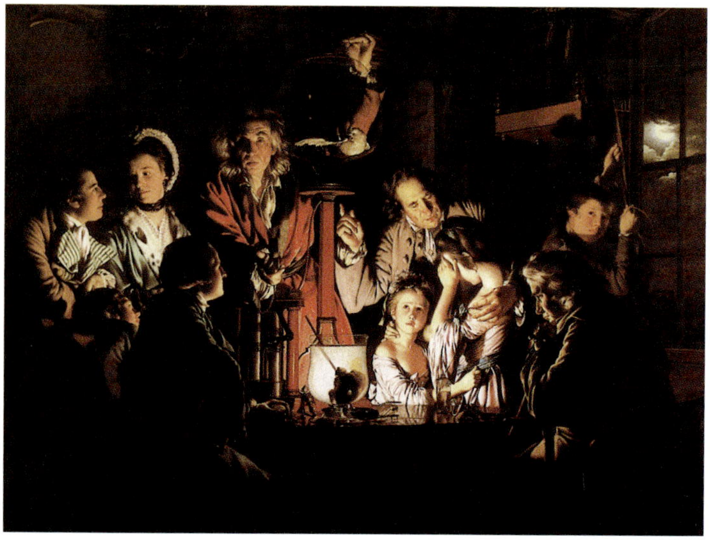

10

10. JOSEPH WRIGHT OF DERBY

An Experiment on a Bird in the Airpump
1768, Oil on canvas, 183 x 244 cm
London, The National Gallery

11. PHILIPPE JACQUES DE LOUTHERBOURG

Coalbrookdale by Night
1801, Oil on canvas, 67.9 x 106.7 cm
London, Science Museum

and medieval towns as idyllic symbols of communal life. The rainbow, symbol of God's grace, links heaven and earth, classical and Christian forms of existence, into a harmonious, cosmic unity. Melancholy and sweet, the sense of the past binds itself to the present, as Friedrich Schiller once wrote. In contrast, Koch's *Schmadribach Falls* (1821/22; Munich, Neue Pinakothek) exhibits a sharp-focus verisimilitude that would bear fruit less for Romantic art than for the naturalistic streams of the nineteenth century.

The most promising point of departure for the Romantic painters was eighteenth-century art into which aspects of the sublime had already entered, especially depictions of terrifyingly beautiful mountain vastnesses. Such pictures of a visionary and quite Romantic cast were painted by the Swiss artist Caspar Wolf (1735–1798), who had worked for a period with Loutherbourg in Paris.

Fichte's philosophy, which raised the self-conscious ego to the measure of all things; Goethe's *Wilhelm Meister*, a "Bildungsroman" with its voyages of discovery into the human soul; and the French Revolution – these three were declared the greatest tendencies of the age by Friedrich Schlegel in 1798. The intellectuals of Germany, a land hobbled by particularism that still bore the pompous title of Holy Roman Empire, a feudal country without capital or cultural center, without a politically responsible middle class or industry, initially saw in the French Revolution of 1789 a chance not only for political but for spiritual renewal. The emancipated citizen, they thought, would join ranks with the people of other nations to form a cosmopolitan society, breaking down all intellectual and emotional frontiers. Schlegel, again, stated that it was a revolutionary mission to establish the Kingdom of God, which would be identical with the beginning of progressive development and modern history.

Yet disappointment soon set in as the consequences of the revolution became ever clearer. The subsequent wars of liberation against Napoleon demanded thinking in terms not of universal but of national politics. Still, with the early Romantics, the idea of the nation-state remained bound up with the desire for bourgeois emancipation and for a new, progressive attitude to life, as when Friedrich Schleiermacher, in 1807, linked the Neo-Protestant movement with the emergence of the German nation.

The usual distinction made in German Romanticism between a Protestant northern and a Catholic southern stream is superfically correct; it is true to say that much of southern German painting was strongly determined by Catholic subject matter and aims, and therefore was relatively conservative in orientation. Still, painters in northern Germany saw themselves beholden not so much to Protestantism as a confessional dogma as to a religiosity that was universal in the sense described above – that is, humane and cosmopolitan. A revealing example in this regard is Friedrich's *Tetschen Altarpiece* of 1807/08 (Dresden, Gemäldegalerie), which after many alterations of plan was finally installed in the palace chapel of a Catholic prince, without artist or liberal-minded buyer seeing any obstacle in the sacred content of the painting.

Friedrich's mind was not beclouded by mysticism to nearly the extent that some of his contemporaries and many of his modern commentators maintain. Certainly he was a Romantic – but one who kept his eyes open to his environment and era. Nor was it simply Teutomania that made Friedrich a Francophobe. It was the conviction that Napoleon had betrayed the French Revolution (which admittedly many Romantics initially idealized) and had humbled Germany. At this point, such motifs as cliffs, boulders, oak, fir, and pine trees began to take on

1802 — Novalis' *Heinrich von Ofterdingen* ("blue flower") is posthumously published

1803 — The United States of America purchases the Louisiana Territory from France, thereby doubling its size

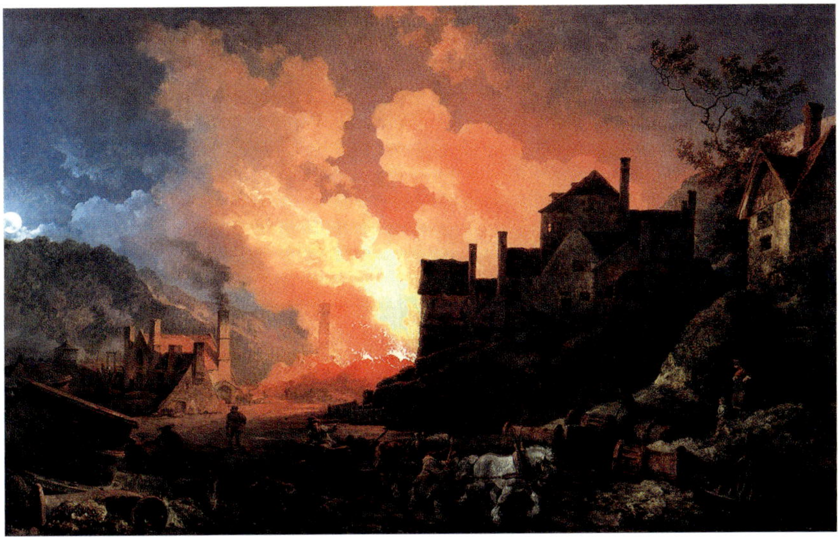

11

a new prominence in Friedrich's art. These were allusions to things German, if very covert ones, since French censorship had continually to be reckoned with. The call to arms ardently followed by his artist and poet friends Kersting, Theodor Körner (1791–1813), Friedrich de la Motte Fouqué (1777–1843), Philipp Veit (1793–1877), and Ferdinand Olivier (1784–1841) was not for Friedrich, however, who considered himself too old to fight. But he did sponsor a portion of the equipment for the Voluntary Corps formed to oust Napoleon.

Friedrich's example made Dresden one of the key centers of Romantic art. For Johan Christian Clausen Dahl (1788–1857), Carus, Kersting, Ernst Ferdinand Oehme (1797–1855), and many others, the landscape of the region was the prime theme, in which individual mental powers, a divine, cosmic omnipotence, and the utopia of a harmonious future coverged. Most of these artists were initially receptive to the ideal of a progressive human and political development, as propagated at the start of the century by the Jena circle of philosophers and writers.

It was Philipp Otto Runge, who lived in Hamburg, who provided the most detailed theoretical underpinning for the new, Romantic painting, declaring landscape to be its foremost mission. Landscape, Runge said in effect, was not simply the visual compilation of a natural scenery, but revelation through sensation or sentience. By the same token, even a human face or a scene with figures could become a "sentient landscape."

This perhaps explains why he considered the pure colors to be symbols of a limitless, divine illumination of the universe, which unfurled itself between the poles of light and darkness. Runge developed visual allegories whose pantheism, the belief that God was inherent in every element of the self-existing universe, was most clearly expressed in his cycle of *Four Seasons* (ill. p. 37), conceived in 1802/03. The planned cycle united Christian and classical mythological motifs, plants and landscape in ornamental compositions intended as metaphors for human existence. For obvious reasons, Runge's cerebral and frequently mystical art would not find successors to nearly the same extent as did Friedrich's more cogent symbolism.

The Nazarenes, the Catholic branch of the German Romantic Movement, envisioned a national art based on medieval Christian traditions. For the generally sentimental treatment of their nostalgic and politically conservative themes, they preferred, unlike their northern German colleagues, the linearly contoured, closed form. The story of the Nazarenes began in 1809, when a few students in Vienna, disaffected with the neoclassicism taught at the academy, formed an "order," the first artists' group in the Romantic era to be inspired by the cult of friendship. They called themselves the St. Luke's Brotherhood, after the Evangelist and patron saint of painters. Conditions for membership were a rejection of academic norms and an adherence to certain ethical and religious principles.

From Vienna, the group moved in 1810 to Rome, where they settled in the secularized monastery S. Isidoro. The founding members, who included Johann Friedrich Overbeck (1789–1869) and Franz Pforr (1788–1812), were joined over the following years by others, such as Peter von Cornelius (1783–1867), Wilhelm von Schadow (1788–1862), Johann and Philipp Veit, Julius Schnorr von Carolsfeld (1794–1872), and Ferdinand and Friedrich Olivier (1791–1859). Due to their long hair parted in the middle, the Romans mocked them as "Nazarenes."

Their appearance and dress amounted to a programmatic statement, for it was not classical antiquity but the "holy" Middle Ages they

1803 — The Imperial Deputation calls for the secularization of ecclesiastical property in Germany

1804 — Bonaparte crowns himself emperor of France, as Napoleon I

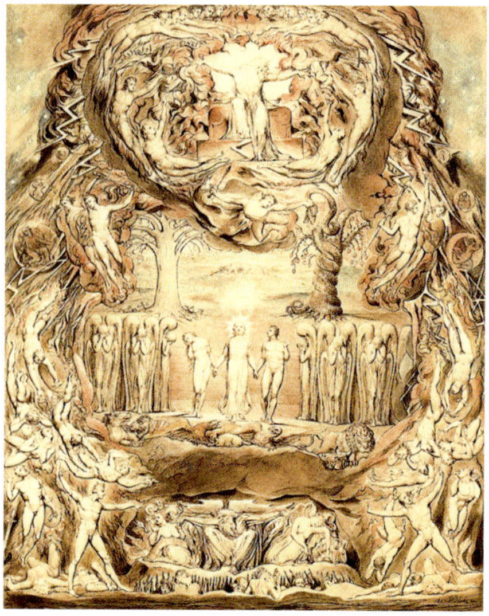

12

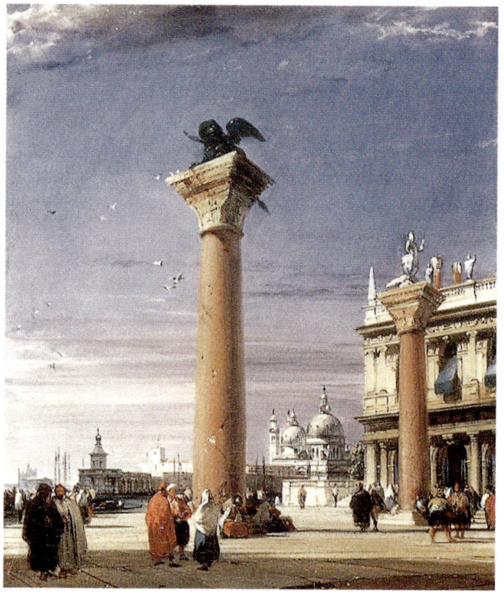

13

sought in Rome. The contemporaries of Albrecht Dürer (1471–1528) and the Italian painters before Raphael, especially Fra Angelico (c. 1387–1455) and Perugino (c. 1445–1523), became the models for the Nazarenes' attempt to revitalize painting by infusing it with profound sacred feeling and a Catholicism accessible to the people. This religious emotion was accompanied by a "Neo-German" patriotism supposedly rooted in the people. Thus until about 1830, the Nazarenes embodied a form of Romanticism that, its eyes turned back to the utopian ideal of the medieval caste society, fought the republican ideas introduced by the Enlightenment and French Revolution. Their subjects, biblical, symbolic, or taken from ancient German history and legends, were treated in a naive, popular, gracefully linear, narrative style.

The Nazarene's prime aim was to exalt mural painting in this style to a new, grand, and national art. They were able to put it into practice to only a modest extent, in projects such as the frescoes for the Palazzo Zuccaro, residence of the Prussian Consul General Bartholdy in Rome (1816–1817), and thereafter frescoes in the Casino Massimo. Cornelius was the only member of the group to work on a monumental scale, from 1818 in Munich and then in Berlin.

Still, in pursuit of their ideal of a revitalized religious mural painting, for a few decades the Nazarenes received greater international attention than any other movement in German Romantic art. Their significance for cultural history lies not least in their contribution to a rediscovery of German medieval and early Renaissance painting, which, for example, was given a prominent place in the museum by Philipp Veit, director of the Städelsches Kunstinstitut in Frankfurt from 1830.

Apart from the two key movements mentioned, there were many other German artists who pursued Romantic or partially Romantic aims on their own. The two most significant were Karl Blechen (1798–1840) and Carl Anton Joseph Rottmann (1797–1850). Blechen, after an early influence from Friedrich, gradually developed a more realistic and daring plein air approach to landscape (ill. p. 71). Rottmann's idealistic landscapes (ill. pp. 13, 61) developed from Romantic beginnings into a monumental picturesqueness, a dramatic, painterly approach that ultimately eludes stylistic classification.

After the fall of Napoleon, Metternich marshaled the forces of restoration at the 1815 Congress of Vienna, and the "Carlsbad Edicts" led to a "persecution of demagogues," that is, of university staff and journalists suspected of fomenting revolution. The two great German powers – the Austrian empire and the Prussian monarchy – maintained the old feudal and clerical prerogatives, as the congeries of small and miniscule states cultivated a mind set of submissive parochialism. Not until the German Uprising of March 1848 – the same year as Marx and Engels published their *Communist Manifesto* – would the parliamentary idea enjoy a brief heyday.

However, the preceding "Vormärz" period had seen the defeat of the great national and democratic tendencies, as the bourgeoisie ensconced itself in submissive humility and forsook the public sphere for the private. In 1848, Victor von Scheffel (1826–1886) published two poems in the Munich satirical magazine *Fliegende Blätter,* whose titles translate as "Biedermann's Cozy Evenings" and "Bummelmaier's Lament." A few years later some other author telescoped these into "Biedermaier," a pseudonym under which he launched a vitriolic attack upon the petty bourgeois complacency of the pre-1848 period. This philistine "new inwardness" also suffused the painting of the time, which can be characterized not so much in terms of a definite style as in terms of its underlying attitude. It was humble and unambitious,

1804 — Beethoven removes from his Symphony No. 3, Eroica, his dedication to Napoleon

1805 — Battles of Austerlitz and Trafalgar

1807 — Fichte writes his anti-Napoleon *Speeches to the German Nation*

12. WILLIAM BLAKE

The Fall of Man
1807, Watercolor, 49.6 x 39.3 cm
London, Victoria and Albert Museum

13. RICHARD PARKES BONINGTON

St. Mark's Column in Venice
c. 1826–1828, Oil on canvas, 45.7 x 44 cm
London, Tate Gallery

14. JOHN CONSTABLE

Old Sarum
1834, Watercolor, 30 x 48.7 cm
London, Victoria and Albert Museum

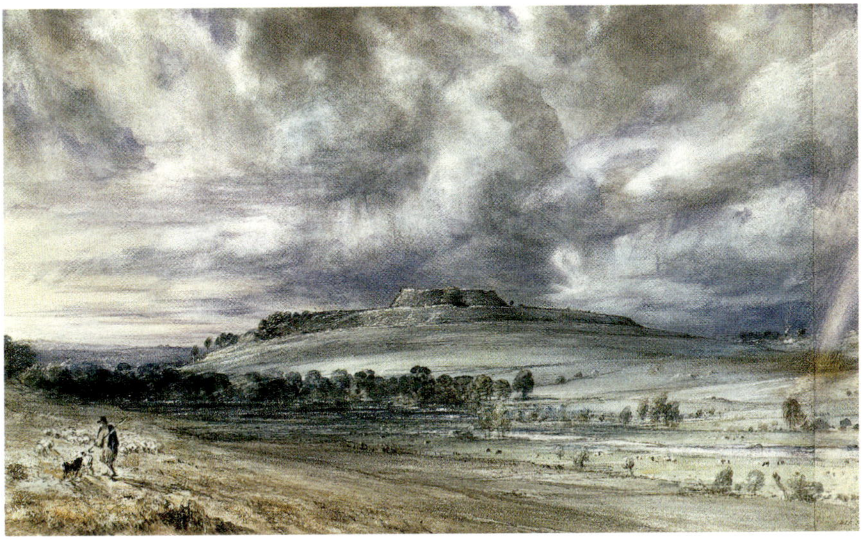

14

expressing itself in small-format compositions for sitting rooms, featuring tightly framed portrayals of local landscapes or towns with figurative staffage, or in individual and group portraits infused with reserved if somewhat prosaic dignity. It was in such work that Biedermeier painters gave their best.

Romanticism blended seamlessly into Biedermeier. This is just as true of the genre scenes in constricted interiors painted by Kersting as it is of the landscapes and fairy-tale subjects done by Adrian Ludwig Richter (1803–1884) and Moritz von Schwind (1804–1871). In paintings that have lost none of their general appeal even today, Richter transformed the early Romantic, cosmically evocative landscape of the soul into the "garden arbour idyll," a genre named after the then popular household journal *Die Gartenlaube*. In Richter's pictures, nature enfolds people like a charming ornament, a domesticated nature in which they feel just as at home as within their own four walls. Peace and quiet is the prime civil right; and where better to find it than out of doors, though not so far out of doors that one loses sight of home. Too much strangeness or unfamiliarity would have disturbed one's recuperation after a long day at the mills. Two of Richter's print sequences were indicatively titled *Beschauliches und Erbauliches* and *Fürs Haus*, or Things Tranquil and Edifying and for the Home.

Even greater popularity was attained by Schwind, be it through his frescoes in the Munich Residence (begun 1832) and a series of watercolor designs for Hohenschwangau Castle, for the Wartburg in Thuringia (begun 1853), or for the Vienna Opera House (begun 1866), or be it through his fairy-tale cycles and paintings, such as *Rübezahl* of 1851–1859. The most popular and beloved Biedermeier artist of all, however, was Carl Spitzweg (1808–1859), whose whimsical visual anecdotes, for all their idyllic character, tacitly caricatured the narrow-mindedness of his fellow citizens. His humorously ironic themes should not blind us to the free, well-nigh impressionist paint handling that came to the fore especially in Spitzweg's late period.

The Romantic vision of a continual progress from the finite to the infinite entailed a rejection of every self-contained, classical view of the world, in favor of both formally and substantially open compositions. Many of the artists' contemporaries dismissed this openness as being tantamount to mere indulgence in mysticism. A number of Romantic artists in fact became tragic outsiders. The failure of their utopian goals plunged them into melancholy, into a cult of friendship with a handful of kindred spirits, into a retreat to solitude in nature. At such existential extremes, these attitudes remained limited to the "pure" Romanticism of the first two or three decades of the century. Still, Romantic traits continued to suffuse a large part of German painting throughout the nineteenth century, being present in the Biedermeier, but above all in the more naturalistic landscape tendencies to follow.

The final third of the century, however, witnessed a true burgeoning of the Romantic attitude. Examples are the paintings of Arnold Böcklin (1827–1901), shot through with melancholy, a mood of death, and mythological symbolism, as well as and especially the artistic program of the Bavarian "fairy-tale king," Ludwig II. In the spirit of Richard Wagner's musical dramas, Ludwig began in 1868 to have his neoromantic Neuschwanstein Castle decorated with scenes from *Tristan and Isolde, Lohengrin, Tannhäuser*, and *Parsifal*. Though the Romantic attitude does not fully explain Ludwig's palaces, it does explain his immersion in a built dreamworld, as well as his wish that it be demolished after his death.

But there can be no doubt that all this was a far cry from early German Romanticism around 1800 and its political and prophetic

1807 — London's streets are illuminated by gas lighting
1808 — Beginning of Spain's War of Independence against Napoleon
1809 — Birth of Charles Darwin
1810 — Johann Wolfgang von Goethe writes his *Theory of Color*

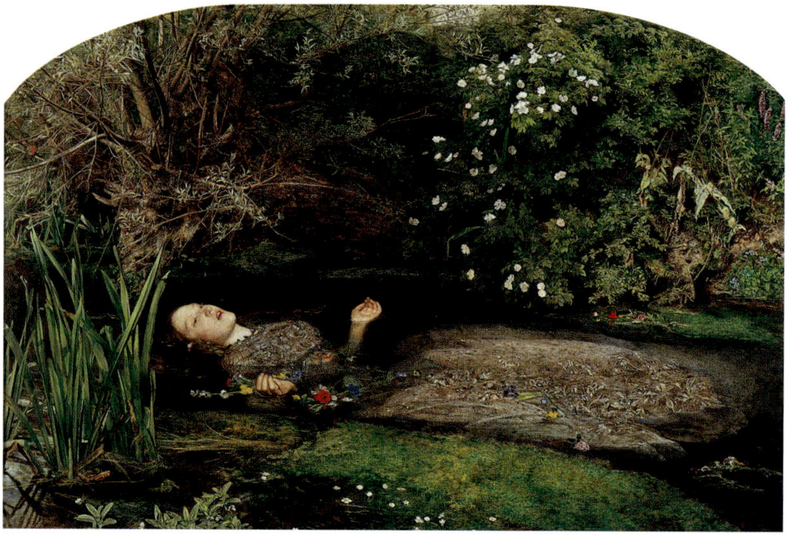

15

15. JOHN EVERETT MILLAIS
Ophelia
1852, Oil on canvas, 76 x 112 cm
London, Tate Gallery

16. DANTE GABRIEL ROSSETTI
The Bride
1865, Oil on canvas, 80 x 76 cm
London, Tate Gallery

17. EDWARD BURNE-JONES
The Baleful Head
1886/87, Oil on canvas, 155 x 130 cm
Stuttgart, Staatsgalerie Stuttgart

aspects. Now Romanticism merely served as a means of escape from a disenchanted reality, and into the magic realm of distant times and climes, an escape in which the nouveau riche bourgeoisie increasingly began to participate from 1850 onwards. Sitting rooms were plunged in dimness by pseudo-oriental curtains that kept banality at bay; knick-knacks and travel souvenirs embodied middle-class visions of escape and meaning, or reminiscences of a medieval era of leaded-glass and knights' manors. Home was a place for reverie, while real life took place outside, in the counting-houses and mills, the barracks and government offices.

Great Britain

The nineteenth-century English Romantics, as I noted above, were able to recur to an incomparably rich heritage of romantic tendencies in the art of the foregoing period. The landscaped garden was a repository of picturesqueness and sentiment, and its exotic accoutrements conveyed a longing for the charm of the faraway and bygone. The Neo-Gothic structures or ruins with which the gardens were fitted out were often associated with the settings of those tales of terror whose Gothic Romance tradition continued without interruption into the industrial century.

In the Ossian epic, in John Milton's *Paradise Lost* (1667), and in Edward Young's *Night Thoughts* (1742–1745), Britain had produced literary works whose mythicizing and demonizing of Christian themes and exploration of the depths of the human psyche were to make them unfailing sources for all of Continental Romanticism. The highly regarded Shakespeare belonged inalienably to the cultural heritage of a nation which, in Burke, could also boast the foremost propagator of the sublime. With the doctrine of sensualism, English philosophy at the start of the eighteenth century had paved the way for the psychological penetration of human art and culture.

Like no other nation, England forced the transition from manual craftsmanship to mass production based on a division of labor. Despite Adam Smith's (1723–1790) complaint, in 1763, that this caused what we today would call a dumbing down of workers, the Industrial Revolution was inexorably underway. It led to an enormous growth of cities, complete with slum housing for the equally rapidly growing proletariat. The more brutal working life and the conditions of existence became, the more writers and artists reacted to the prosaic and impoverished industrial world by celebrating the power of the imagination and individual creativity. When the Frenchman Philippe Jacques de Loutherbourg, a painter of dramatic natural scenes who settled in London in 1771, began to lend the new industrial plants a grandiosely sinister effect, he both demonized and romanticized them, a reaction to the new situation shared by many artists in England.

In a picture like *The Experiment with the Airpump* of 1768 (ill. p. 14), Joseph Wright of Derby (1734–1797) summed up the intentions behind the art of the era in an exemplary way. The well-nigh demoniacally emphasized experimentor in the center has just created a vacuum in a glass receptacle. To him falls the godlike decision whether or not to revive the laboratory animal, a pigeon that has already collapsed. In the faces of the spectators of this nocturnal spectacle are reflected, depending on age and degree of sensibility, a range of feelings extending from curiosity and fascination to sadness and concern, from an acceptance of the new possibilities of science to their rejection.

1811 — Heinrich von Kleist commits suicide
1812 — Napoleon leads his Russian campaign
1813 — Battle of the Nations at Leipzig
1814 — Napoleon is banished to Elba

"conception, my boy, fundamental brain work, is what makes all the difference in art."

Dante Gabriel Rossetti

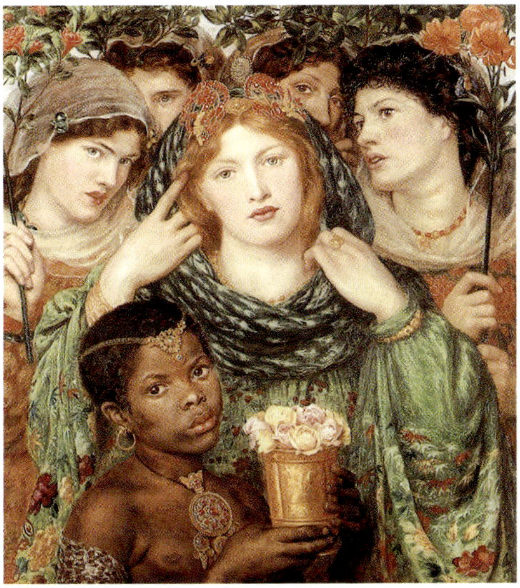

16

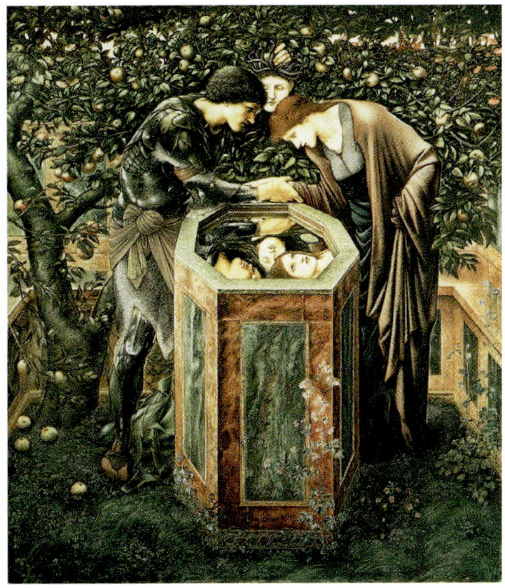

17

A broad current of imaginative, fantastic – in a word, pre-Romantic – paintings flows through English art of the eighteenth century. A few examples will have to suffice for many: the landscapes of Richard Wilson (1714–1782), the pictures of John Runciman (1744–1768), and those of an American artist working in England, Benjamin West (1738–1820).

Johann Heinrich Füssli (1741–1825), a Swiss who as Henry Fuseli lived in England from 1778 until his death, illustrated Dante, Milton, and Shakespeare, and, after 1800, the Nordic saga of the Edda, the Nibelungenlied, and Friedrich de la Motte Fouqué's fairy-tale *Undine*. But he was best known for his various versions of the *Nightmare* (ill. p. 27), in which the unreal and eerie were given compelling form. Figments and outgrowths of the imagination determined Fuseli's œuvre and led, in his paintings, to distortions of the classical canon and an abandonment of familiar spatial logic.

The transition to a demoniacal Romanticism took place in his work almost to the extent that it did in that of William Blake (1757–1827). Blake was both poet and painter, providing superb and idiosyncratic illustrations to his own writings, to editions of the Bible, and to the works of Dante, Milton, and Young (ill. p. 16). He has justifiably been called the great myth-creator and visionary of English Romanticism. The creative and destructive passions of the human soul, capable of throwing open the doors to Heaven and Hell, were the forces underlying Blake's compositions, which burst through formal conventions even more strongly than Fuseli's.

In the field of landscape painting, the transition from the eighteenth century to Romanticism took place more gradually, and initially in a concentration on much more peaceful moods. With landscape views in oil or watercolor, artists projected another type of counter-world to the Industrial Revolution, a world in which the schism between man and nature seemed to have been overcome.

The point of departure for this development was the eighteenth-century fashion of rounding off the education of young aristocrats by a journey to Italy. Often they were accompanied on this Grand Tour by watercolorists, whose series of pictures served a purpose not unlike the tourist snapshots of today. Travels to picturesque attractions, as well as a new interest in the moods of local sites and sceneries, led to an unprecedented upswing in English landscape painting from about 1800 to 1840.

Among the artists involved, such as Thomas Girtin (1775–1802), followed by John Crome (1768–1821), Richard Parkes Bonington (1802–1828; ill. p. 16), and John Sell Cotman (1782–1842), the outstanding figure was John Constable (1776–1821), whose atmospheric depictions of the natural scene, rendered in loose, unconventional brushwork, excited Delacroix and Théodore Géricault (1791–1824), and later influenced the masters of Barbizon and even the Impressionists (ill. p. 17).

Yet greater than them all was William Turner, whose motifs dissolved in sheer color and light were passionately defended against their detractors by John Ruskin (1819–1900), the leading theoretician of Romanticism in England, in his 1843 book *Modern Painters*. Turner, member and professor of the Royal Academy, initially oriented himself to the classical landscape style of Claude Lorrain, as well as to Burke's reflections on the beautiful and the sublime. In 1802, he took his first journey to the Continent, to Switzerland. Two years thereafter Turner opened his own gallery, and began to make ever more daring experiments in watercolor and drawing that culminated in the virtuoso sophistication of his late work. In the course of his career, based on

1814 — Reestablishment of the Jesuit order and the inquisition within the Papal States

1815 — Final defeat of Napoleon at Waterloo and his exile to Helena

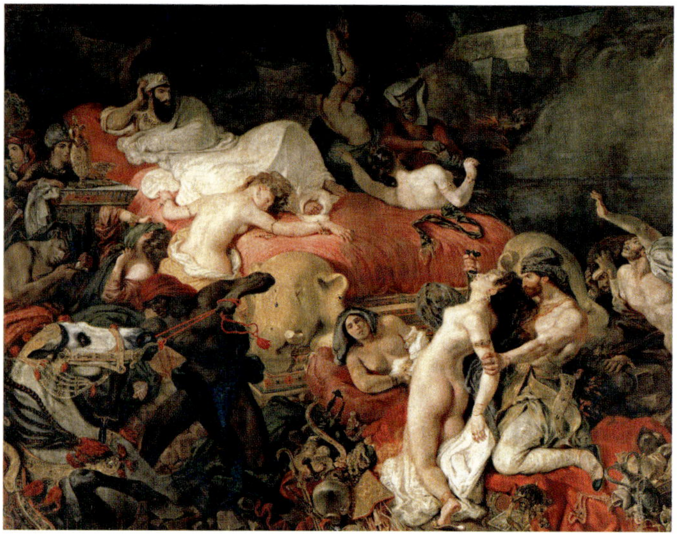

18

> **"The truth is revealed only to the genius, and the genius is therefore always alone."**
>
> **Eugène Delacroix**

18. EUGÈNE DELACROIX

The Death of Sardanapalus
1827/28, Oil on canvas, 395 x 495 cm
Paris, Musée National du Louvre

19. THÉODORE GÉRICAULT

The Charging Light Cavalry Officer (Chasseur)
1812, Oil on canvas, 292 x 194 cm
Paris, Musée National du Louvre

20. PAUL DELAROCHE

The Sons of Edward IV
1830, Oil on canvas, 181 x 215 cm
Paris, Musée National du Louvre

Goethe's color theory, Turner developed a revolutionary handling of light and color, producing textures and structures that had an impressionistic, sometimes practically abstract effect, as seen particularly in the Venice paintings of the 1840s. Turner looked upon unbounded nature as an insoluble mystery, which he envisioned in a series of mythical landscape scenes in terms of cosmic destiny. Seeing the universe as extending between the poles of light and darkness, he found visual correspondences to the processes of creation and destruction, birth and decay, of a visionary power that far surpassed the poetic landscapes of other Romantic artists.

As in Germany and other countries, later Romantic painting in England tended to drift into the uncommittal, or attempted to make up for a dearth of profundity by theatricality or melodrama. A case in point are the compositions of John Martin (1789–1854), which often seem forced and occasionally recall the pomp of Hollywood technicolor movie epics (ill. p. 79).

Yet with the Pre-Raphaelites, England experienced a belated but impressive culmination of the Romantic approach (ill. pp. 18, 19). In the 1820s, under the leadership of Benjamin Robert Haydon (1786–1846), a few admirers of Blake founded a secluded artists' society. Like the German Nazarenes, of whom they were aware, these artists rejected modern materialism and, recurring to Italian Early Renaissance painting before Raphael, they emulated the religious fervor of the Middle Ages. These were the premises on which the Pre-Raphaelite Brotherhood was founded in London in 1848. An anti-academic protest united artists such as John Everett Millais (1829–1896), William Holman Hunt (1827–1910), and the brothers William and Dante Gabriel Rossetti (1828–1882) into a group that lasted until 1853, and whose aims were shared, though they were not official members, by William Dyce (1806–1864), Edward Burne-Jones (1833–1898), and Ford Madox Brown (1821–1893).

All of these artists adopted themes of deep symbolic and socially relevant meaning, which they found preformulated in medieval legends and literature, in the Bible, and in Shakespeare. Their ideals, however, were not exhausted in a retrospective view, for they grew out of an earnest moral involvement with the conditions of the contemporary age.

In an antiquarian and allegorical guise, the Pre-Raphaelites addressed, for instance, morbid psychological and sexual themes that to Victorian moralism were taboo. This lent their pictures a unique tenor, a blend of evocative symbolism with intense color combinations recalling Gothic stained glass, and an incredible fidelity to detail in the drawing. Such an unconventional combination of social message with realistically observed objects and lighting effects was also propagated by John Ruskin, the most influential English critic of the nineteenth century, who defended the Pre-Raphaelites in these terms against their many critical detractors.

The works of the Pre-Raphaelites are located between romantically escapist musing, idealistic ethics, and a realistic interpretation tending almost to the surreal. Their fidelity of detail combined with intense palette and ornamental composition found application in the latter half of the nineteenth century in the decorative arts of England. Brown, Burne-Jones, Rossetti, and others supplied product designs to the firm established in 1861 by the social reformer William Morris (1834–1896). The founder of the Arts and Crafts Movement envisioned a revival of solid, handmade home furnishings to supplant the shoddy, mechanically mass-produced merchandise of the day, and with his associate artists developed an ornamental approach that would become a forerunner of Art Nouveau.

1816 — Lord Byron: *The Siege of Corinth*; Johann Wolfgang von Goethe: *The Italian Journey* (until 1829)

1816 — E. T. A. Hoffmann publishes this novel *The Devil's Elixirs*

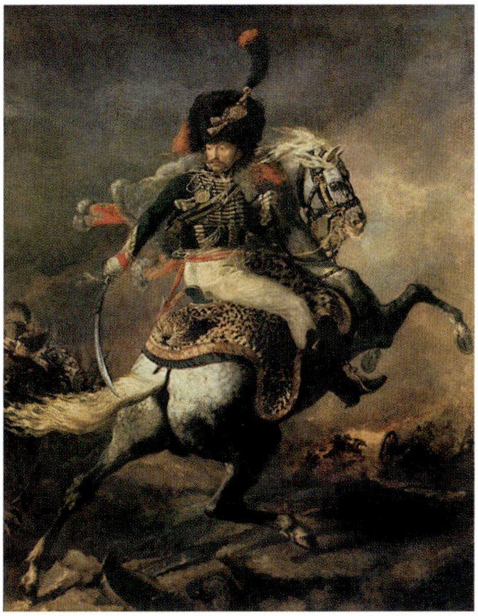

19

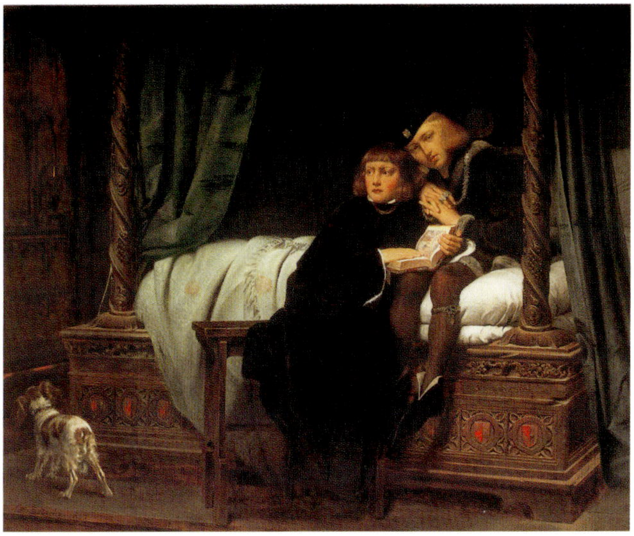

20

France

France, too, produced artists and works in the eighteenth century that seemed to anticipate Romanticism proper, for instance the dramatic seascapes of a Vernet, several of the history paintings of François-André Vincent (1746–1816), or a few of the depictions of ruins by Hubert Robert (1733–1808).

The writings and novels of the philosopher Jean-Jacques Rousseau exerted an enormous influence on European thought. Rousseau argued that with the advance of civilization, humanity had let itself in for continually worsening symptoms of decay and degeneration. His famous cry, "Back to Nature," did not mean returning to man's primitive beginnings, but it did draw fresh attention to everything primitive and archaic. And it basically implied the same thing as the widespread appeal to overcome the alienation of man from nature, an alienation described and decried by Denis Diderot, Enlightenment philosopher and co-editor of the ***Encyclopedia***. It was precisely its emphasis on reason that enabled the French Enlightenment to arrive at new insights into individual psychology on the one hand and nature on the other. Besides advances in empirical science, it helped paved the way for new sensibilities in the arts.

This development in the direction of Romantic attitudes, however, was interrupted in 1789 by the French Revolution. The artists who served it could not, or would not, countenance any journey into the mysterious depths of the individual mind, for it was more important to champion the victorious republican ideals and supply visual propaganda for collective political goals. In terms of content, this painting adopted the ancient Roman catalogue of virtues, and conveyed these in formal terms by means of a rigorously composed neoclassicism and in the medium of history painting. When Napoleon launched into his campaign to vanquish all Europe, teeming history works or allegories continued to be employed to celebrate the triumphs of the commander, and subsequent emperor, and his armies. Although this celebratory intent occasionally led to a sort of romanticizing of the image of Napoleon, the beginnings of French Romanticism shortly after 1800 developed in opposition to the emperor and to the neoclassical, Empire style officially propagated by him.

Chateaubriand and Germaine de Staël were among Napoleon's most outspoken critics. Madame de Staël advocated taking German Romanticism as the model of a universalism that transcended all petty power politics and, in the artistic field, as a way to overcome "anemic" neoclassicism. How difficult this proved to be, however, is shown by the long and successful career of the foremost neoclassicist, Jean-Auguste-Dominique Ingres (1780–1867). On first view, his 1862 painting *The Turkish Bath* (ill. p. 91) may appear to bear traces of exotic, oriental romance. Yet the extreme precision of its graceful lineatures, the smoothness of the cool surfaces of color, and the formal purism of the whole, would seem to exclude any deeply felt emotion, any tendency to Romanticism in the narrower sense.

The Salon exhibition of 1827 was extolled in France as marking the victory of true Romanticism over neoclassicism. Yet the extent to which the French version differed from those of Germany or England may be seen from the work of its two main protagonists, Géricault (ill. pp. 21, 55) and Delacroix (ill. pp. 4, 20, 57). Both were profoundly painterly painters, and both were brilliant geniuses who, like all greats in art history, are by nature difficult to categorize in terms of any one style. And both bypassed the landscape genre so preferred throughout the rest of Europe, and turned instead to history painting. The

1819 — The "Carlsbad Edicts" restrict political and intellectual freedom in Germany

1819 — Arthur Schopenhauer writes *The World as Will and Representation* **1821 — Greek War of Independence from the Ottoman Empire**

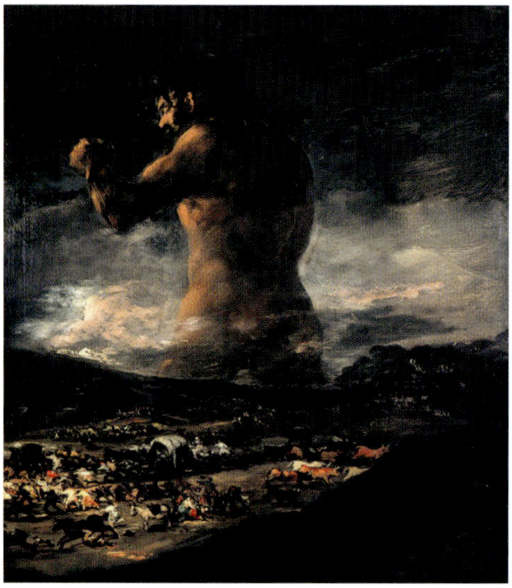

21

"Fantasy, abandoned by reason, produces impossible monsters; united with it, she is the mother of the arts and the origin of marvels."

Francisco de Goya

pathos of their compositions built on color and light, but unlike early history paintings, theirs often focussed on the nameless hero, the individual involved in fateful events or disastrous circumstances. Especially Delacroix, with his liberated, sensitive paint application, with coloristic pictorial symphonies, which largely baffled contemporary audiences, achieved an intensity whose effects were still felt among the Impressionists, and ultimately by Vincent van Gogh, Paul Gauguin, and Paul Cézanne. Even in his highly dramatic subjects, set in the distant past, Delacroix was not concerned with mere fantasy or theatricality, but solely with human passions, which he believed were the catalyst behind historical developments.

The accusation of empty posing, sentimentality, and pathetic national pride can be aimed with more justification at the history paintings of Eugène Devéria (1805–1865) or Paul Delaroche (1797–1856; ill. p. 21), which well served the taste of the petty bourgeois masses for "the interesting," for an escape from the drudgery of everyday life. The orientalism that was concurrently the fad in France, as well as the genre of Italian folk scenes, produced in their finest examples a new, painterly transformation of subject matter that bore a certain affinity to the discoveries made in English landscape painting, though the weaker examples did not go beyond a superficial sentimentalism.

Landscape became a central concern of nineteenth-century French painters only belatedly, but with all the more impact. The School of Barbizon, led by Camille Corot (1796–1875), often populated their gauzily rendered slices of the natural scene with mythological figures, intended to embody both an archaic and a utopianly envisaged unity of man and nature. These were counterimages to touristically accessible, more or less fleetingly viewed scenic attractions, as well as standing in opposition to nature ravaged by economic exploitation and development. Employing the means of plein air, open air or outdoor, painting, the Barbizon landscapes represented more an overture to Impressionism than a form of Romanticism, despite their evocation of the moods and atmospheric changes in nature.

At the same time, French painting was dominated by a socio-politically oriented Realism in which a distant echo of Romanticism could occasionally be heard, as in Jean-François Millet's (1814–1875) *Angelus* (1858/59; Paris, Musée du Louvre), which struck contemporary critics as the quintessence of sentimental melodrama. In fact, if a comparison be sought, one finds closer parallels to this peasant family at its evening prayers in the Biedermeier work of Ludwig Richter than in the universalism of early Romanticism around 1800. The great Gustave Courbet (1819–1877) cannot be accused of sentimentality, but perhaps it was something of the late Romantic heritage that led him to place at the very center of his grand allegory on his political, cultural, and artistic environment, *The Painter's Studio* (1855; Paris, Musée d'Orsay), a moody landscape on which he is just working, watched by a small boy and a nude model, personifications of unspoiled natural life.

Romantic Painting in other European countries

As the previous review has shown, Romantic painting was doubtless centered in Germany and England, where, in the field of landscape painting especially, theoreticians' advocacy of the liberation of the individual from social constraints and his becoming one with the universe found clearest expression. France, on the other hand, evinced a quite unique development in which genre and history pictures pre-

1821 — Thomas de Quincey publishes *Confessions of an English Opium Eater*

1822 — French scholar Jean-François Champollion deciphers Egyptian hieroglyphics

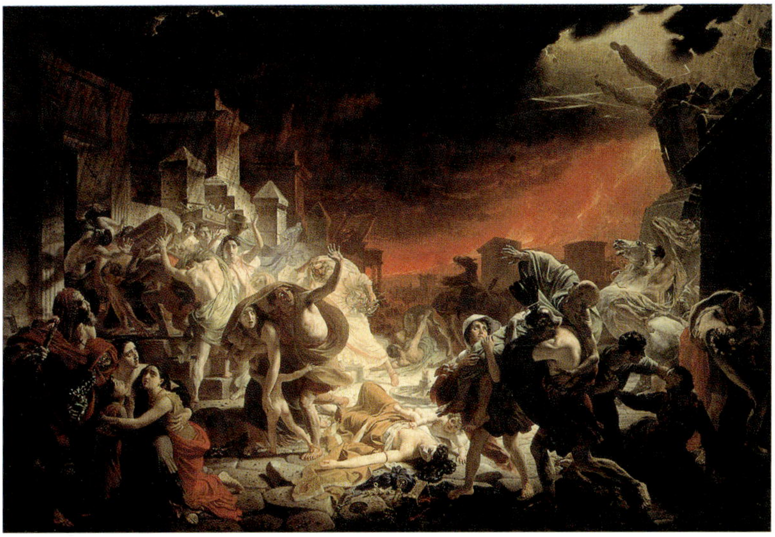

22

21. FRANCISCO DE GOYA

El Gigante
c. 1808/09, Oil on canvas, 116 x 105 cm
Madrid, Museo Nacional del Prado

22. KARL PAVLOVIC BRÜLLOW

The Last Day of Pompeii
1830–1833, Oil on canvas, 456 x 651 cm
Moscow, Tretyakov Gallery

dominated and to which stylistic classifications are very difficult to apply. This difficulty also often confronts us when we look further, to the painting of other European countries.

Scandinavia, however, poses no problem in this regard. The source of Romanticism there was the Copenhagen Academy. Although Nicolai Abraham Abildgaard (1743–1809) was a friend of Fuseli and Alexander Runciman in Rome, and adopted many of their subjective traits and formal distortions to increase the expressiveness of his motifs, he nevertheless ran his academy classes along largely neo-classical lines. The academy's director, Jens Juel (1745–1802), was likewise beholden to this tradition, yet in small landscapes done around 1800 (ill. p. 24) he anticipated the naturalism that would soon come to the fore in Germany, in the work, for instance, of Wilhelm von Kobell (1766–1856). The Copenhagen Academy was able to provide key German Romantics, Friedrich and Runge, with a training, the excellence of which they continually emphasized. Also, it was there that their first contacts were made with the indubitable master of Scandinavian Romantic painting, the Norwegian Johan Christian Clausen Dahl, who in 1818 settled in the immediate neighborhood of his friend, Friedrich, in Dresden and frankly admitted that Friedrich was his ideal.

Belgian Romanticism, as far as one can speak of such, was limited entirely to the field of history painting. Its leader, Gustave Wappers (1803–1874), whose works caused waves of enthusiasm not only in his homeland, was content with a patriotic concentration on the history of Flanders, unlike, say, the painters of early German Romanticism, who attempted to combine national consciousness with universalistic aims. Accordingly, Wappers had no qualms about imitating Rubens. He was surpassed in this by Antoine Wiertz (1806–1865), whose admiration for the great Flemish master took on a veritably pathological character. In the Netherlands, too, the work of Wijnand Jaan Joseph Nuyen (1813–1839), to name only one, documented the extent to which Romantic tendencies in the Lowlands were linked with a recurrence to national painting of the Baroque.

It is a strange phenomenon that Spain and Italy remained largely unsusceptible to the Romantic attitude, which would seem to support the argument that the movement was largely a "Nordic" one after all. At the turn of the eighteenth to the nineteenth century, Spain possessed, with Francisco de Goya (1746–1828), one of the most outstanding figures in the history of European art (ill. pp. 22, 45). Only in its Rococo beginnings is Goya's work classifiable in stylistic terms, for its later phases are marked by sovereign originality. Nor can Goya be called a Romantic by any stretch of the term. Still, the way in which, in paintings and prints, he pilloried human stupidity and superstition, the clerical narrow-mindedness of his countrymen, the degeneracy of the Spanish royal family, the barbarian depths to which both individuals and fanatic masses sank in the war against Napoleon's troops, and the visions and nightmares with which Goya filled his Madrid house around 1820 – all of these exist in an orbit not unfamiliar to Romanticism. Yet obviously Goya's views about the world and humankind were too merciless, too harsh, to trigger any merely pleasurable sense of horror. By comparison to his attitude, Romantic "Weltschmerz" has the look of superficial cant.

Spanish artists such as Leonardo Alenza (1807–1845) and Eugenio Lucas y Padilla (1824–1870) subsequently exploited Goya and romanticized him, whereas Francisco Lameyer (1825–1854) and Jenaro Pérez Villaamil (1807–1854) took their cues from the landscape painting of English Romanticism.

1824 — Lord Byron dies in Greece
1829 — Greece is liberated from Turkish rule, becoming a monarchy several years
1830 — July Revolution in Paris

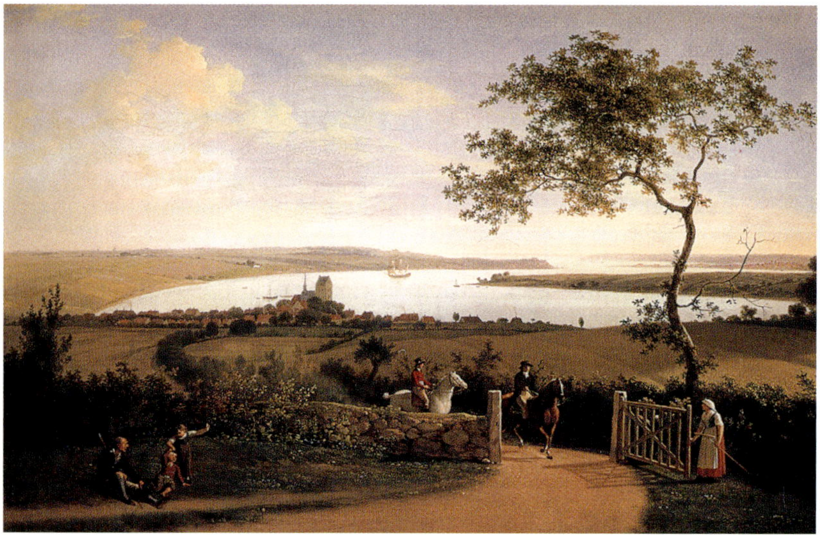

23

23. JENS JUEL

View over the Lesser Belt
c. 1800, Oil on canvas, 42.3 x 62.5 cm
Copenhagen, Thorvaldsens Museum

24. THOMAS COLE

The Ages of Life: Youth
1842, Oil on canvas, 134 x 194.9 cm
Washington, DC, National Gallery of Art

Italy, the prime land of Romantic yearnings, was like Spain in only very gradually opening itself to the movement. In the first place, the classical heritage, including poets like Dante and Tasso, who were elsewhere considered "anti-classical," still carried too much weight there. And second, Italian painting had long lost its international rank by around 1800. Nevertheless, it had still had artists like Tommaso Minardi (1787–1871; ill. p. 33), whose brilliant early work combined harsh realism with empathy, and Francesco Hayez (1791–1881), whose accomplished neoclassical figure paintings were suffused with restrained emotion. Those were roughly the poles between which Italian Romanticism, including an artist like Giovanni Migliara (1785–1837), moved. Then there were the "Purists," with Luigi Mussini (1815–1888) at the helm. Orienting themselves among other models to the German Nazarenes, this group published a manifesto in Rome in 1843 in which they advocated a return to quattrocento painting. Another indication that in Italy, as throughout Europe in the nineteenth-century, Romantic tendencies surfaced again and again and suffused a great variety of other developments.

A link between Russia and the pacesetting centers of European history painting was formed by Karl Pavlovic Brüllow (1799–1852). With *The Last Day of Pompeii* (ill. p. 23), Brüllow created a melodramatic, apocalyptic vision that was enthusiastically described by Alexander Pushkin (1799–1837) and Nikolai Gogol (1809–1852), who, like many of their countrymen, saw the painting as at long last bringing Russian art up to international standards. While Romantic reverberations were felt in the work of Alexei Venezianov (1780–1847) and Alexandr Ivanov (1806–1852), Russian painting as a whole, apart from historical themes, soon turned to a naturalistic depiction of everyday life, which occasionally had emotional and sometimes even sentimental traits without really striving for a Romantic liberation of individual feeling. Similarly to developments in Russia, the tentative emergence of Romantic painting in Poland – Piotr Michalovski (1800–1855) deserves mention here – was increasingly overborne by realism from the 1830s onwards.

Raden Saleh Ben Jaggia (c. 1801–c. 1880/81), a Javanese prince, studied painting in Holland and traveled through Europe from 1841 to 1846. Initially influenced by Delacroix, he was deeply impressed, when he came to Dresden, with Dahl, and with him the Friedrich school. With Ben Jaggia's return to Batavia, the spirit of German Romanticism was wafted to a distant, exotic land of the kind to which it had always felt attracted – and that not only theoretically.

Romantic Painting in the United States

When the Pilgrim Fathers left England for America to escape religious persecution in the early seventeenth century, they not only brought their settlements to the New World but also their doctrine of salvation. They envisioned creating a Nation of God in New England, or New Canaan, as they called it. Their emigration, their passage through the wilderness, the foundation of a Kingdom of God on earth, bore parallels in the Puritans' minds with the Exodus of the Jews to the Promised Land. New England was part and parcel of the Christian history foreordained by the Lord; the settlers claimed the privilege of being a chosen people, and their belief in a possible earthly paradise determined their vision of America's destiny. In consequence, they propagated the American present as the point of departure for an unlimited secular progress.

1837 — Queen Victoria's accession to the English throne ushers in the Victorian Era, a period marked by the rise of the bourgeoisie
1840 — Great Britain takes possession of Hong Kong

“The sky is the soul of all scenery. It makes the earth lovely at sunrise and splendid at sunset. In the one it breathes over the earth a crystal-like ether, in the other a liquid gold.”

Thomas Cole

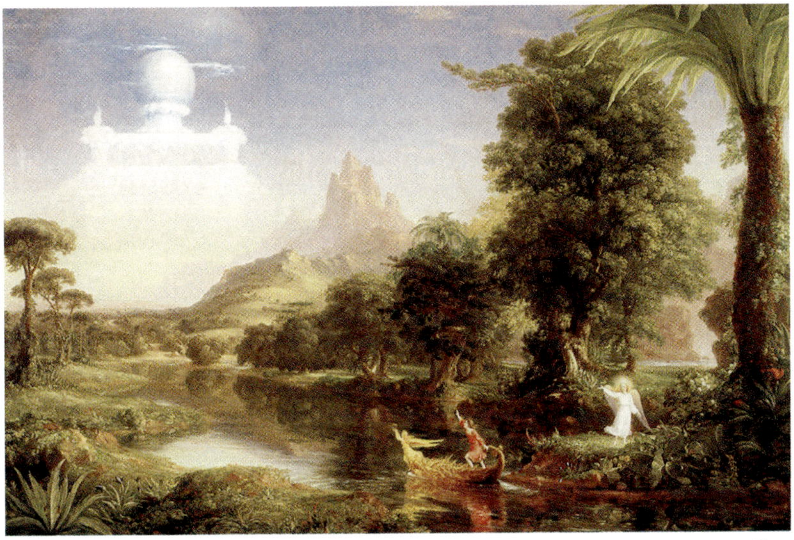

24

Ideas of this kind retained their underlying validity in many subsequent guises. Wild and unspoiled nature, in particular, figured in America as a sublime manifestation of divinity. It was revered with well-nigh religious fervor and at the same time raised to a patriotic symbol. This perhaps explains why, around 1800, landscape became the preferred medium of Romantic painting in the United States, as well as an emblem of America as an earthly paradise. Painters there frequently took as their model Claude Lorrain, with his prospects leading the eye to an idealized and hazy horizon, and his moods of color and light that evoked a paradise in the here and now.

Claude's arcadias were transformed into a vision of America. It was in this vein that Thomas Cole (1801–1848), an emigrant from England who founded the Hudson River School, extolled the New World wilderness as a divine creation in his 1836 *Study on the American Landscape*. In the same vein, Cole's pupil Frederic Edwin Church (1826–1900), in his 1857 painting *Niagara Falls* (ill. p. 89), raised the natural wonder to a symbol of the political energy of “God's own” people and their country. In parallel, Cole's pictures of the South American tropics presented the spectacle of an exotic paradise. At the same period, the German-born Albert Bierstadt (1830–1902) discovered the American West for painting in romantically visionary compositions.

Yet the artistic appropriation of the frontier West or the tropics also had an escapist aspect, because the more unspoiled regions in the United States were overrun by civilization, the more artists had to turn to exotic landscape preserves if they wished to continue dreaming the dream of a “promised land,” to continue to believe in the Romantic utopia of a reconciliation between elemental nature and modern man.

1848 — *The Communist Manifesto* of Karl Marx and Friedrich Engels is published

1848 — The Frankfurt parliament held in the city's Church of St. Paul's

The Nightmare

Oil on canvas, 76.5 x 63.5 cm
Frankfurt am Main, Freies Deutsches Hochstift – Frankfurter Goethe-Museum

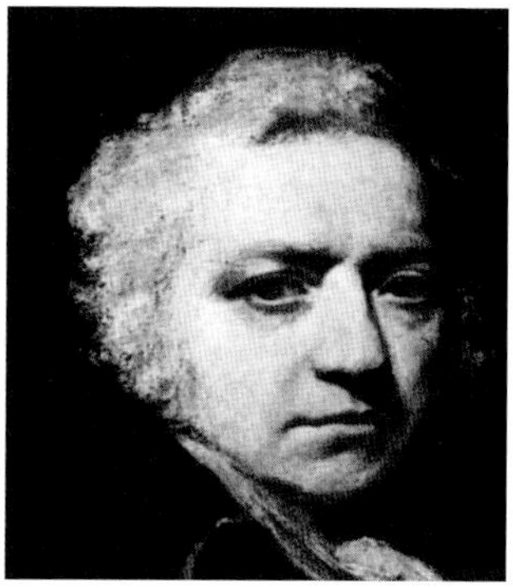

b. 1741 Zurich
d. 1825 Putney Hill (near London)

Fuseli was the second son of the Zurich portraitist and author Johann Caspar Füssli. His early contact with the teachings of Johann Jakob Bodmer familiarized him with the figures of world literature, which were to remain a major source of inspiration throughout his career. Ordained in 1761 as a pastor in the Zwinglian Reformed Church, he left Zurich two years later for political reasons, traveling by way of Berlin to London, where he settled. Initially, Fuseli made his living by writing, while engaged in illustrating the works of his favorite authors, particularly William Shakespeare.

It was Joshua Reynolds who persuaded him to concentrate entirely on fine art. He traveled through Italy, visiting Florence, Venice and Naples, and lived for eight years in Rome. This period, during which Michelangelo's monumental style left a deep impression on him, became a lasting influence. After a short stay in Zurich on his return to London from Italy, Fuseli began to paint extensively. *The Nightmare* (Detroit, Institute of Arts, and Frankfurt am Main, Goethe-Museum), probably his most popular work, excited great attention when it was exhibited at the Royal Academy, to which Fuseli was elected in 1790.

In the history of style, Fuseli's significance lies in the strain of early Romanticism he injected into the classical revival repertoire, the eerie, larger-than-life presence of his dreamlike, sometimes macabre figures and scenes. His often overrated importance as colorist probably derives from his novel, draftsman-like treatment of color.

Fuseli did a total of four variations on *The Nightmare*, probably his best-known theme. The example in Frankfurt is the second variation. Though the motif was not inspired by any specific literary model, it would be unthinkable without a knowledge of ghost stories, especially English ones. The figure of the woman lying asleep or unconscious is extremely elongated and distorted, not because Fuseli could do no better, but in order to visualize the horrible oppressiveness of the gnome crouched on the woman's breast, a nightmare and incarnation of unconscious terrors. In the gap between the curtains in the background appears the ghostly head of a blind horse, which anticipates the demoniac aspect given this animal especially in later French Romanticism.

"some open the gates of art with a golden key and, with dignity, count themselves among the demigods of fame; others beat the gates down using violence, thrusting themselves hastily onto a pedestal; thousands waste their time clinking useless keys and directing futile blows at the unyielding gates."

Henry Fuseli

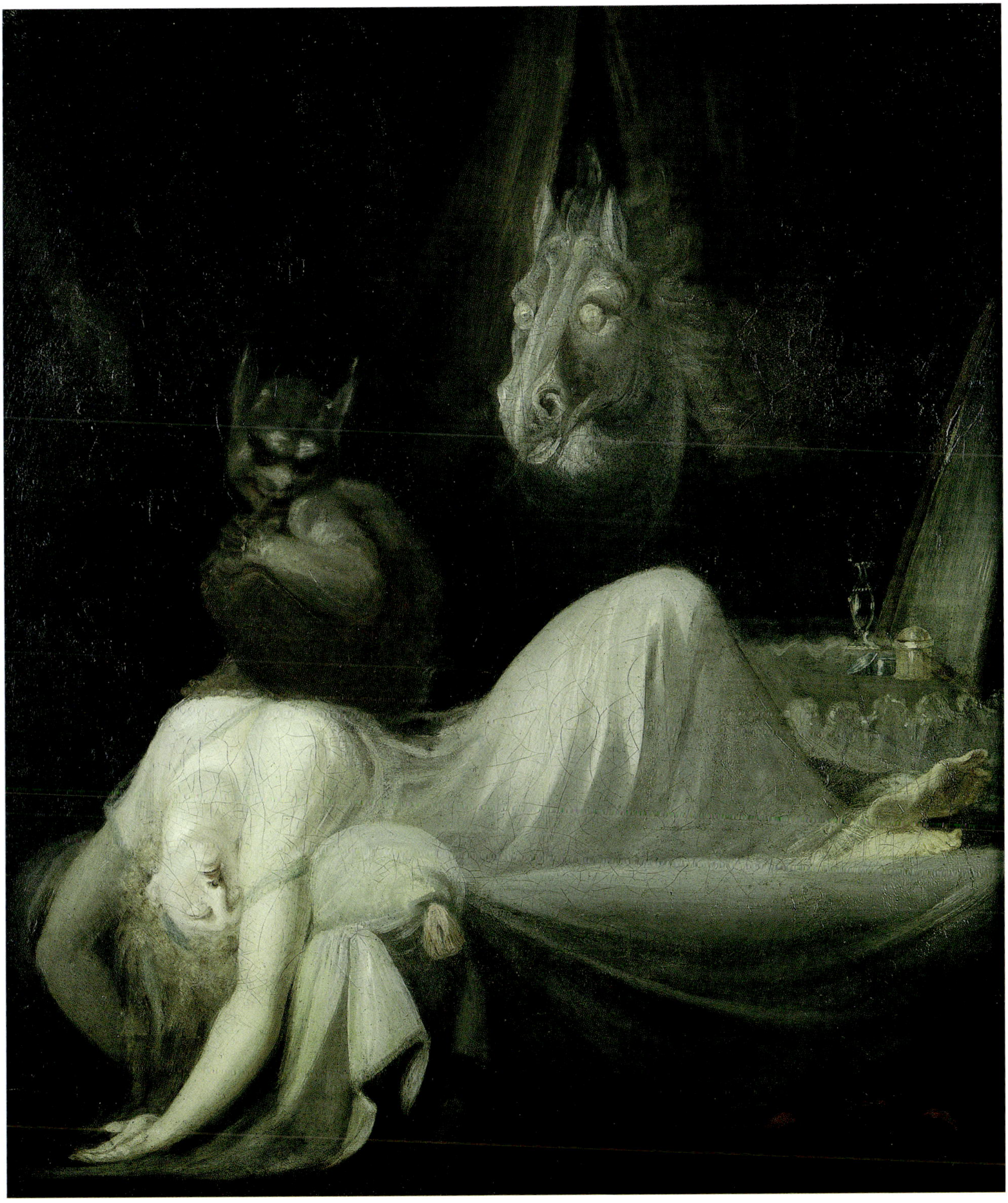

The night of Enitharmon's Joy (formerly called "Hecate")

Color print finished in ink and watercolor on paper, 43.9 x 58.1 cm
London, Tate Gallery

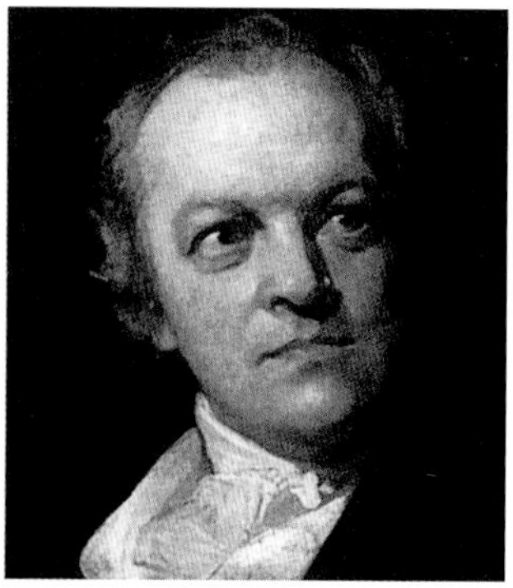

b. 1757 London
d. 1827 London

Blake, the son of a stocking weaver, already had visionary experiences in childhood, which anticipated the prophetic character of his singular combination of visual art and poetry. At the age of ten he received drawing lessons from Henry Pars, then was taught engraving by James Basire, for whom he produced medievalist pictures. His early works were influenced especially by Michelangelo, whose monumental human figures were to lastingly shape Blake's style. While attending the Royal Academy (from 1778), he became embroiled in an argument with Joshua Reynolds about the relative importance of color and drawing.

Blake took the classical view, and his entire œuvre shows his disinclination to use color for effect. In his illustrations to the Bible, the works of Dante Allighieri, or his own writings, the traditional relation between picture and text was abandoned, and a symbolic unity of word and image was achieved, which would not be accepted until decades after Blake's death.

In Greek mythology, Hecate was a goddess of the moon, earth, and underground realm of the dead, and was later regarded as the goddess of sorcery and witchcraft. Blake emphasizes this latter role, showing Hecate reigning in a gloomy nocturnal realm, her hand resting on an open book, accompanied at the left and in the background by uncanny, threatening animals.

This monotype, a color print created using a technique that had been invented by Blake himself, was not intended as a book illustration like most of the English artist's other work. It formed part of a 1795 trilogy, devoted to the subjects of superstition, the evils of an overemphasis on reason, and the power of sensuality, which holds an outstanding place in Blake's œuvre.

The image evinces certain formal and substantial influences, recalling the work of the German artist Asmus Jakob Carstens, but even more that of Fuseli and, by way of him, the phantasmagorical animal realm of Goya's *Caprichos*. Elements of neoclassicism and hallucinatory Romanticism are combined into a compelling image rife with subjective mystical symbolism.

Like his friend Fuseli, Blake developed a highly subjective religious philosophy and, in an abstracted linear style that seemingly ignored the laws of gravity, lent it a radically visionary expression that sent all familiar traditions by the board. This new, spiritually nurtured "mythology" perfectly conformed with the Romantic desire to derive a universal scheme of things from an interplay of opposing forces. After 1790, in the wake of two profound revolutions, the French and the American, the story of Genesis would be rewritten for a modern Western world and under the sign of a new cosmology.

"colouring does not depend on where the colours are put, but on where the lights and darks are put, and all depends on form and outline, on where that is put."

William Blake

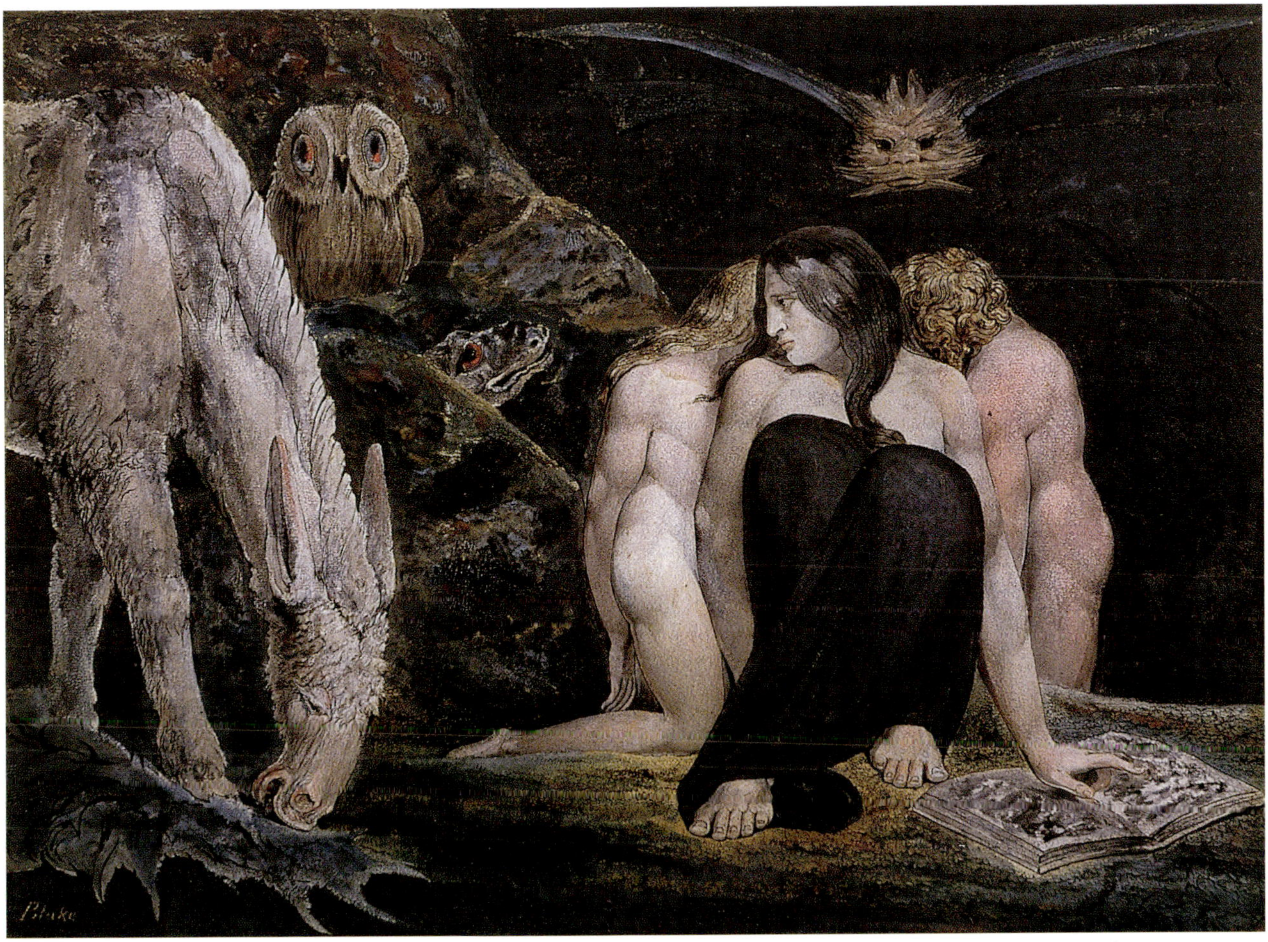
Blake

Madame Récamier

Oil on canvas, 225 x 145 cm
Paris, Musée Carnavalet

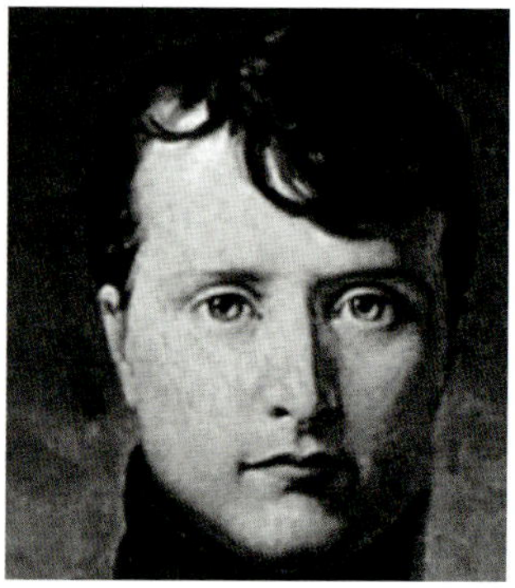

b. 1770 Rome
d. 1837 Paris

Gérard's family lived until 1780 in Rome, where his father served as steward at various courts. After the family's return to Paris, Gérard entered the atelier of Jacques-Louis David at the age of sixteen and soon became his favorite pupil. In 1790, he traveled to Rome to sort out family affairs after his father's death, and there married one of his mother's younger sisters. Soon Gérard had to return to Paris to avoid being registered as an emigrant.

When the French Revolution deprived him of the portrait commissions by which he made a living, he began illustrating the works of Racine and Virgil. He also became a successful painter of historical scenes, winning the competition to commemorate the meeting of the National Assembly of 10 August 1792. However, he soon returned to portraits, which were much sought-after on account of their careful preparation and classical detachment. Gérard's reputation remained high through the Restoration period. In 1817, he became court painter to Louis XVIII, and was ennobled in 1819.

The Paris salon of Juliette Bernard, who married the much older Jacques Rose Récamier in 1793, was a gathering place for artists and intellectuals opposed to Napoleon. Due to her celebrated beauty, she was also much in demand as a portrait model.

A few years before Gérard, his teacher Jacques-Louis David, the neoclassical painter of the Revolution, had done a portrait of her in an empty room, reclining on the type of couch named after her, the *récamier*. She was dissatisfied with David's classical revival, low-key depiction, which therefore remained unfinished. Madame Récamier commissioned Gérard, the most popular portraitist of the day, to do a new portrait, showing her in a more natural setting, in which the graceful curves of her figure and the hues of her complexion are echoed in the forms and colors of the surroundings. The slight twist of her body, the low neckline of the Empire dress that barely covers her breasts, and the naked feet make for a highly effective pose quite beyond the norms of the time. The erotic magnetism of her appearance is both mitigated and made more suggestive by the musing pose and the stillness of the room, isolated from the hurly-burly of the outside world. At the time, Madame Récamier's pose was considered intimate and thoughtful – sentimental in the best sense of the word. This aspect of sentimentality played its part in the development of the Romantic attitude.

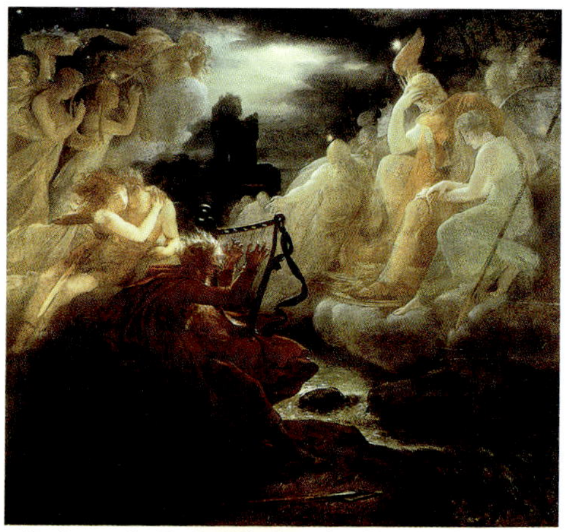

Ossian on the Bank of the Lora, Invoking the Gods to the Strains of a Harp, undated

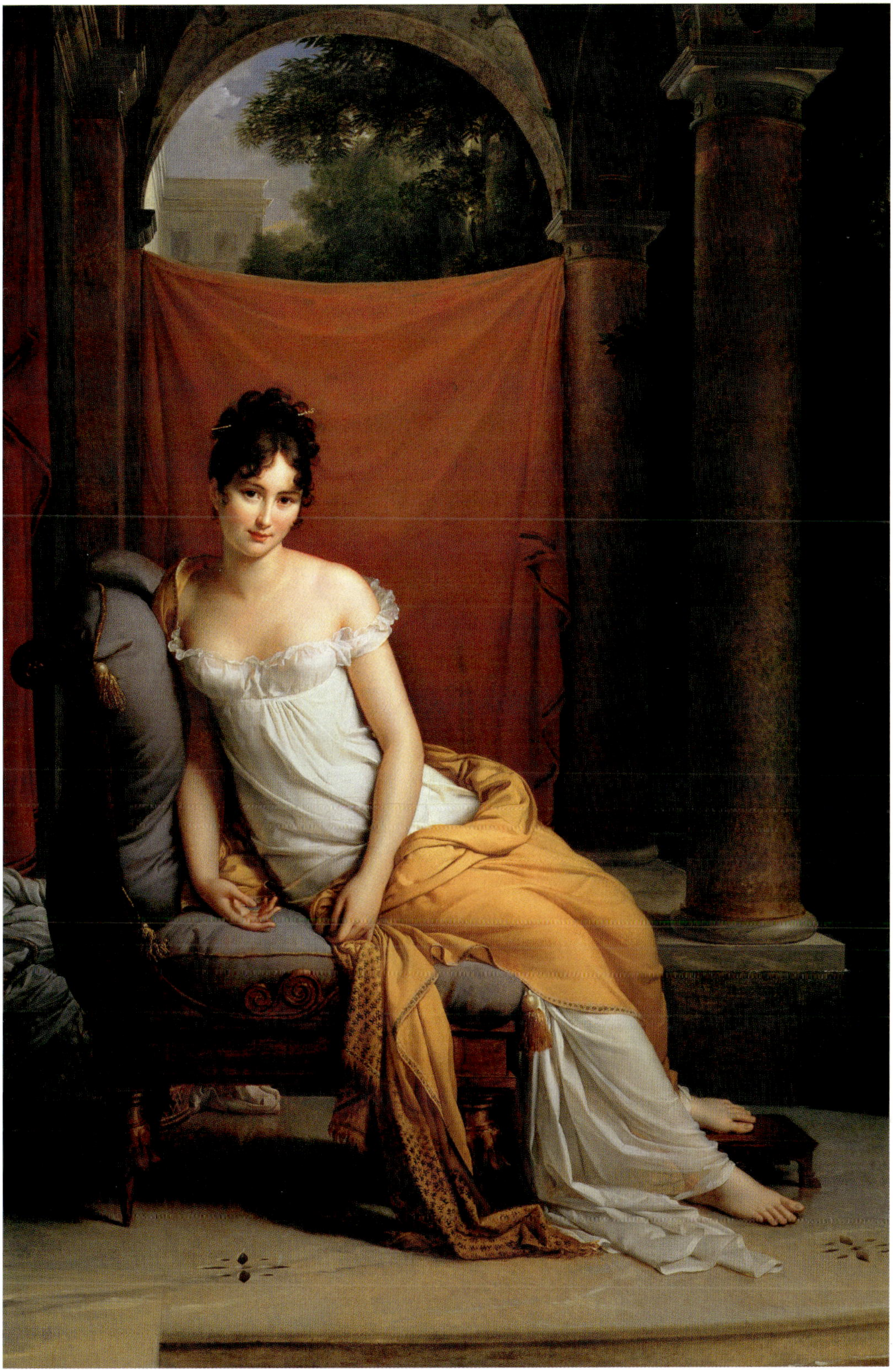

self-portrait

Oil on canvas, 37 x 33 cm
Florence, Galleria d'Arte Moderna

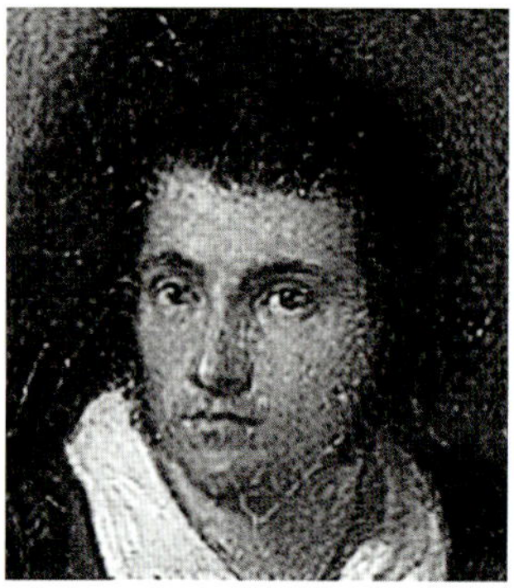

b. 1787 Faenza
d. 1871 Rome

A painter, illustrator, and author, Tommaso Minardi began his career as a pupil of Giuseppe Zauli. His initial activity in Rome consisted in ten years of employment with the engraver Giuseppe Longhi, for whom he did reproduction drawings of Michelangelo's ***Last Judgment*** in the Sistine Chapel; in addition, he studied the works of Leonardo and Raphael. In 1819, on behest of the neoclassical sculptor Antonio Canova, Minardi was named director of the Academy in Perugia. From 1821 to 1858, he was employed as an instructor at the Accademia di San Luca in Rome.

The brilliant early work of Minardi combines merciless realism with that profound suffering at the state of the world, which was so characteristic of Romantic art.

In his *Self-Portrait*, the artist depicts himself sitting on a mattress, wrapped in his coat, in a humble but tidy room. The oblique wooden ceiling of the mansard room forms the strongest diagonal accent in a composition that is otherwise determined by a quiet contrast of horizontals and verticals. On the back wall of the room, there is a full bookcase, and books are piled on the desk at the left. A number of other everyday things are distributed picturesquely around the room.

Light falls into the interior from two windows on opposite walls whose shutters open into the room. A death's head and an animal skull serve to underscore the melancholy mood of the as yet unrecognized, starving genius. This motif would later be treated by the German artist Carl Spitzweg (ill. p. 79) with an ironic, eccentric twist. Minardi himself subsequently adopted the style propagated by the German Nazarenes.

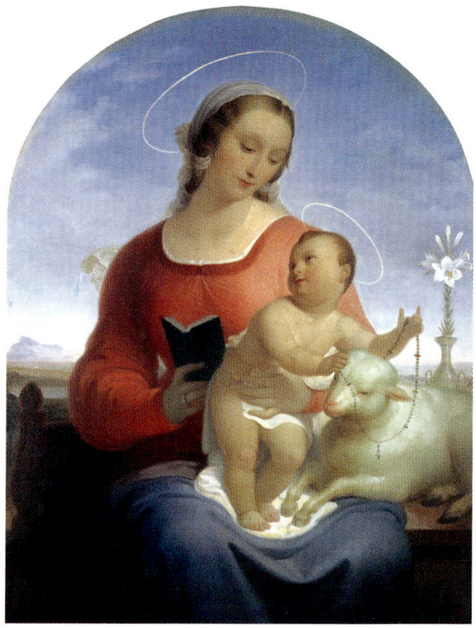

Madonna of the Rosary, 1841

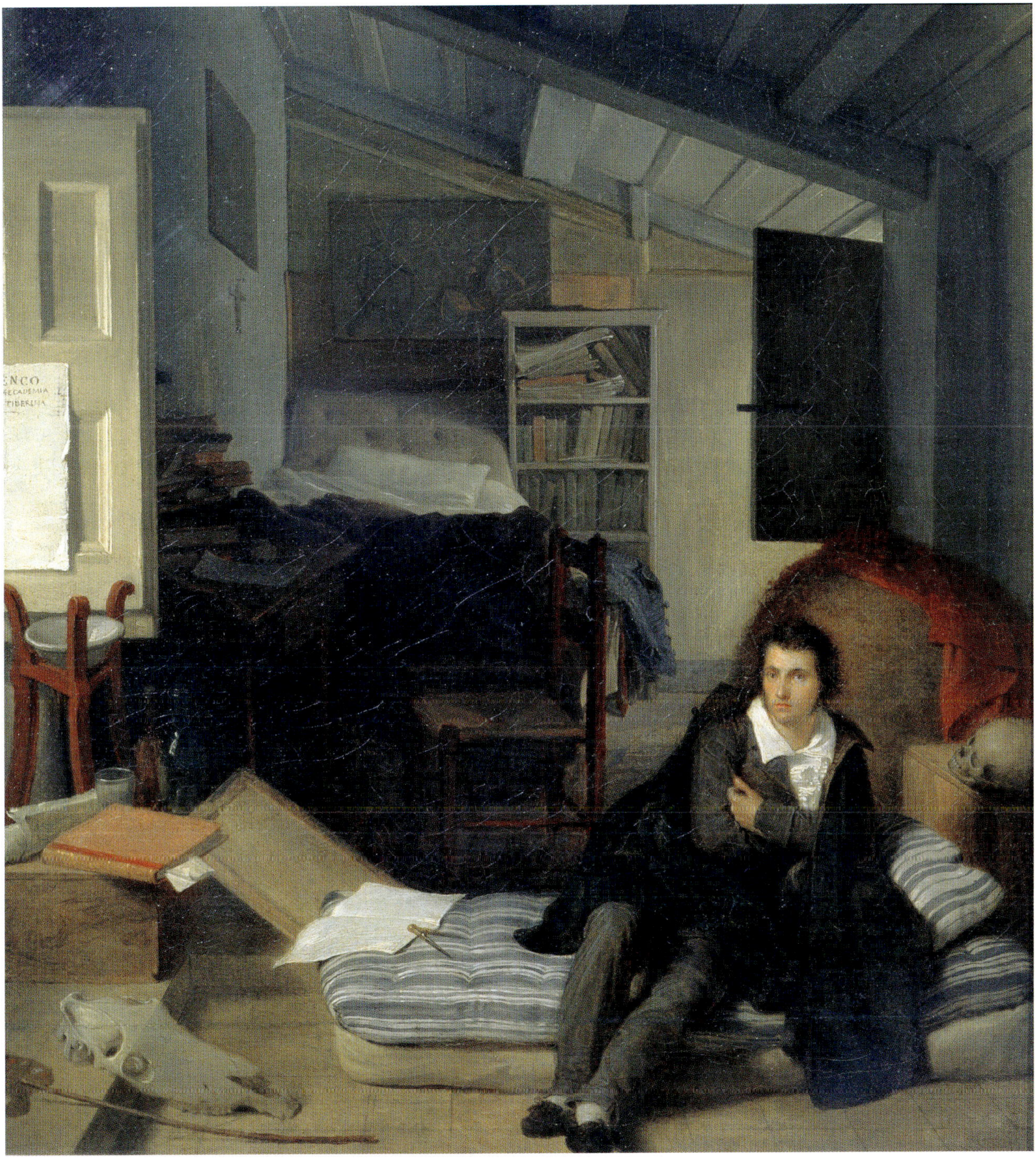

Justice and Divine Vengeance Pursuing Crime

Oil on canvas, 243 x 292 cm
Paris, Musée National du Louvre

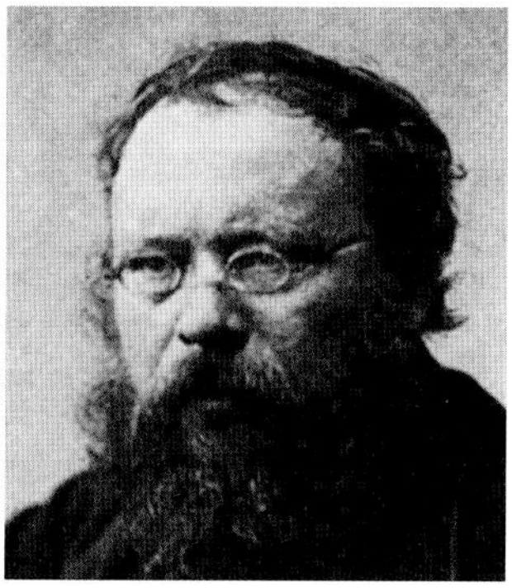

b. 1758 Cluny
d. 1823 Paris

Prud'hon began his career at the Dijon Academy under François Devosge and continued his studies at the Paris Academy. In 1784, he won the Prix de Rome, which took him to Italy from 1785 to 1788. Although this period coincided with David's triumphs in Rome, Prud'hon remained unimpressed by his countryman's neoclassicism. He became a friend of the sculptor Antonio Canova and studied the art of antiquity, but was most lastingly influenced by the Renaissance masters, especially Leonardo and Correggio.

On his return to France he settled in Paris, supporting himself with the sale of drawings and miniatures. His first important commission came in 1798, a ceiling painting in the palace of Saint-Cloud. This was followed by similar orders, devoted to allegorical themes. The Empress Joséphine was his most influential patron, and Prud'hon became the portrait painter of the royal family. Napoleon's second wife, Marie-Louise, also admired his work, securing many commissions for him and employing him as her drawing master. In an art scene dominated by austere neoclassicism, Prud'hon held a rather isolated position, yet his sensitive handling of color and composition helped to usher in Romanticism.

In 1805, Prud'hon received a commission to execute a monumental painting for the council chamber of the Palace of Justice in Paris. After several changes of plan, he finally exhibited *Justice and Divine Vengeance Pursuing Crime* at the 1808 Salon, drawing the highest praise from Napoleon and accolades from a public that had grown jaded to the neoclassical coolness represented by Jacques-Louis David's compositions. Though the clarity of lineature and the relief-like arrangement of the figures in the foremost picture plane still recalled David, the overall emotionally charged impression created by dramatic poses, illumination, and coloring amounted to a daring innovativeness in approach.

In the midst of a stark, rocky landscape, a thief and murderer looks anxiously back at the naked body of his victim, garishly illuminated by the full moon, as the goddesses of vengeance swoop down upon him from the upper right. The wasteland in which this takes place represents the "classical" site for such events. The bush and cliffs in the background run parallel to the figure on the ground, while the diagonal of the fleeing figure is likewise compositionally underscored by the dark rock formation behind him to the left. The overall configuration of the allegories of supernatural powers has a semicircular contour that corresponds with the zone where the victim lies on the one hand, and with the line of the criminal's back on the other.

Though it would be mistaken to describe this impassioned and somewhat pathetic visualization of the mental state of a man who has stooped to crime as "romantic" in the narrower sense of the word, the way everything in the scene is suffused with a sense of dread does indeed mark the transmission of the French tradition of romantic horror into the nineteenth century.

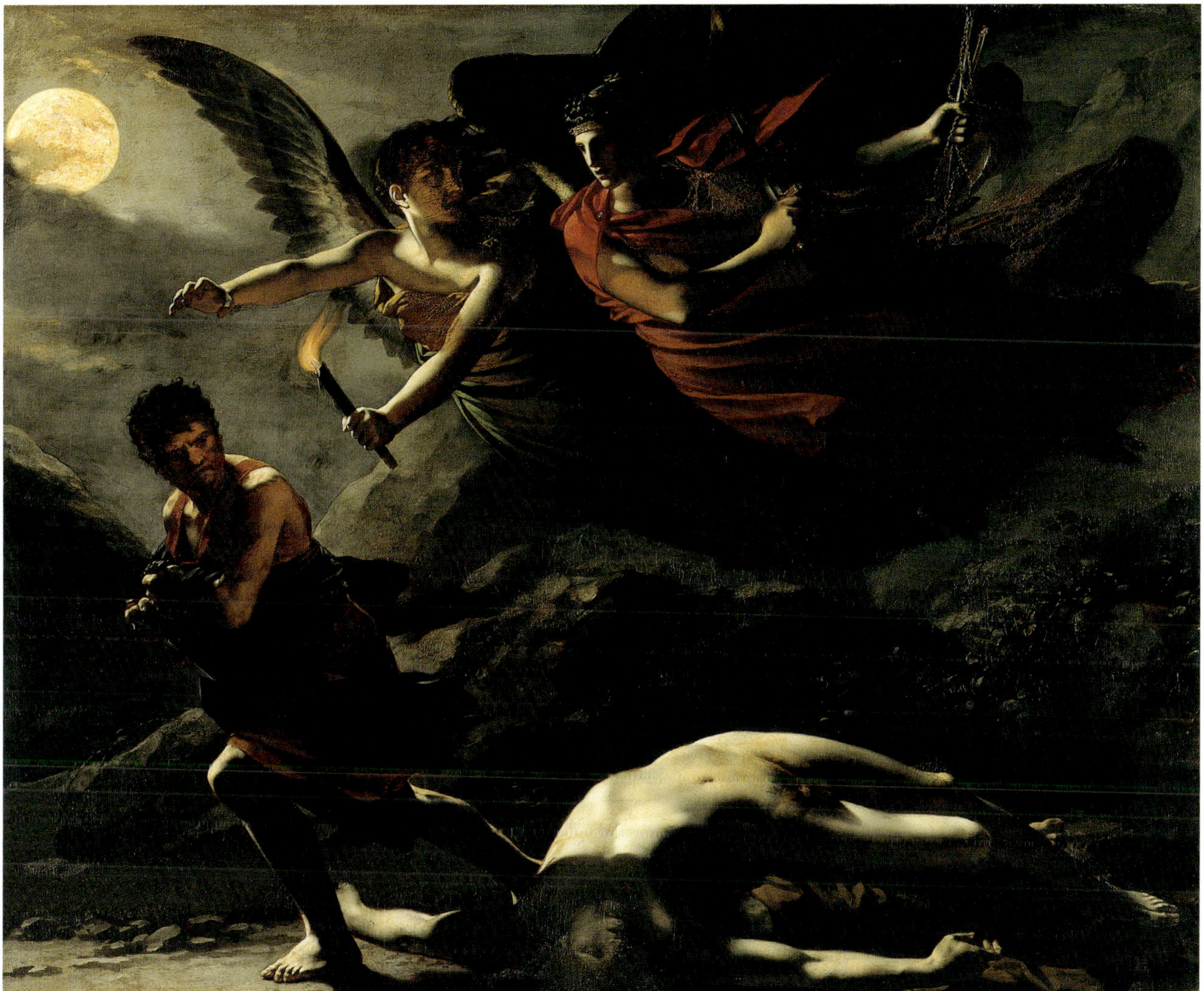

MORNING (FIRST VERSION)

Oil on canvas, 109 x 85.5 cm
Hamburg, Hamburger Kunsthalle

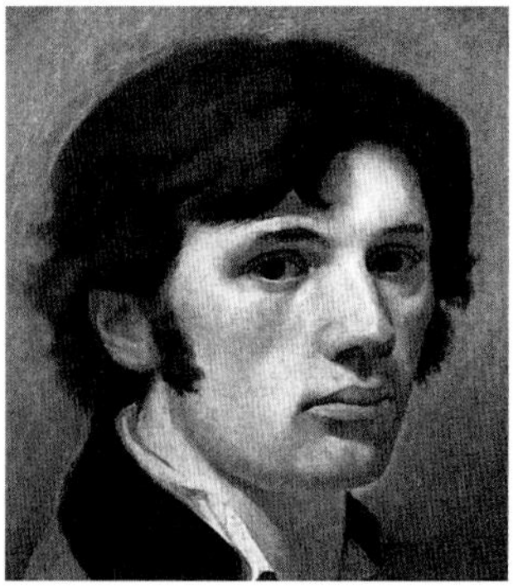

b. 1777 Wolgast (Pomerania)
d. 1810 Hamburg

Runge's father was a grain merchant and shipowner. In boyhood, Runge already displayed an extraordinary talent at cutout silhouettes. His brother Daniel greatly furthered his career, introducing him to artists and financially supporting him through his Hamburg trading company.

After attending the Copenhagen Academy, from 1799 to 1801, Runge visited Caspar David Friedrich at Greifswald and went to Dresden. He immersed himself in the works of the poet and dramatist Ludwig Tieck, whom he visited in Berlin. He fell in love with Pauline Bassenge, a love that would prove fundamental to him not only personally but artistically. After their marriage in 1804, the couple returned together to Wolgast. Runge often suffered from ill health, and from 1807 he and his family lived with his brother in Hamburg.

In Runge's drawings, etchings, and paintings, real objects serve as mere physical embodiments of a metaphysical world imbued with the spirit of God. Here, matter and light represent two different levels, the material and the immaterial, of an all-embracing spiritual unity. His investigations into color theory formed the basis for Runge's metaphysical treatment of light and color, supplemented by symbolic elements drawn from Protestant Baroque mysticism.

Morning was originally intended as part of a painting sequence on the times of day, as evidenced by a series of preparatory drawings and etchings. The four planned paintings were to encompass, moreover, the themes of the seasons, the ages of life, and the human temperaments, and were envisioned as monumental decorations for a central building whose design would be based on plant forms.

In the central field of the small version of *Morning*, which was followed a short time later by a larger version in oil (fragment; Hamburg, Kunsthalle), a nude female figure rises above the sea, which extends beyond a plain dotted with flowers and bushes. This figure, alluding to Venus and Aurora as well as to the Virgin, ultimately embodies the forces of nature striving toward the sunlight. From her right hand, directly over her head, a lily with pairs of embracing children seems to grow. Above this appears a star with three cherubs' heads. The child lying on the ground – Eros and Christ Child in one – may be interpreted as representing a pure incarnation of light.

The painted frame bears more depictions of children and plants, which, with the interior image, Runge said represented "the limitless illumination of the universe."

"Art is a pure celestial sphere to which few have truly raised themselves; indeed, art can be recognized and fully comprehended only through faith."

Philipp Otto Runge

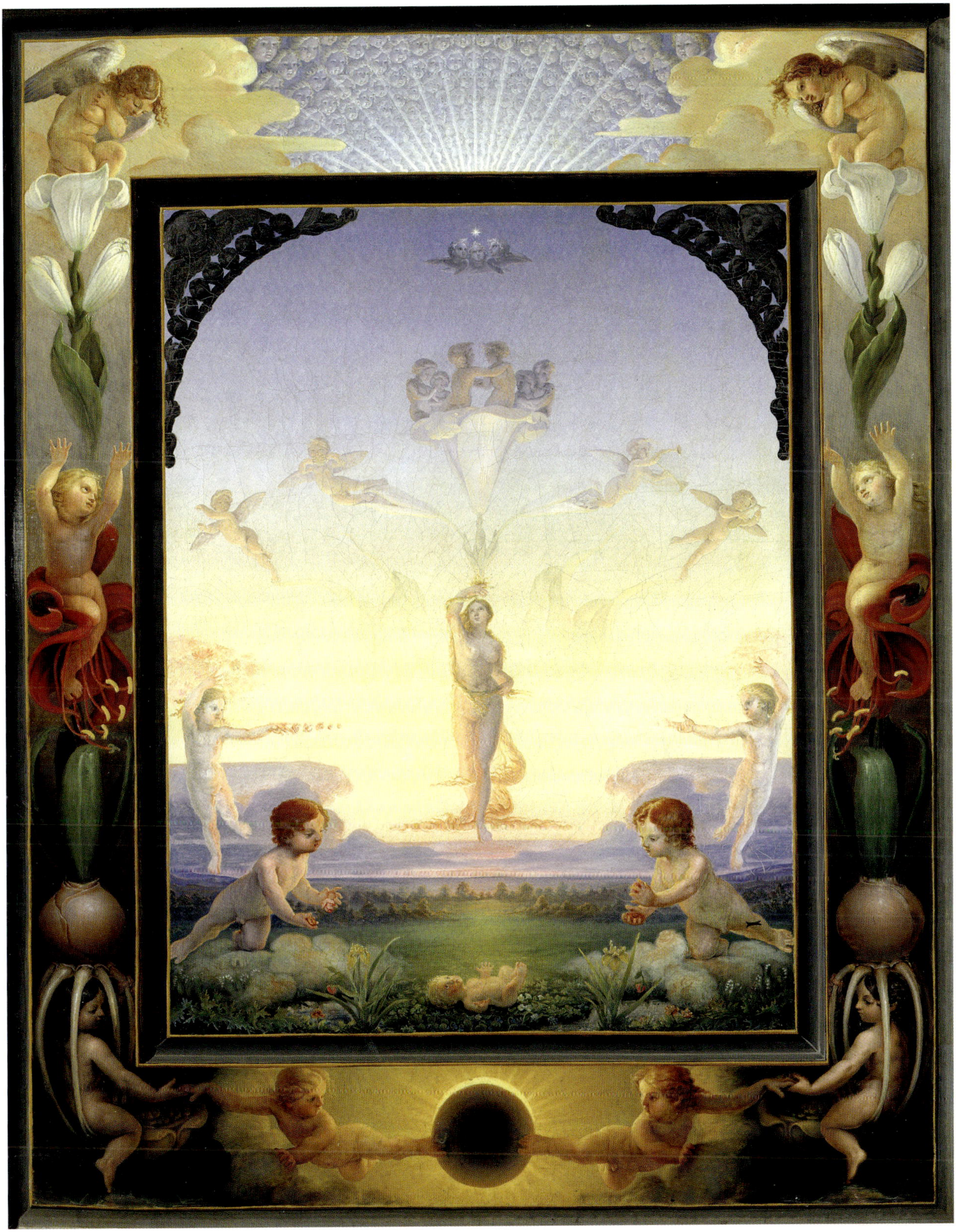

portrait of the second Lieutenant charles Legrand

Oil on canvas, 248.9 x 161.9 cm

Los Angeles, CA, Los Angeles County Museum of Art, Gift of California Charities Foundation

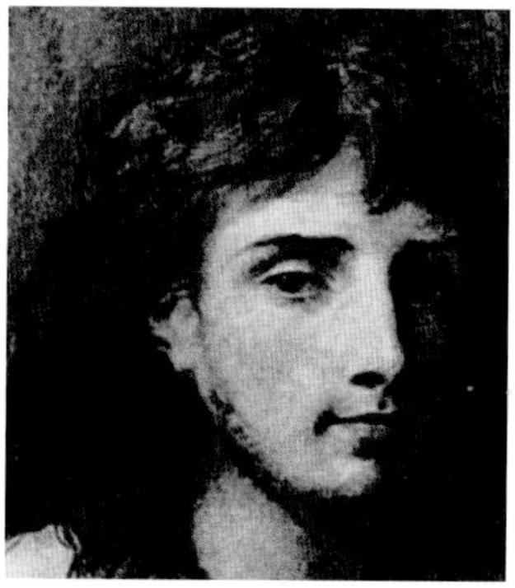

b. 1771 Paris
d. 1835 Bas-Meudon (near Paris)

Gros was only fourteen when he became a pupil of Jaques-Louis David, after having received instruction from his father, a miniature painter. In 1793, accused of royalist tendencies, he had to flee to Italy, where he lived mainly in Florence and Genoa, making a living from miniatures and portraits.

In 1796, an introduction to Napoleon in Milan established Gros's career. His first commission was *Napoleon at Arcola* (1796; Paris, Musée du Louvre), a work whose dynamic approach already set it apart from David's cool severity. After returning to France in 1799, Gros painted colossal and highly acclaimed battle scenes to celebrate Napoleon's martial prowess, including *Bonaparte Visiting the Plague-Stricken at Jaffa* (1804; Paris, Musée du Louvre) and *Napoleon on the Battlefield at Eylau.*

Under Rubens' influence, his compositions took on increasing vitality and his palette grew more intense. The Romantics, especially Eugène Delacroix, were impressed by the freshness and vigor of his work. As under Napoleon, during the Restoration Gros remained the official portraitist of high society. In 1824, he was made a baron. When David went into exile to Brussels in 1816, he handed over his studio to Gros and, as head of the Classical School, urged him to continue the good fight against Romanticism. The lifeless compositions on mythological subjects that ensued were rejected not only by the Romantics but by Gros's own pupils, who turned to the great Classicist Ingres. At the age of sixty-five, depressed by his failures, Gros committed suicide.

Charles Legrand was killed on 1 May 1801 in Madrid, when rebelling peasants attacked a regiment of Napoleon's curassiers on the Puerta del Sol, tore the men from their horses, and knived them. Legrand was the son of a French general. In his memory, his parents commissioned Gros to execute a life-size portrait. The result was the artist's masterpiece.

The lieutenant has dismounted and led his horse to the trough. The path descends to the right, where a view opens out of a peaceful, classically stylized landscape. Legrand stands nearly frontally to the viewer, slightly off the central axis of the picture, in a relaxed attitude. He rests his right arm on the rump of his black horse, whose neck and head are silhouetted in a beautiful curve against the sky. Holding the reins in one hand, with the other he supports his magnificent helmet with horsetail and peacock feathers against his hip. Legrand's handsome young face is turned slightly aside as he gazes into the distance with a musing look. Such works with their cultivated, painterly coloration and true depth of feeling placed Gros at the inception of French Romanticism.

"If all the kings of the earth could view such a spectacle, they would be less keen on wars and conquest."

Napoleon about Gros's work "Napoleon on the Battlefield at Eylau"

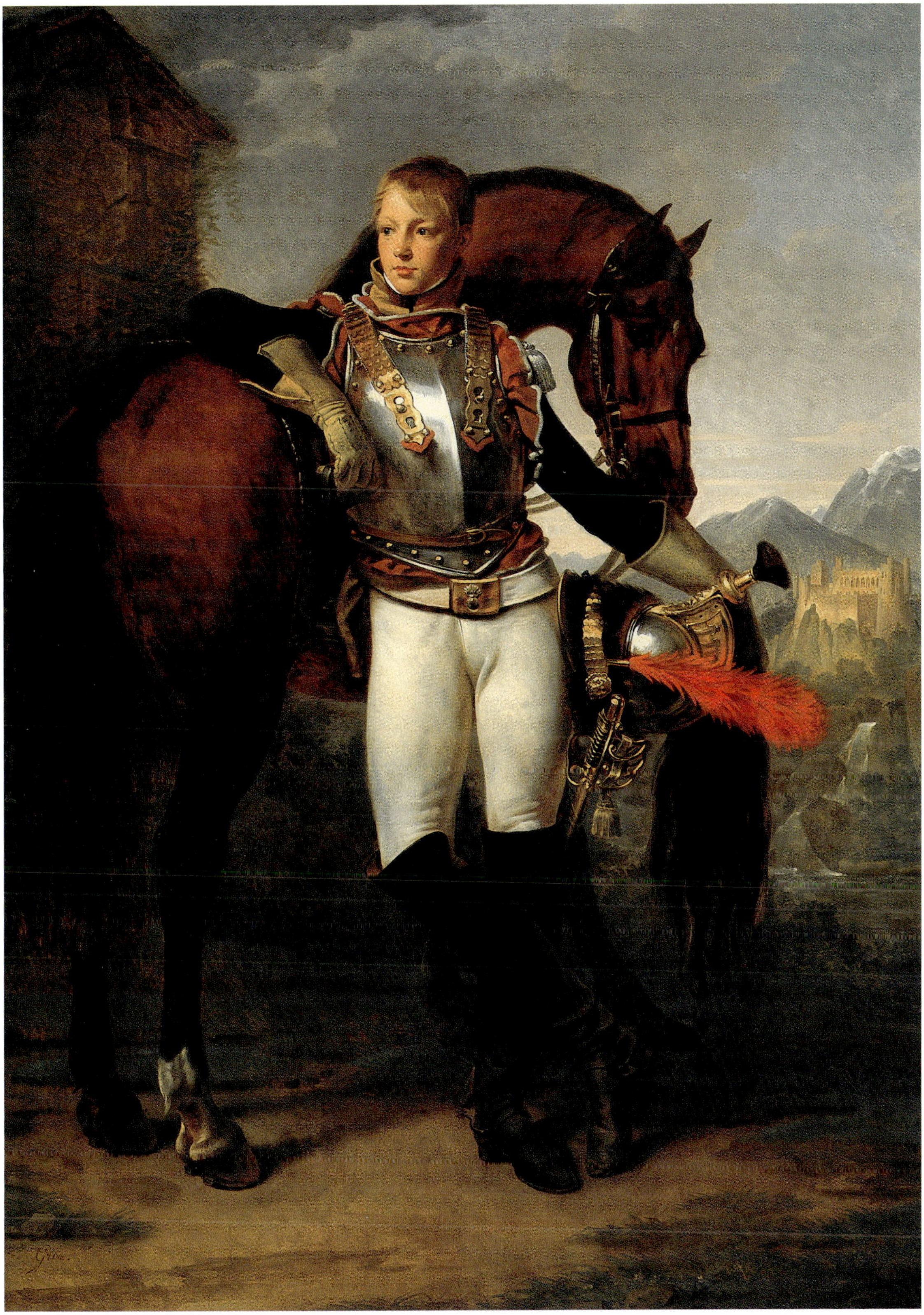

shulamit and Mary

Oil on panel, 34 x 32 cm
Schweinfurt, Georg Schäfer Collection

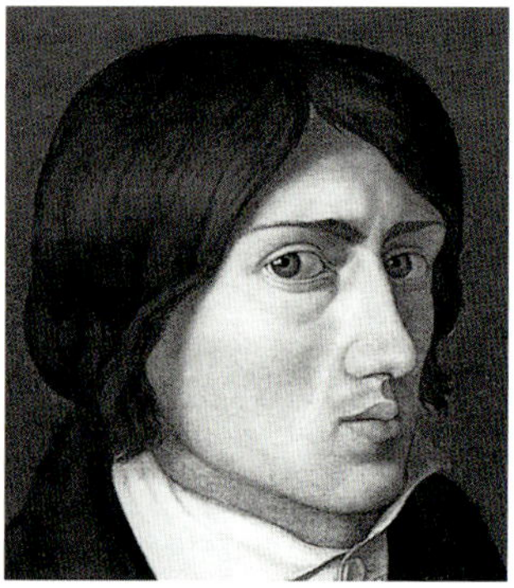

b. 1788 Frankfurt am Main
d. 1812 Albano

From 1805, Pforr attended the Vienna Academy, where he and Johann Friedrich Overbeck, Joseph Wintergerst, Ludwig Vogel, Johann Konrad Hottinger, and Joseph Sutter in 1809 founded the "Lukasbund," or St. Luke's Brotherhood, an anti-academic group dedicated to a renascence of German art out of the spirit of religion. After arriving in Rome in 1810, Pforr initially lived at Villa Malta, then moved with other members of the group into an abandoned monastery, S. Isidoro. In 1811, he traveled to Nemi and Naples, and in 1812 to Albano, where tuberculosis ended the young life of one of the most outstanding representatives of Nazarene art.

Pforr's small panel in the shape of a medieval two-winged altarpiece stands in the tradition of the Romantic friendship picture. The female figure of Shulamit, on the left, symbolically represents the artist's friend and fellow painter, Friedrich Overbeck, while Pforr associates himself with Mary, on the right. Shulamit's name, calling to mind the Song of Solomon in the Old Testament, signifies riches, a love of luxury, and the worldliness and beauty of the South.

On the right panel, the figure of Mary serves as an image of contrast. She is depicted in an interior whose bull's-eye panes and exposed-beam ceiling characterize it as an Old German parlor of the type seen, for instance, in Albrecht Dürer's engravings. Pforr's ideal of feminine beauty is the blonde, upstanding German maiden. The canopy over her bears the comforting symbols of death: cross and wreath. Next to her perches a dove, evoking the flight of yearning. Shulamit's canopy, in contrast, with its entwined flowers and dove, contains the joyful symbols of life and fertility.

"My predilections draw me to the medieval era, where the dignity of man still showed itself in full force." With this confession, Pforr not only stated the credo of his own art but of that of the Nazarene group as a whole. Pforr's rendering of the ***Entry of Emperor Rudolf of Habsburg into Basel*** reflects this enthusiasm for the Middle Ages, which was simultaneously a patriotic enthusiasm.

> **"Art has greatly deteriorated. considering to what end it is used, one can only regret that its decline is so universal."**
>
> **Franz Pforr**

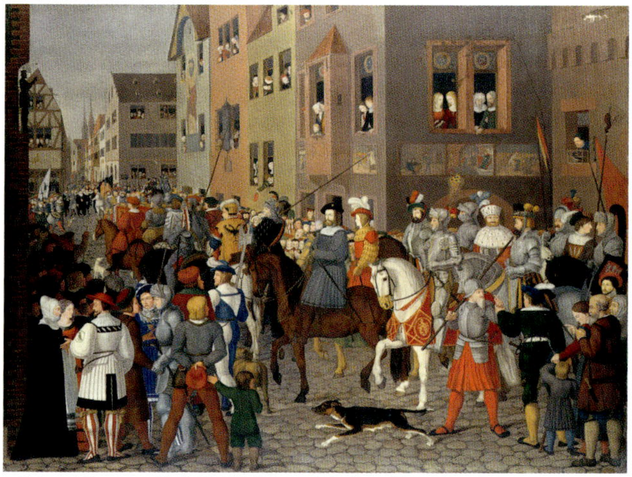

Entry of Emperor Rudolf of Habsburg into Basel in 1273, 1808–1810

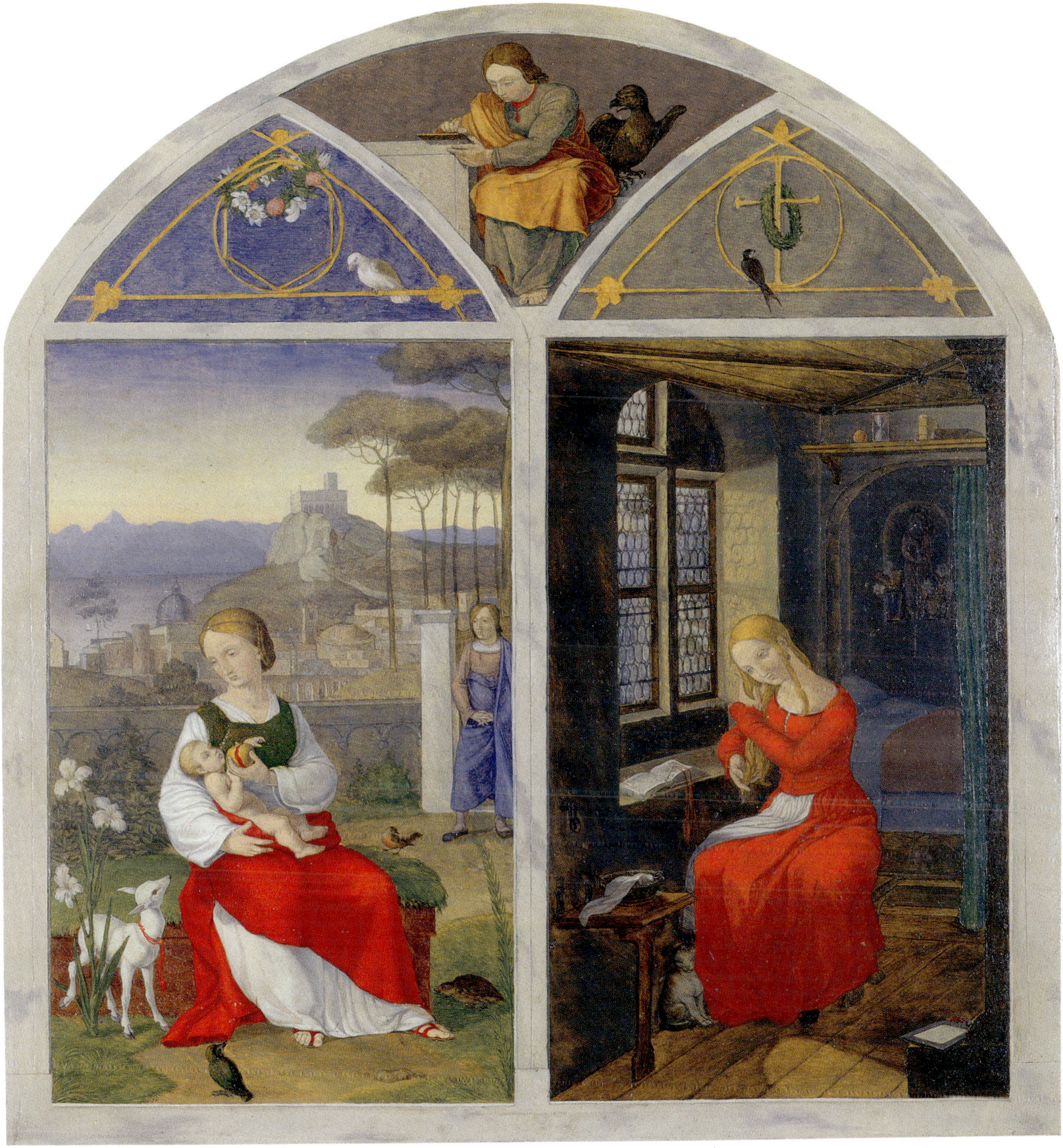

Man Reading at Lamplight

Oil on canvas, 47.5 x 37 cm
Winterthur, Oskar Reinhart Collection

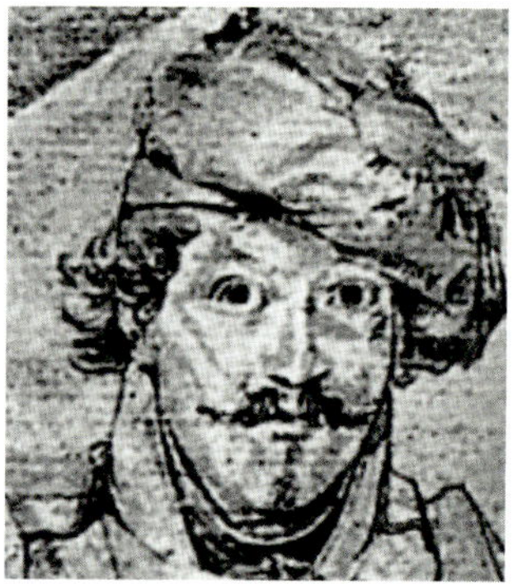

b. 1785 Güstrow
d. 1847 Meißen

Like many German artists of his time, Kersting hailed from a humble lower-middle-class background. After the death of his father, a glazier and glass painter, a well-to-do relative sent Kersting to the Copenhagen Academy, which he attended from 1805 to 1808. He then settled in Dresden, where he was befriended by Gerhard von Kügelgen and Caspar David Friedrich. With the latter, he embarked on a walking tour through Silesia and Bohemia.

Kersting concentrated exclusively on interiors, a genre established in seventeenth-century Netherlandish art. His pictures often show humble, even spartanic working and living quarters, redolent of the concentrated spiritual life led by their inhabitants, who are often occupied with reading. This was Kersting's favorite subject apart from portrayals of his friend, Friedrich, and quite in tune with his unemphatic but delicately colored compositions.

Among Kersting's finest accomplishments were interiors, which, unlike later Biedermeier depictions of domestic comfort and self-sufficiency, captured the mood of individual rooms and the way they reflected the thoughts and feelings of their occupants.

In the present picture *Man Reading at Lamplight*, it is the mental world of reading that determines the overall impression. The concentration of the man immersed in his book is echoed in the spartanic simplicity of the furnishings and the way the bookshelves serve to delimit the room formally. Contemplative thought, which is just as capable of opening up new worlds as an actual journey to exotic lands, has been translated into compositional elements and visual signs. The light cast by the reading lamp on the empty back wall, where it congeals into strange configurations, becomes an outward expression of the inward illumination that, at that period, forged knowledge into a weapon of the educated German middle class against censorship and suppression of freedom of opinion.

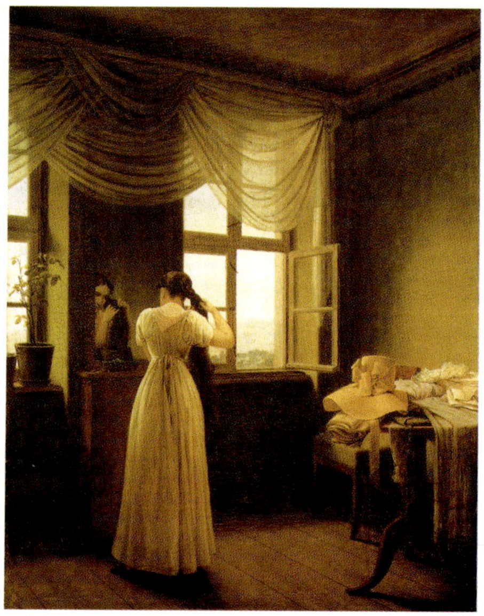

Before the Mirror, 1827

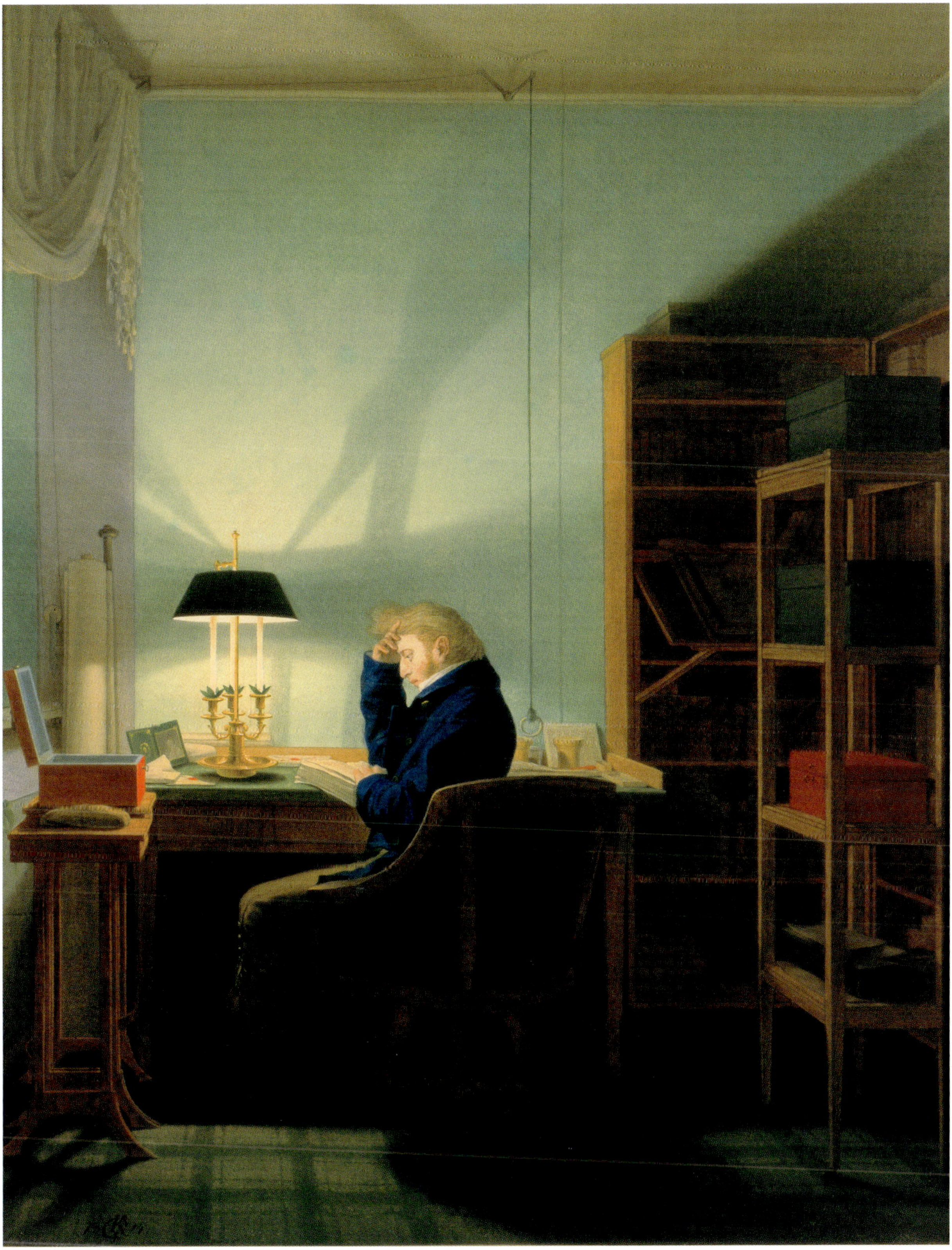

The Execution of the Rebels of 3 May 1808

Oil on canvas, 265 x 345 cm
Madrid, Museo Nacional del Prado

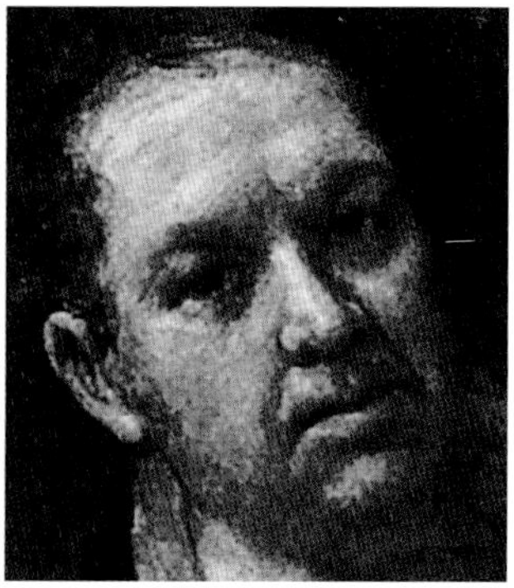

b. 1746 Fuendetodos (near Saragossa); d. 1828 Bordeaux

Goya was trained in Saragossa by José Luzan, a pupil of Giordano and Solimena, before going to Madrid. There, he entered the studio of Francisco Bayeu, his future brother-in-law, who worked under Mengs at the court of Charles III. After visiting Italy in 1770 to 1771, Goya was asked to provide designs for the royal tapestry works. In 1780, he became a member of the Real Academia de San Fernando, which he would subsequently serve as deputy principal and principal. After carrying out court commissions from 1781, he was appointed court painter in 1786, painter to the royal chamber in 1789, and principal court painter in 1799. Goya began in the Spanish version of the Rococo manner, intermingled with French and Italian elements, but in 1792, when a severe illness resulted in permanent deafness, his style changed drastically. In a series of uncommissioned paintings, Goya began, under the mask of ordinary genre scenes, to invoke a world of terror and nightmares (*Funeral of the Sardine, Procession of the Flagellants; The Madhouse; Session of the Inquisition* – all Madrid, Academia de San Fernando). During the same period emerged *Los Caprichos*, a series of eighty etchings published in 1799, intended to "scourge human vices and errors," as Goya wrote. With his "black paintings" of the Quinta del Sordo (Madrid, Museo Nacional del Prado) he reached the pitch of his portrayal of the negative and unaccountable aspects of human existence. Under the pressure of the Restoration, Goya left Spain and emigrated to Bordeaux. His evocations of the deeply dubious side of human nature, also reflected in the portraits, would not find full recognition until the twentieth century.

The Execution of the Rebels of 3 May 1808 is one of Goya's most famous paintings. It represents the shooting of Spanish patriots who had attacked French occupation troops in Madrid on the preceding day. At the right of the large-format composition, the firing squad is depicted as a group of faceless, anoymous figures seen from behind. Standing in a perfectly straight rank, as if welded into a blind machine of destruction, a uniform mass, the soldiers lower their rifles to aim at close range at their victims, who await the fatal salvo. Visible in the middle ground are other condemned men being led to the place of execution. The diagonally sloping mound of earth and the buildings of Madrid with city gate stand out against an oppressively dark night sky. The only visible source of illumination in the picture, the large lantern at the French soldiers' feet, casts a garish light on the figure of a peasant in a white shirt. Together with his raised arms – a gesture of resistance that simultaneously exposes his chest to the bullet – this dramatic lighting makes him the compositional center of interest and meaning. The other rebels, including a trembling monk murmuring a prayer for the dead, are depicted in various stages of despair, from dull submission to sheer terror. In the left foreground, executed men lie in pools of blood.

This red is the only unbroken color in a scene pervaded by subdued tones. Though the gloom reflects the early morning hour at which the executions actually took place, its principal effect is symbolic. Even more frighteningly than in Delacroix's later *Massacre of Chios* (1827/28), this darkness seems to convey the blackest side of human nature. Goya, one of the most significant artists of all time, cannot be strictly classified in terms of style. Still, his œuvre does contain the key elements of that transitional epoch around the year 1800: neoclassicist, realistic, and indeed romantic, as seen in his painterly approach, a predilection for fantastically heightened shock-effects, and a visionary sense of the unreal that always lurks just beneath the real. Yet in terms of the existential power of its statements and its aesthetic qualities, Goya's work far surpasses all of these currents.

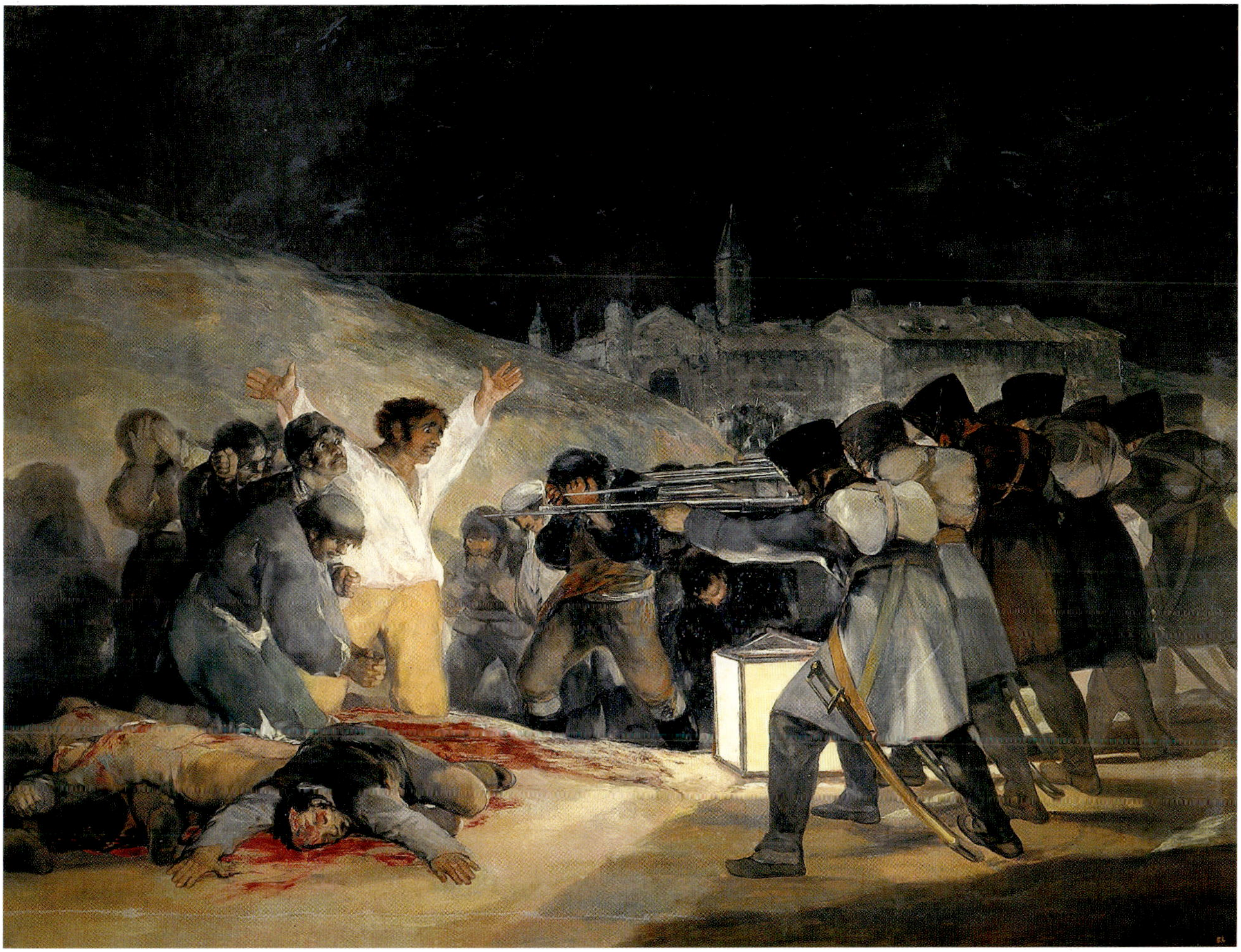

Set Design for "The Magic Flute": Starry Sky for the Queen of the Night

Gouache, 46.3 x 61.6 cm
Berlin, Staatliche Museen zu Berlin – Preussischer Kulturbesitz, Kupferstichkabinett

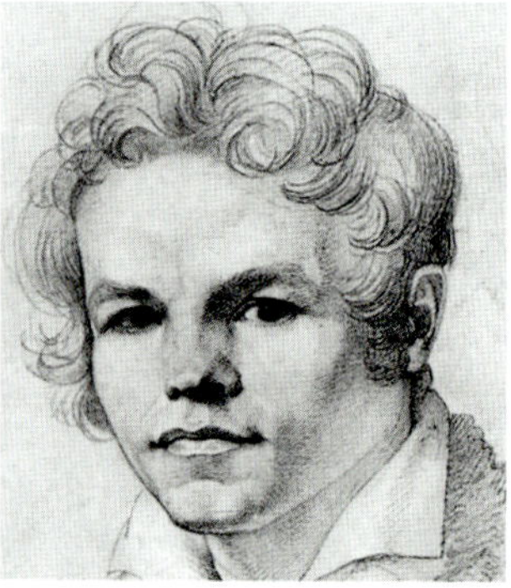

b. 1781 Neuruppin
d. 1841 Berlin

A pupil of the architect Friedrich Gilly and a student at the Bauakademie, or Building Academy, in Berlin, Schinkel developed a neoclassical architectural style that materially shaped the face of Berlin in the first half of the nineteenth century. A journey to Italy in 1803–1805 took him to Rome, Naples, and Sicily. In Rome, he met Wilhelm von Humboldt and the artists Gottlieb Schick and Joseph Anton Koch.

His own landscapes and architectural depictions evinced Schinkel's lasting interest in medieval buildings and romantic scenery, which supplemented his basic neoclassical vocabulary. While serving as chief building supervisor in Berlin from 1815, he made a crucial contribution to the field of maintenance of public and national monuments.

Schinkel is known as one of the most outstanding neoclassical architects of Germany, and indeed of Europe. But at the onset of his career, when the French occupation precluded large building projects, he was active as a painter, inspired especially by Dresden Romanticism and its major proponent, Caspar David Friedrich.

In addition to oils, Schinkel executed a series of set designs for Wolfgang Amadeus Mozart's opera *Die Zauberflöte* (*The Magic Flute*) (1791), in a new performance held at the Royal Opera House, Berlin, on 18 January 1816. In making the designs, Schinkel attempted to put into practice his key idea for theater reform, the demand that word, visual image, and performance form a unity. His stage backdrops, painted on canvas, were unique in the context of contemporaneous set design as regards the monumentality of their architectural or landscape motifs. The premiere in the presence of the king was a dazzling success, not least due to Schinkel's sets.

In his design for the palace of the Queen of the Night, the diminutive female figure standing on a crescent moon is overarched by a brilliant dark blue firmament whose bands of stars create the impression of a cupola or even of a planetarium. It is a profoundly Romantic notion that expands the queen's uncanny nocturnal kingdom into a cosmic, universal symbol and confronts it, in the other designs, with Sarastro's kingdom of light. At the time, the poet E.T. A. Hoffmann praised the scene in a newspaper review as Schinkel's "most sublime and brilliant."

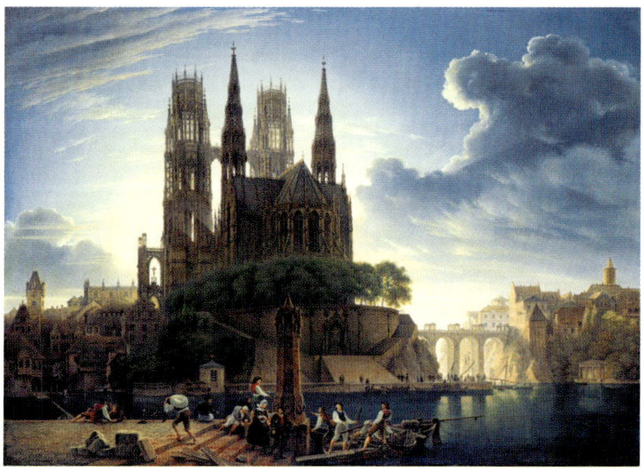

Gothic Cathedral by the Waterside, c. 1813/14

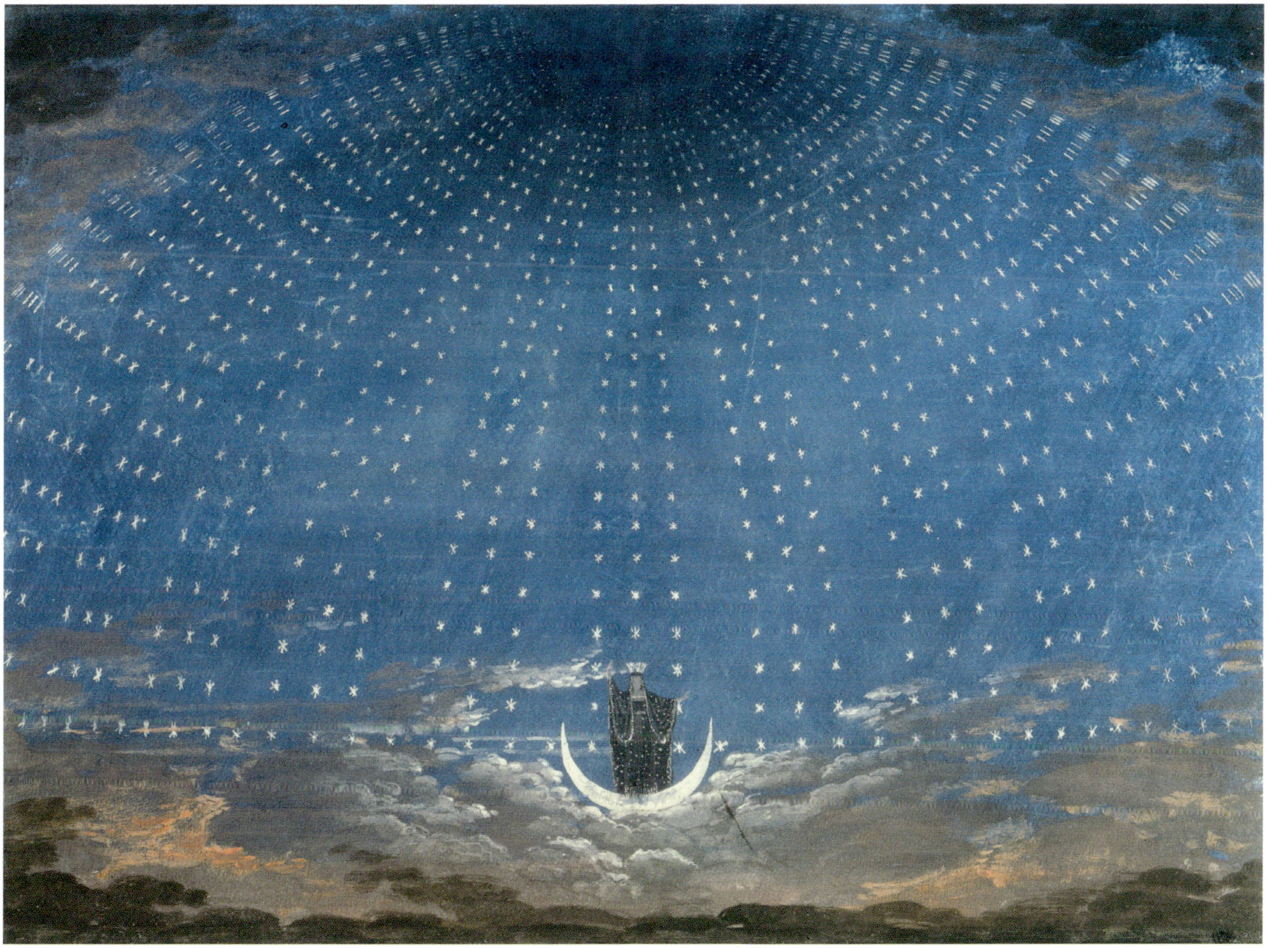

Joseph Reveals himself to his Brothers

Fresco, 236 x 290 cm
Berlin, Staatliche Museen zu Berlin – Preussischer Kulturbesitz, Gemäldegalerie (formerly Palazzo Zuccaro, Rome)

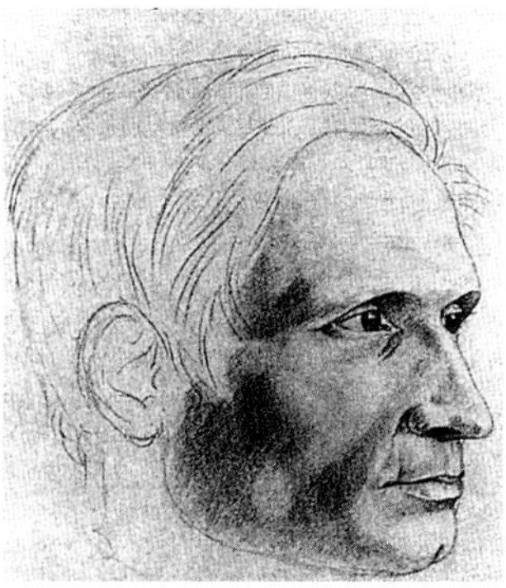

b. 1783 Düsseldorf
d. 1867 Berlin

Peter von Cornelius was one of several nineteenth-century German artists involved in a revival of idealistic fresco painting. In 1811, he joined the Nazarene group in Rome, having already made early German art his model at the encouragement of the Boisserée brothers and Consul Wallraf. In 1816, he painted two frescoes of the Old Testament story of the life of Joseph for the Prussian Consul General Bartholdy at Palazzo Zuccaro. These were so well received that Cornelius was called both to the Düsseldorf and Munich Academies simultaneously in 1819. He accepted both appointments, commuting between these cities, but finally deciding on Munich. Here he was appointed director of the Academy in 1824 and given an opportunity he had not been given in Düsseldorf – to paint large-scale frescoes.

However, after a falling out with King Ludwig I of Bavaria over his murals in the Ludwigskirche in Munich, Cornelius went in 1840 to Berlin, where he made the designs for the planned Campo santo. When these were exhibited in 1859 in Berlin and Düsseldorf, idealist religious art celebrated a late triumph.

In his Roman period, from 1811 to 1819, Cornelius became a member of the artists' brotherhood of the Nazarenes and untiringly propagated its foremost aim: to revive large-scale Christian art, that is, fresco painting, and at the same time to make it the basis of a popular, patriotic art.

The first culmination of Cornelius' work in this regard came with frescoes in the Palazzo Zuccaro and the Casa Bartholdy in Rome, whose subjects were taken from the Old Testament story of Joseph. By comparison to his passionate and ambitious words, the Roman frescoes are surprisingly straightforward. On a relatively narrow proscenium in an open loggia, a frieze-like sequence is devoted to the scene in which Joseph, in the meantime a high dignitary at the Pharaoh's court, reveals himself to his brothers, who had sold him as a boy to Egyptian slave-traders.

"But now I have finally arrived at that, which I hold to be the most forceful and unfailing means to give German art a foundation for a new direction, adequate to the great era and the spirit of the nation: This would be none other than the reintroduction of fresco painting… (it concentrates), as in a focal point, the vital rays flowing out from God into a brilliant flame that benificiently illuminates and warms the world."

Peter von Cornelius

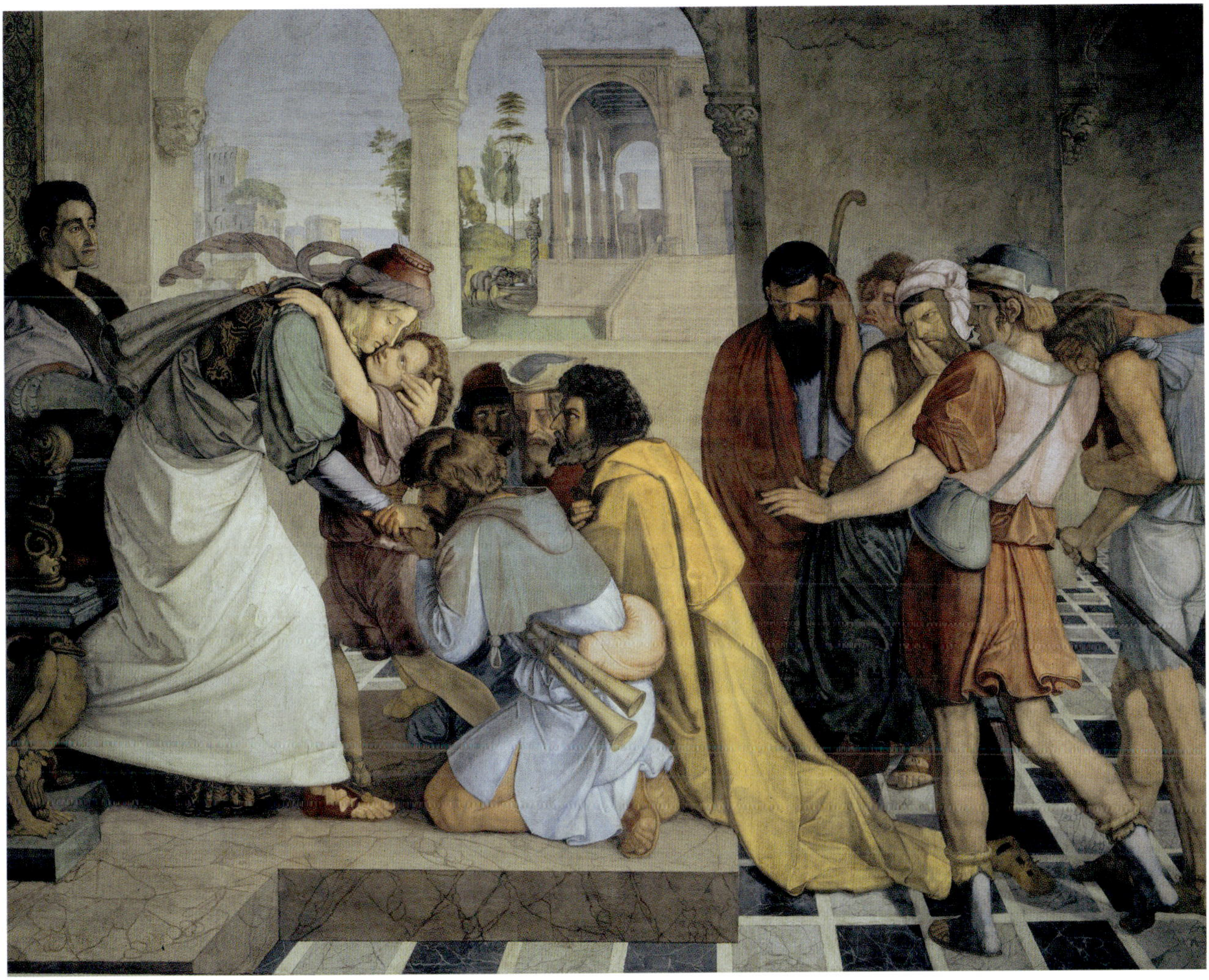

wanderer watching a sea of FOG

Oil on canvas, 98.4 x 74.8 cm
Hamburg, Hamburger Kunsthalle

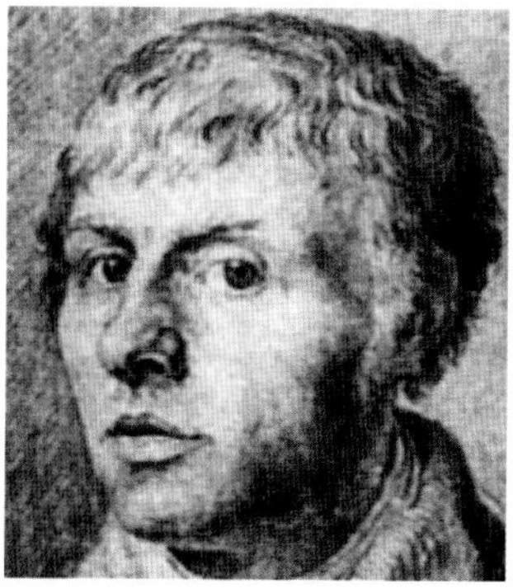

b. 1774 Greifswald
d. 1840 Dresden

Friedrich was the son of a soapmaker and chandler, and studied under Jens Juel at the Copenhagen Academy from 1794 to 1798. That year brought him to Dresden, where he would spend his entire life, interrupted only by journeys to Greifswald, Rügen, Neubrandenburg, the Harz Mountains, and northern Bohemia. In 1816, he became a member of the Dresden Academy, and in 1824 professor extraordinary. Friedrich was the founder of German Romantic landscape painting. His style combined an unprecedented fidelity to reality, based on his travel experiences, with a metaphysical illumination inspired by Christian Neoplatonic ideas.

The origins of his landscape art lay in the eighteenth-century *veduta*, or view. Already in evidence here were the foreground with observer's standpoint, set against an interesting background landscape, in some cases already that type of grand natural scenery which in the nineteenth century would be termed "the sublime" – lonely mountain ranges or ocean vastnesses that, in the sensitive viewer, aroused feelings of religious awe and insight. But Friedrich's pictures have none of the travelogue character found so frequently in eighteenth-century landscapes. His views of nature are externalized embodiments of the mood of the figures in the foreground, "atmospheric landscapes," to use the nineteenth-century term. They are invariably determined by two elements: the observed environmental situation and the attitude of the person or persons observing it, figures usually seen from behind and often magnified in proportion to the scene. Friedrich's contrast of boundless distance with the bounded position of the onlooker in the foreground evokes the two sides of human existence – body and soul, the earthbound and the divine – which from ancient times have comprised the fundamental dichotomy of Christian and Neoplatonist thinking. Friedrich was an intelligent and contemplative artist. His friends included not only painters such as Philipp Otto Runge, Johan Christian Clausen Dahl, Friedrich Kersting, and Gerhard van Kügelgen, but also poets like Ludwig Tieck as well as scientists and philosophers. He was also a fervent patriot, which explains the symbolism in many of his pictures alluding to the German wars of independence against French occupation.

In the foreground, on a dark, craggy, sharply silhouetted outcrop, a wanderer in medieval-style German costume stands with his back to the spectator. He gazes out over clouds of fog rising from the depths and the bare sharp rocks emerging here and there, toward distant peaks and mountain ridges. High above them lies a bank of clouds.

The composition reflects a tendency seen in Friedrich's work after 1816 to create continuous transitions between near and distant spaces, between the finite and the infinite. Also, it perfectly illustrates the principles of the Sublime as formulated, for instance, by the English poet, Lord Byron, who once asked whether mountains, hills and clouds were not part of himself and his soul, just as he was a part of them. The figure seen from behind was probably intended as a patriotic memorial to a man killed in the war. Yet he also stands proxy for the spectator and leads the eye over the distant fog banks, which here evoke the cyclical processes of nature. In this way, precisely rendered natural phenomena become objects of religious meditation.

"Art is infinite, finite all artists' knowledge and ability."

Caspar David Friedrich

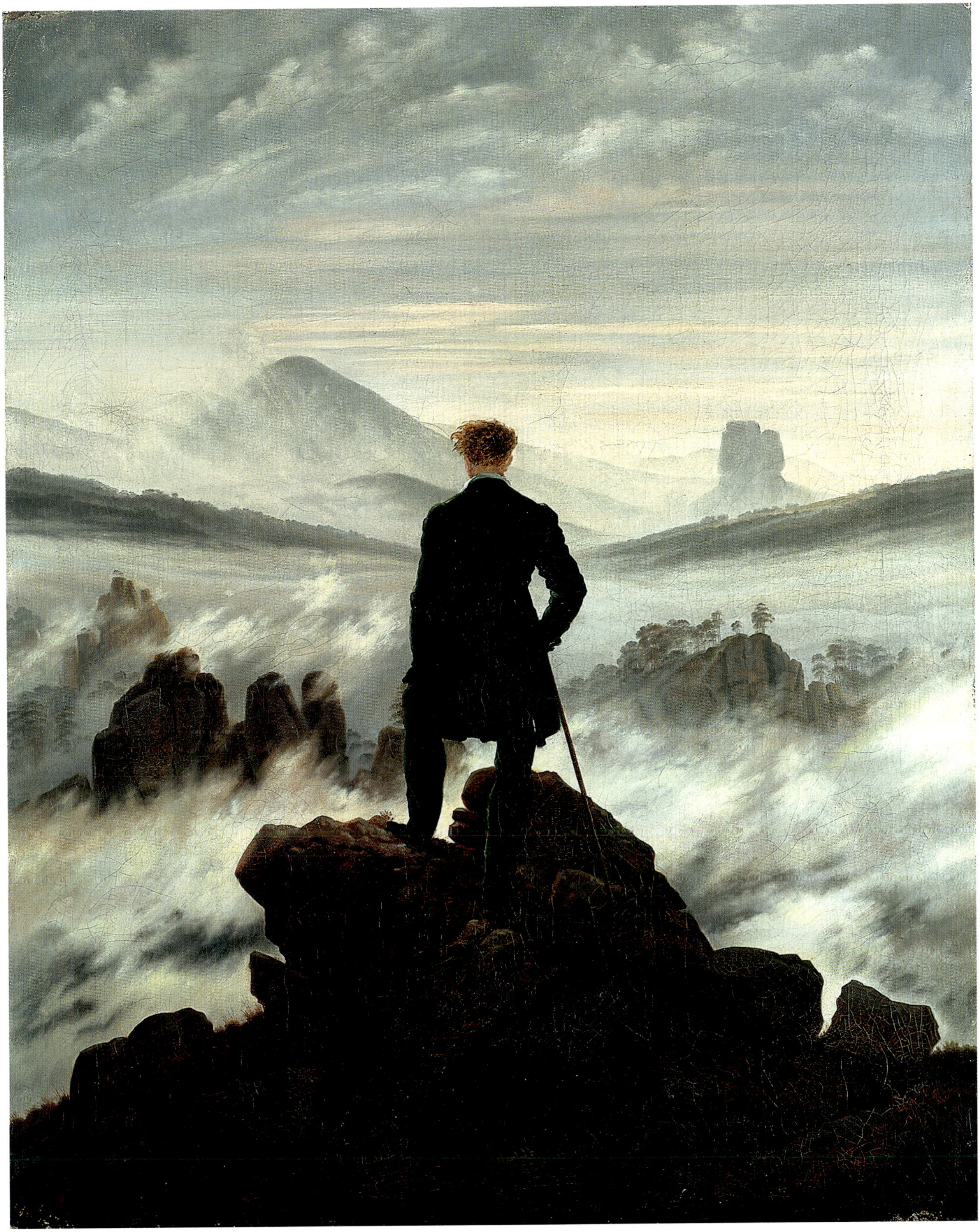

Ideal Landscape near Rocca Canterana

Oil on canvas, 98 x 135 cm
Eichenzell (near Fulda), Museum Schloss Fasanerie

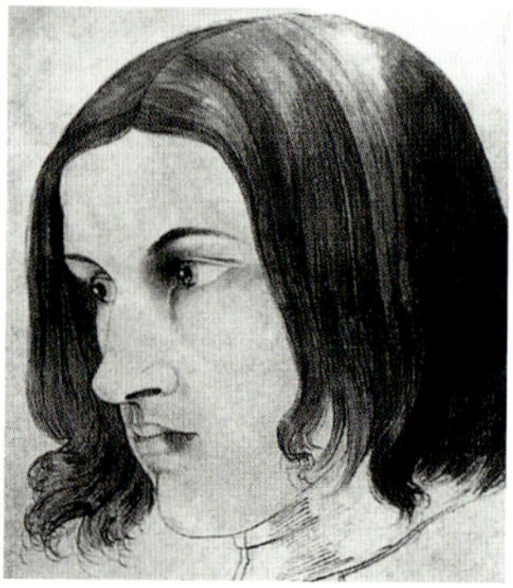

b. 1795 Heidelberg
d. 1818 Rome

Fohr trained first with the genre and *veduta* painter Carl Rottmann and, from 1810, with Georg Wilhelm Issel in Darmstadt, then attended the Munich Academy. In 1815, a walking tour took him by way of Tyrol to Verona and Venice. After a brief return to his home town, he went back to Italy, where, in 1816, he joined the group around his friend Joseph Anton Koch and the Romantics in Rome. The young artist's medieval-style German frock coat, worn as a sign of patriotism, was reputedly the talk of the town. In addition to many portrait studies of his artist colleagues, Fohr devoted himself largely to Romantic landscapes. He drowned in 1818 while swimming in the Tiber.

The *Ideal Landscape near Rocca Canterana* of the year 1818 is one of Fohr's best-known paintings. To a greater extent than many other Nazarenes, Fohr turned to the tradition, cultivated since the eighteenth century, of a stylized depiction of nature derived from the classical ideal. The composition shows a rocky pastoral landscape in the central mountains of Italy. In the foreground, a path winds past craggy rocks and old, gnarled trees. Walking along it is a festively clad country girl with a child in her arms, holding the hand of another child balancing a jug on her head. To the right, under the trees, a group of pilgrims passes into a defile, in the direction of a distant, illuminated valley. Ahead of the girl, two shepherds follow the path into the picture, where a peaceful, hilly region rimmed by steep mountains opens out.

This painting stands in the tradition of the Arcadian landscape, which emerged in the Renaissance and inspired countless variations on the theme of a paradise on earth – a paradise that, in this case, due to the presence of pilgrims, also makes allusion to the Christian Heaven. By depicting the various stages of walking and wandering, Fohr evokes the transience of all earthly things and the journey into the future, which is the true goal of human existence.

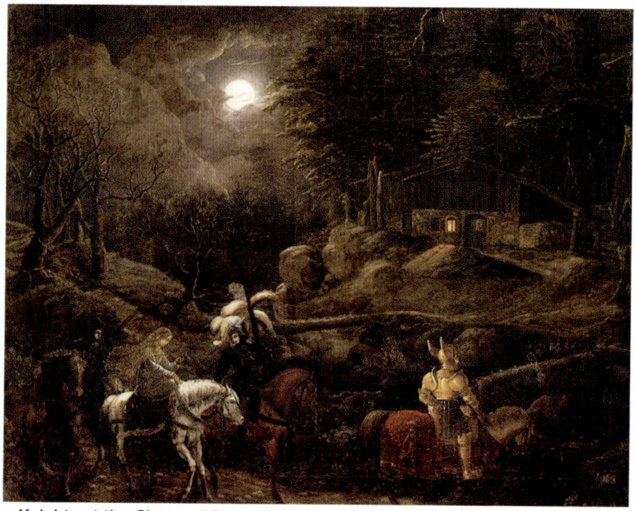

Knights at the Charcoal Burner's Hut, 1816

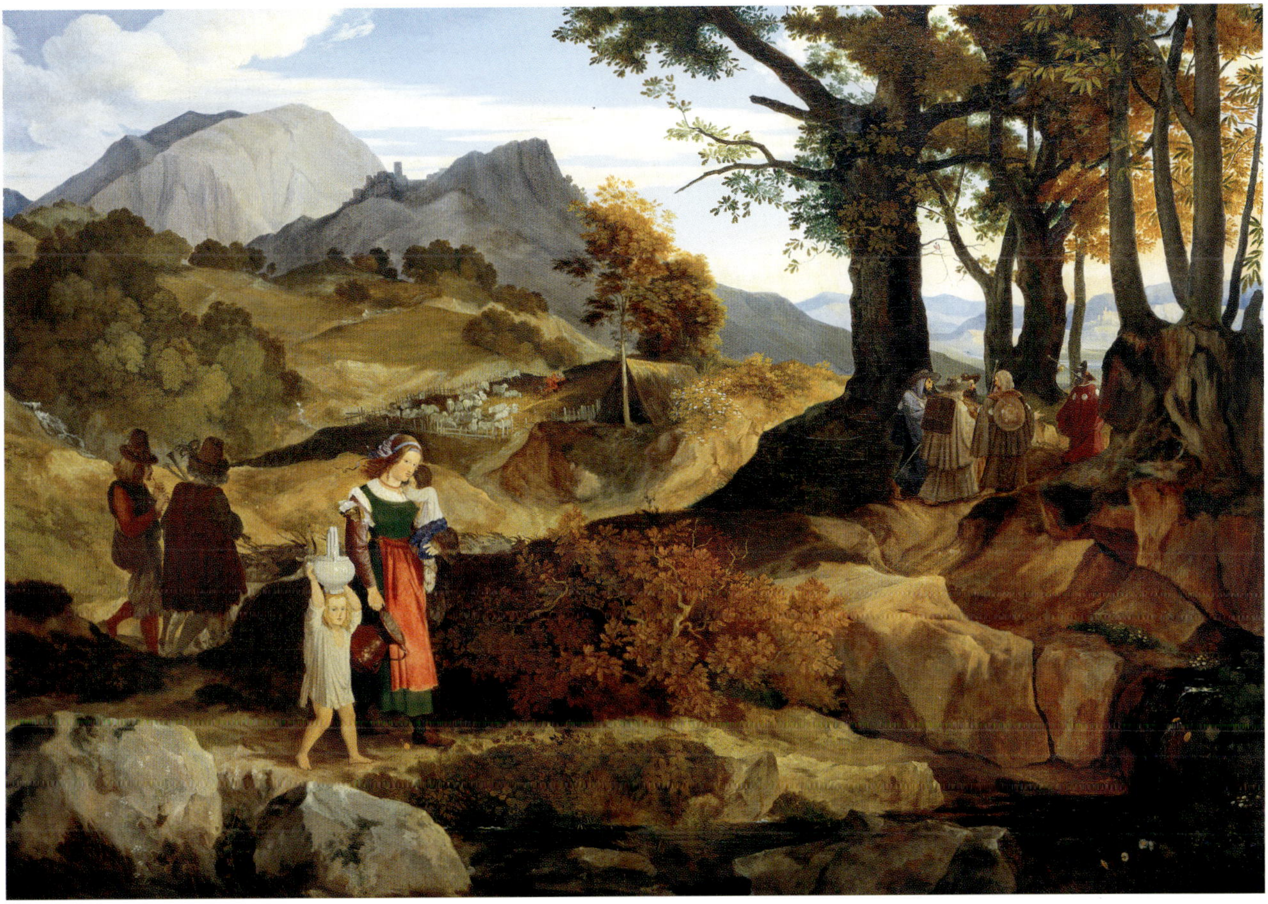

The Raft of the Medusa

Oil on canvas, 491 x 716 cm
Paris, Musée National du Louvre

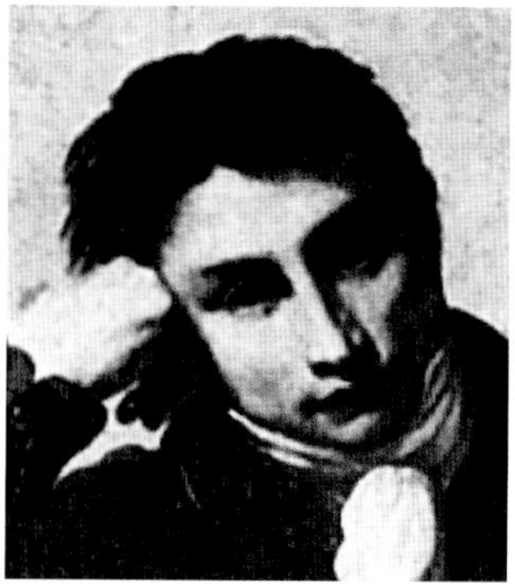

b. 1791 Rouen
d. 1824 Paris

Géricault's extensive œuvre came into being during a period of creative activity lasting only twelve years. His love of horses and riding was reflected in great numbers of sketches and paintings on the subject whose vividness and realism remain unsurpassed. It was one of these equestrian pictures that established his fame, *Charging Light Cavalry Officer*, which in 1812 became the first of his works to be exhibited at the Salon. The passionate, impetuous treatment of the theme amounted to a renunciation of neoclassicism and heralded the onset of the Romantic era. With *The Epsom Derby*, painted just a few years before his death, Géricault paved the way for Impressionism. Géricault entered the studio of the equestrian artist and battle painter Carle Vernet in 1808, then in 1810 went to Guérin, only to find his neoclassicism stifling. The crucial impetus came from an immersion in Greco-Roman art and the masters of the sixteenth and seventeenth centuries. While in Italy in 1816/17, he was particularly impressed by Michelangelo. In England, where he lived from 1820 to 1822, Constable became important, as did Wilkie and Hogarth. Still, the unprecedented realism of his portraits and pictures of animals was founded on an intensive study of life. At the age of only thirty-three, Géricault died in great pain, of injuries incurred in a riding accident.

Géricault exhibited *The Raft of the Medusa* at the Salon of 1819. The monumental canvas enraged most of those who saw it, despite the fact that the perfect modeling of the figures and the strong *chiaroscuro* must have been familiar to the public from neoclassical art. Nor were dramatic depictions of shipwrecks with survivors drifting helplessly in lifeboats anything particularly innovative at the time. What caused the audience's anger was the artist's presumption in using a huge format without, as academic rules demanded, depicting anything classical, heroic, or edifying. Nor was his treatment of the subject sufficiently idealized and thus non-committal. Depictions of disasters were supposed to evoke a universal human fate, not become too concrete or personal, not get under one's skin.

Géricault, in contrast, turned with shock and shame to an actual event that involved human error on the part of the French navy. On 2 June 1816, the frigate *Medusa* had sunk off the West African coast. The crew had left 150 passengers to their fate on a raft. They drifted for thirteen days, in the course of which horrifying scenes of madness, death, murder, and cannibalism took place. When the raft was finally sighted, only fifteen survivors remained, five of whom died after the rescue. The affair was suppressed in official echelons. Then, in the autumn of 1817, a report by the survivors was published, which caused waves of revulsion and was immediately confiscated.

With an artist's obstinacy Géricault launched into an attempt to transform this governmentally, tabooed scandal into a composition that far surpassed reportage or genre to evoke human behavior under extreme conditions and sum it up in an existential parable. With the pyramid of men and women clinging to the raft, whose figures were in many cases based on Michelangelo, at its peak a black man waving a cloth to attract the attention of the distant rescuers, the arrangement of figures is lent a solidity that stands in stark contrast to the chaos of the surrounding waves. The prominence Géricault gives to a black figure here may be linked with the efforts to abolish slavery that had been underway since the latter half of the eighteenth century.

When he went to London in 1810, Gérucault had *The Raft of the Medusa* shipped after him, and it attracted great throngs in the English capital. It had less success the following year in Dublin, where a sensational panorama picture, a kind of early precursor of the cinema, devoted to the sinking of the *Medusa* was concurrently on display. A new medium had begun to challenge the reign of painting.

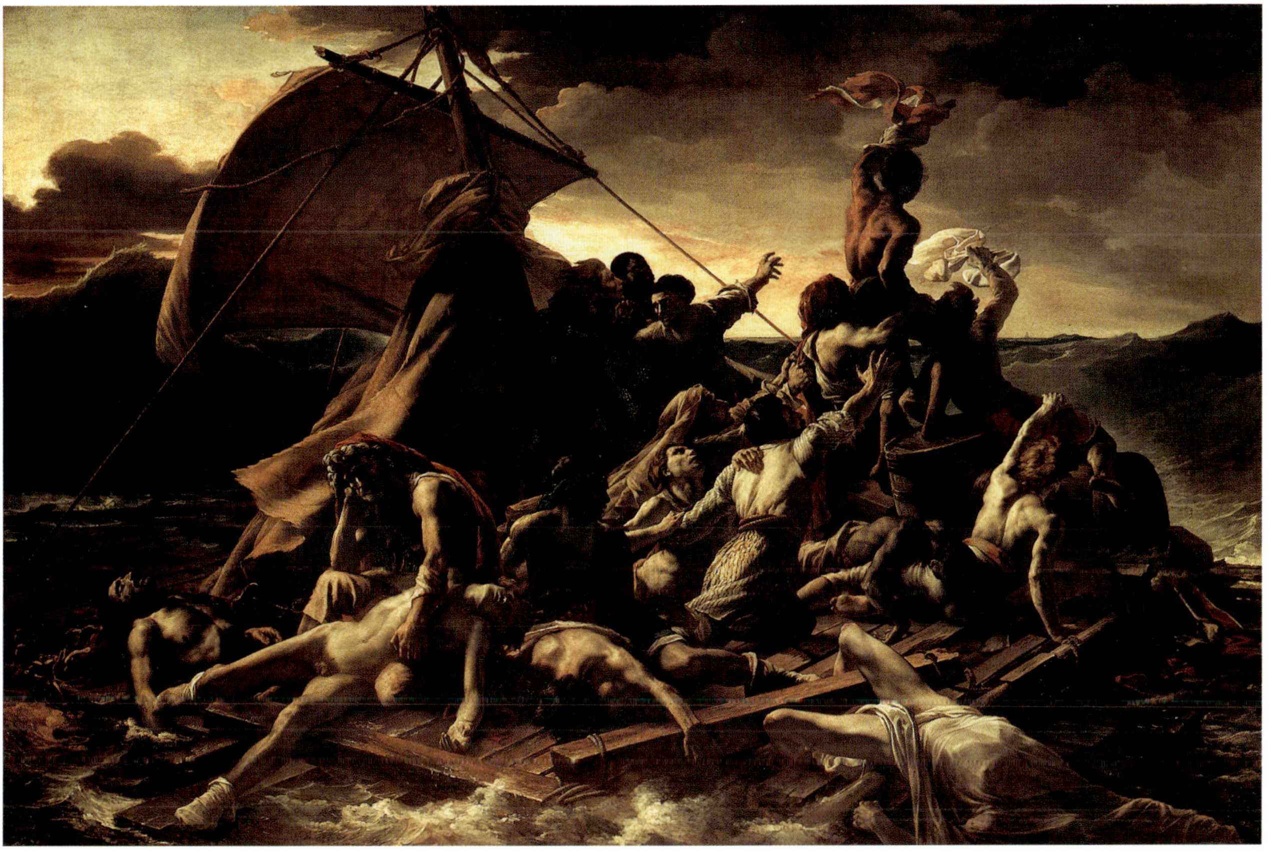

Dante and Vergil in Hell (The Barque of Dante)

Oil on canvas, 189 x 246 cm
Paris, Musée du Louvre

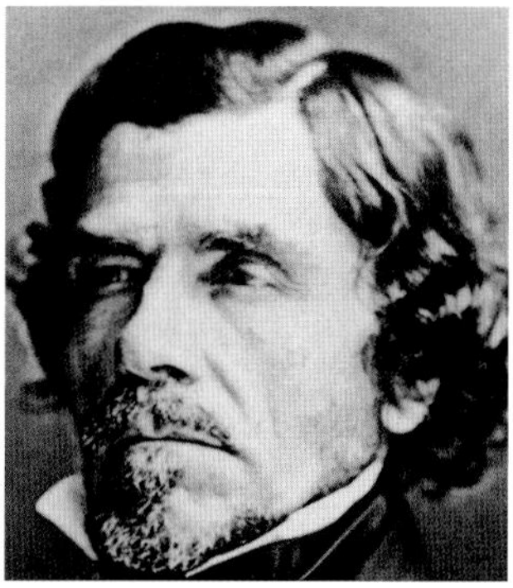

b. 1798 Saint-Maurice-Charenton (near Paris); d. 1863 Paris

After studying music, Delacroix first received instruction in painting at the studio of Pierre-Narcisse Guérin in Paris. In 1816, he entered the École des Beaux-Arts, where he met Théodore Géricault, his junior by seven years, whose work he greatly admired. He was also impressed by Goya's drawings and the paintings of Veronese and Rubens. Delacroix's first major work, *Dante and Virgil in Hell* or *The Barque of Dante*, excited much attention at the Salon in 1822. Two years later, his *Massacre of Chios* led to still greater recognition. Having seen John Constable's pictures at the Salon, Delacroix reworked this painting and added highlights a few days before the exhibition opening. The discovery of Constable, and his friendship with Richard Parkes Bonington, prompted Delacroix to visit London in 1825. Back in Paris, Delacroix found himself acclaimed as the leader of Romantic painting in France, and became the target of criticism on the part of the Classical school, above all Ingres. Delacroix's subject matter was drawn from literary sources, such as Dante, Shakespeare, and Goethe, but also from such Romantic works as the novels of Walter Scott and the poetry of Byron. In 1832, he traveled to Morocco as a member of an ambassadorial mission to the sultan, and also visited Algiers, Oran, Tangiers, and southern Spain. From 1834, he was engaged in large-scale decorative works, including those in the Salon du Roi in the Palais Bourbon (1833–1837), the library in the Palais du Luxembourg (1845–1847), and the church of St. Sulpice (1861). In 1857, he finally became a member of the academy after seven years of candidature. Mounting criticism caused Delacroix to retire into seclusion towards the end of his life, and he died in complete isolation in 1863.

With his first major work, *The Barque of Dante*, 1822, Delacroix introduced a number of innovations in content and painting technique that were to determine his work from that point on. When he presented the painting in the Paris Salon, it was with the hope that the powerful figures, their expression of profound mental torment, and the superb and sumptuous palette would make a deep public impression. Immediately after the Salon *The Barque of Dante* was acquired by the French state for 1,000 francs and taken to the Musée de Luxembourg, at that time the Paris museum of contemporary art. The large format, according to academic conventions, promised a work of history painting, and the subject was in fact taken from Dante's *Divine Comedy*. In her autobiographical novel *Corinna*, which Delacroix admired, Madame de Staël had praised Dante as "a latter-day Homer" gifted with a bizarre and visionary imagination, and described him as a predecessor of the modern, alienated artist. The poet, in a greenish-white cloak with red hood, stands to the left in the boat on the way to Hell. On the fifth level, where the choleric and morose do penance, Dante must cross the muddy underworld river Styx in order to reach Dis, the infernal city. The sight of fellow Florentines wallowing in the bottomless pit triggers a feeling of profound shock and empathy. As if seeking support, Dante extends his left arm to the central figure, the ancient Roman poet Virgil, his guide on the journey through Purgatory and Inferno. Clad in a brown cloak and crowned with laurel, Virgil exudes calm and composure. The boat is steered by the ferryman Phlegias, whose muscular back and blue cloak fluttering in the storm, like the tense, twisted bodies of the damned, one of whom clings by his teeth to the boat at the far left, are redolent of sheer creaturely struggle and existential despair. As if in a spotlight, light-dark contrasts play over the figures and throw their contours into sharp relief. In terms of composition, Delacroix attempts to do justice to traditions, as indicated by his study of Michelangelo, Rubens, and – his most recent model – Géricault's *The Raft of the Medusa* (ill. p. 55), while at the same time introducing daring innovations, particularly as regards the painterly style and the impasto, sketchy paint application.

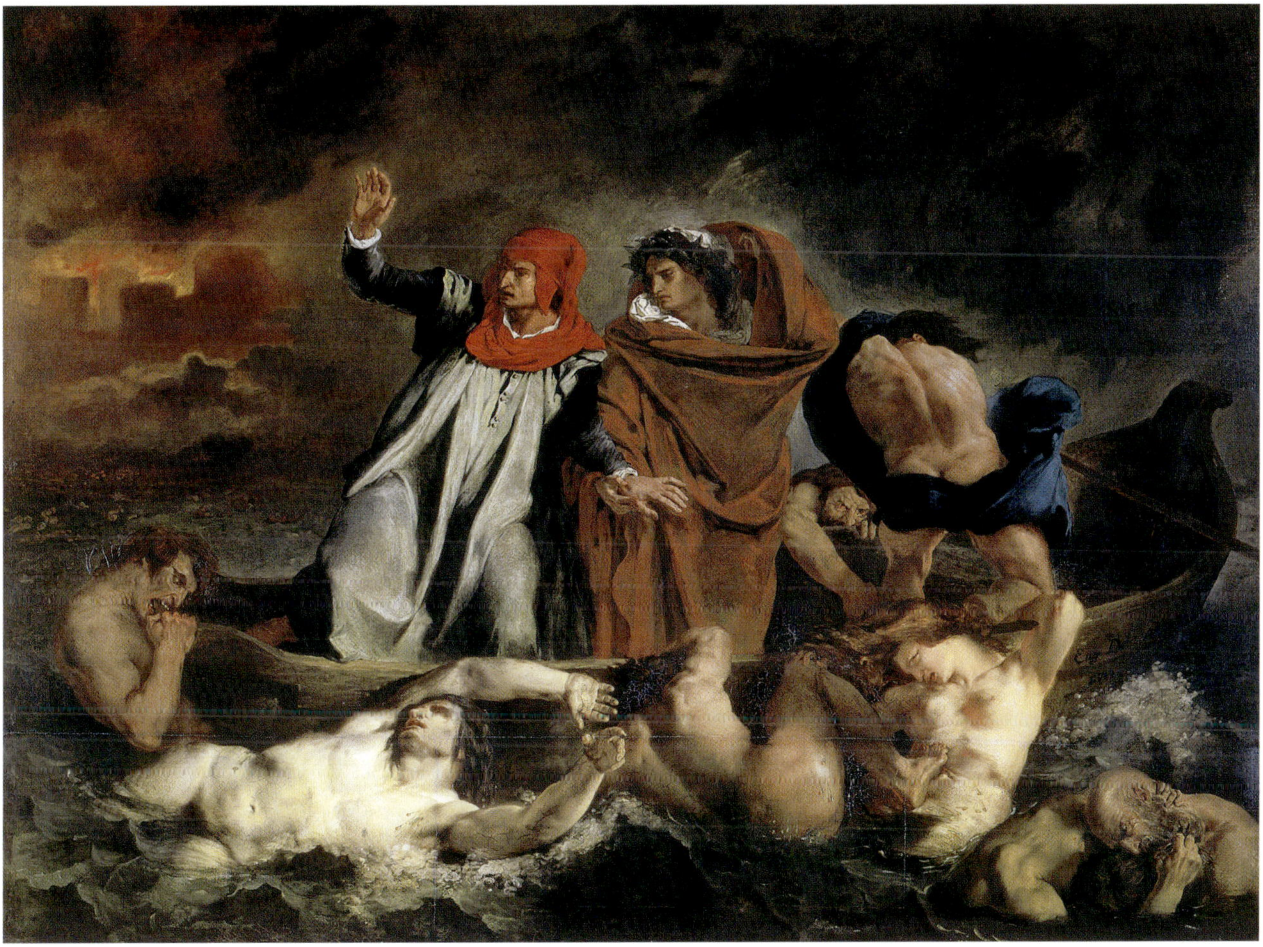

Eruption of the vesuvius

Oil on canvas, 93 x 138 cm
Oslo, Nasjonalgalleriet

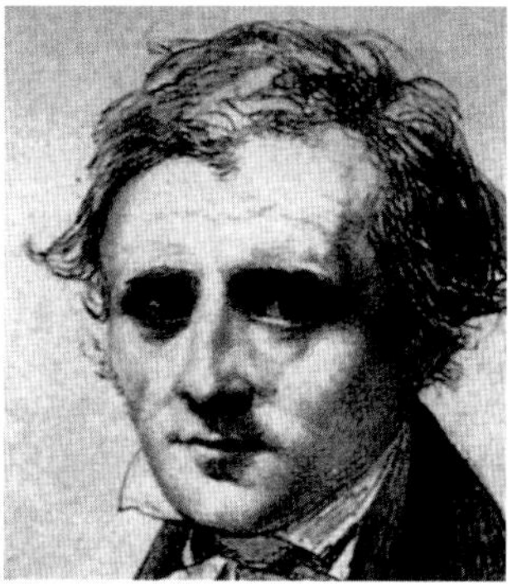

b. 1788 Bergen
d. 1857 Dresden

After working as a decorative painter in his home town of Bergen, Norway, Dahl studied landscape painting at the Copenhagen Academy from 1811 to 1818. Here he was impressed by the work of Jens Juel and Christoffer Wilhelm Eckersberg, but the crucial influence came with a study of the seventeenth-century Dutch masters of landscape. One of them, Allaert Everdingen, had visited Norway and subsequently developed a type of "Nordic landscape" based on his impressions. This style was later taken up by the Norwegian national movement in the nineteenth century. Alongside the "Italian landscape," the "Nordic landscape" also became established on the Continent early in the century.

Stimulated by his first extensive travels through Norway in 1826, Dahl supplemented his previous range of motifs – waterfalls, moving clouds, and windswept trees – with depictions of the bare plateaus of the high mountain regions and their cloud formations, becoming an innovator in Norwegian as well as German landscape painting. In 1818, he settled at Dresden, where he associated with Caspar David Friedrich and Carl Gustav Carus. In 1824, like Friedrich, he was appointed professor at the Dresden Academy. Dresden and its environs began to feature frequently in his compositions, in which the sky often occupied the larger part of the canvas. During a journey to Italy in 1820–1821 he found subject matter for a third range of themes.

In 1820, Dahl made an Italian journey. Staying only briefly in Rome, where the weight of tradition oppressed him, he concentrated on Naples, where the natural scene revealed itself to him in all its multifarity of form and abundance of light. Dahl became completely engrossed in a study of color nuances and effects of illumination. He had little contact with the German artists working in Italy, meeting frequently only Franz Catel, who may have introduced him to Turner's watercolor landscapes, which were exhibited in Rome in 1819.

Dahl looked upon the fresh, spontaneous studies he made in the environs of Naples solely as preliminary works for subsequent oils. When Mt. Vesuvius erupted in December 1820, he was among the first to climb the volcano in order to see and depict the phenomenon at first hand. The Oslo painting goes back to this experience. Already in the eighteenth century, depictions of Vesuvius erupting were among the most popular subjects of pictorial reportage, intended not only to satisfy a public thirst for sensations but to embody the aesthetic ideals of the sublime and the picturesque.

As motif, Dahl chose one of the flowing streams of lava and the emerging windblown flames and smoke clouds. The tiny figures of people observing the natural spectacle stand on the edge of the crater, white at the right, before a panorama of sea and bright sky, a herd of cattle indifferently grazes. As the subject and approach indicate, Dahl did not seek stylized arcadias in the South but viewed the overwhelming forces of nature as picturesquely suspenseful and captured them as elemental experiences in paint. It is as if, like a second creator of the world, he had attempted to participate with his art in the generative forces of nature.

Dahl was certainly not a sober, scientific painter of the kind Carus had envisioned in his late letters on landscape painting. For that, his painterly attack was too expressive and too suffused with atmospheric elements, too filled with pathos. On the other hand, his compositions were not the result of mere sentimental moods.

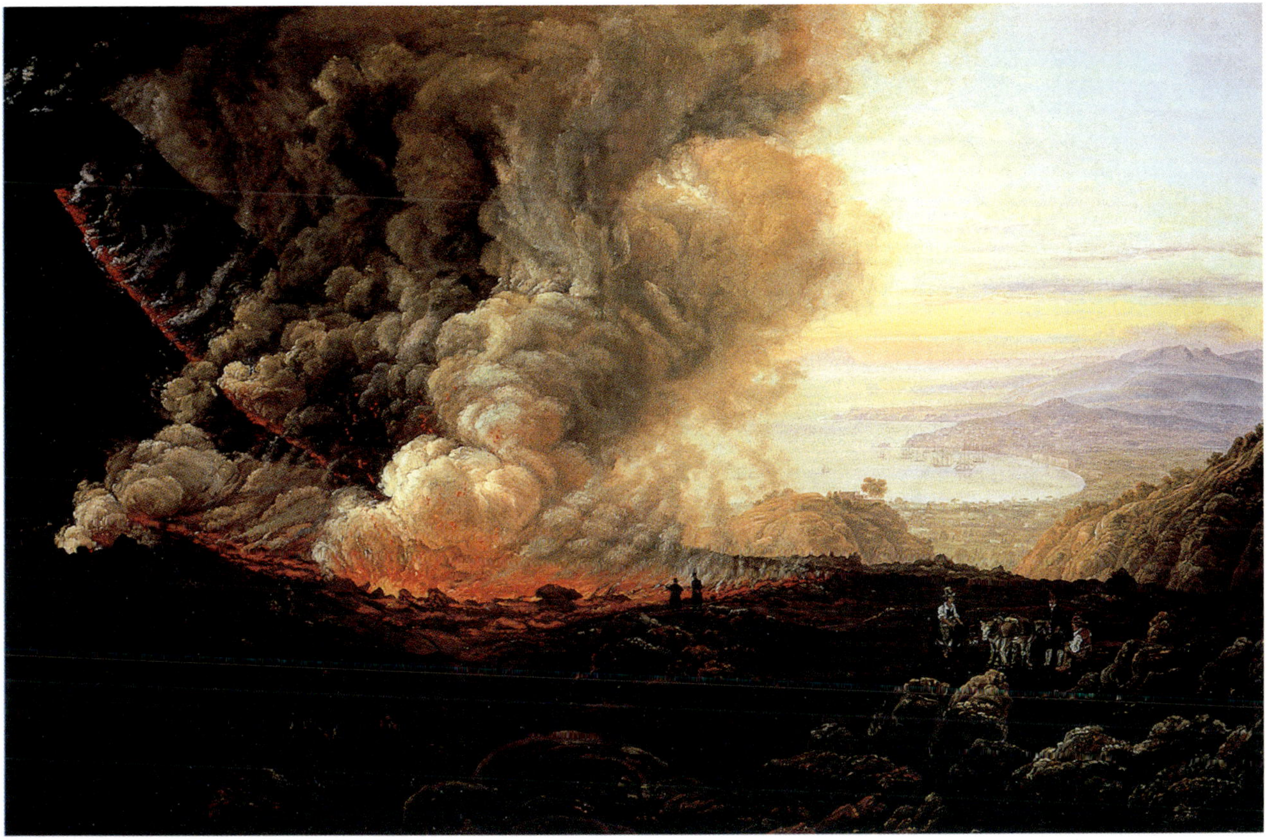

JOHN CONSTABLE 1823

salisbury cathedral, from the Bishop's Grounds

Oil on canvas, 87.6 x 111.8 cm
London, Victoria and Albert Museum, Given by John Sheepshanks, 1857

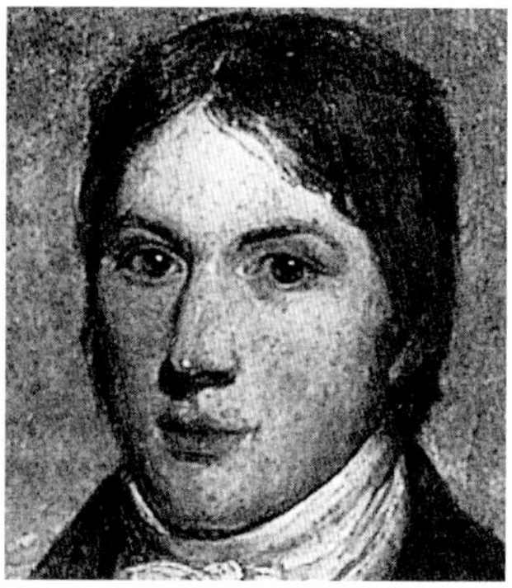

b. 1776 East Bergholt (Suffolk)
d. 1837 London

Constable was the son of a prosperous mill-owner in Suffolk, a county whose scenery became central to his work. Though he took painting lessons in Suffolk, he was largely self-taught. In 1795, he went to London and he entered the Royal Academy schools in 1799. As a student he copied Old Master landscapes, especially those of Jacob van Ruisdael.

Though deeply impressed by the work of Claude Lorrain and the watercolors of Thomas Girtin, Constable believed the actual study of nature was more important than any artistic model. He refused to "learn the truth second-hand." To a greater degree than any other artist before him, Constable based his paintings on precisely drawn sketches made directly from nature. His early work also included portraits and some religious pictures, but from 1820 onwards he devoted himself almost exclusively to landscape painting. His subjects were found in the parts of England that he knew best, mainly Suffolk and Essex, and also Brighton.

Constable inimitably captured the light-and-shade effects of clouded skies and the various moods of landscape. After 1820/21 and a concentration on a series of cloud studies, "wind and weather" and the changing illumination they produced began to determine his landscapes as never before. The fact that his oil sketches were mostly of the same size as the finished picture, if not larger, suggests that Constable considered his studies full-blown works, containing everything that mattered. Yet, despite growing public recognition, the critics never tired of pointing out the sketchy, unfinished character of his works. In 1824, a great exhibition of his paintings in Paris was an instant success, crowned by a gold medal from the Salon. Constable's art became an enduring influence on French painting. In 1829, he was named a member of the Royal Academy.

Constable did this painting on commission from his friend, the Bishop of Salisbury, who also stipulated the point of view and framing of the scene. The Anglican dignitary is depicted with his wife in the left foreground, out for a stroll and pointing to the cathedral.

"My cathedral looks very fine," wrote Constable, then adding that it was the most difficult landscape he had ever had to execute. The view of the Gothic structure with its soaring steeple and stone walls, seemingly dissolved into lacy patterns by the glowing sunlight, is artfully framed by the arching trees. As with the German Romantics of this period, the house of God seems to function here as a symbol of national history and a sign of a harmonious universal order.

A Romantic effect of sorts is produced solely by the rural site, for unlike Gothic churches on the Continent, surrounded by a confusion of urban buildings, those in England were erected in parklike settings, which inevitably carried connotations of the mood of landscape gardens. Yet, by comparison to the works of Caspar David Friedrich, the overall, painterly impression of Constable's canvas is much more objective and oriented to this world rather than to the next. This is underscored by the bishop's reaction to the picture. If only Constable had left out the black clouds, he exclaimed. Clouds were black when it begins to rain. In fine weather the clouds were white, the bishop wrote, and returned the canvas to the artist for reworking.

"There is nothing ugly; I never saw an ugly thing in my life: for let the form of an object be what it may, – light, shade, and perpective will always make it beautiful."

John Constable

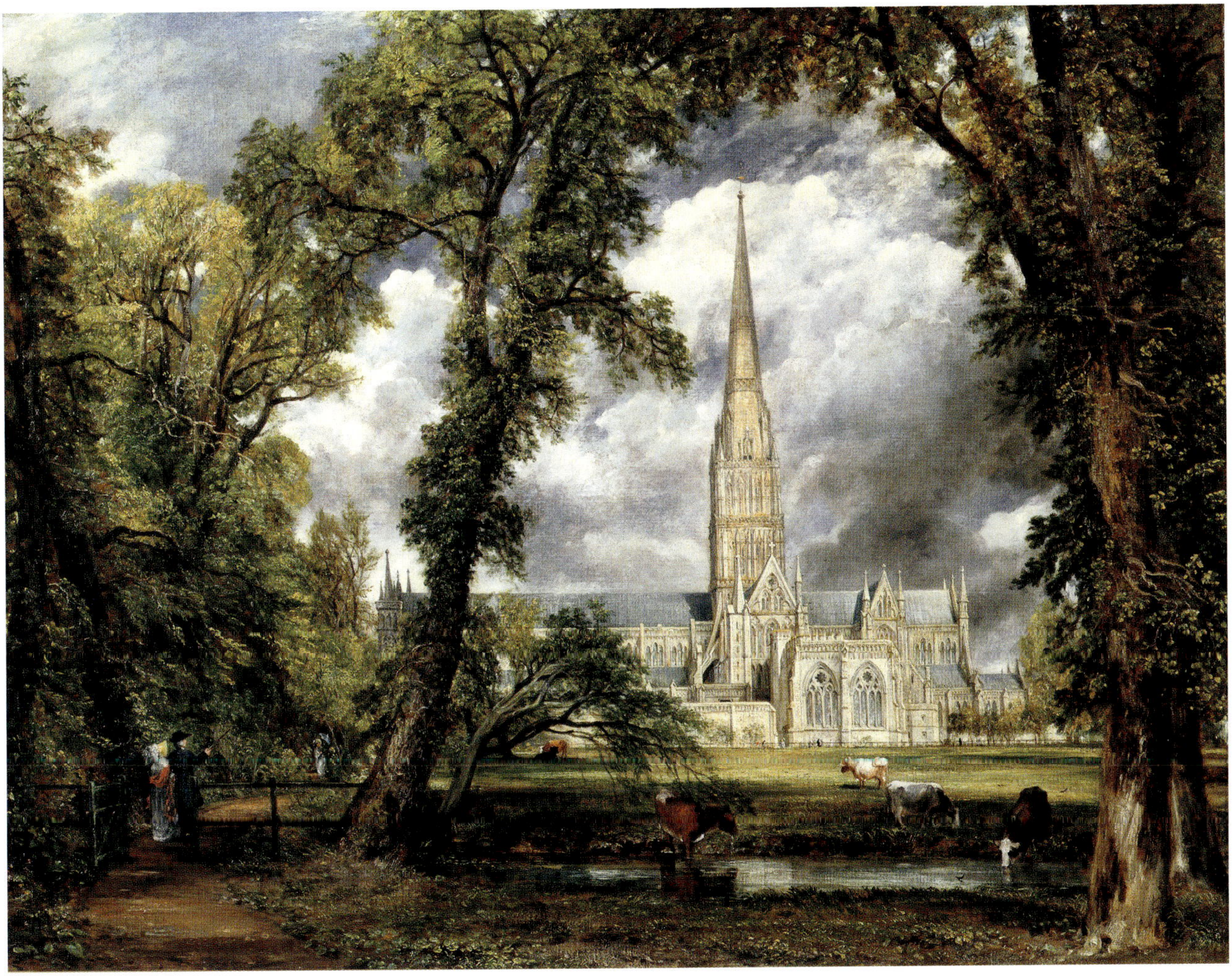

view of the Eibsee

Oil on canvas, 76 x 99.5 cm
Munich, Bayerische Staatsgemäldesammlungen, Neue Pinakothek

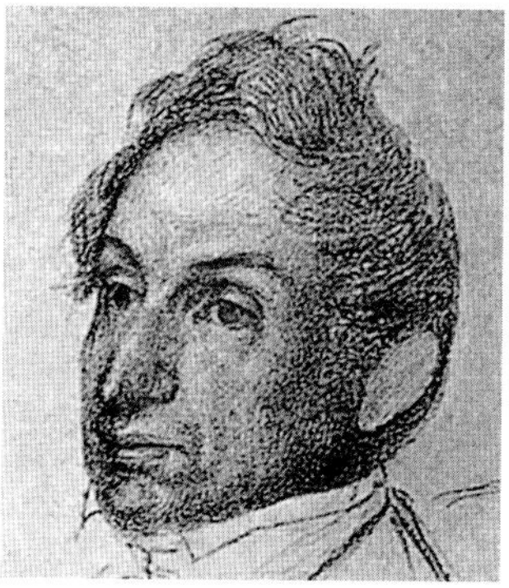

b. 1797 Handschuhsheim (near Heidelberg); d. 1850 Munich

Rottmann came from a family of artists, which brought him into contact with other Heidelberg painters early on. In 1821, he began courses in history painting at the Munich Academy, and went on excursions in the Bavarian mountains to do nature studies. Sojourns in Italy, in 1826–1828, and again in 1829, introduced him to the Roman manner of open-air painting. A key event for his development was his meeting the Bavarian crown prince, the future King Ludwig I, who lived in Rome. Ludwig commissioned Rottmann to paint the Italian Cycle in the Munich Hofgarten Arcades (1830–1833), a series of frescoes depicting Italian landscapes, which would remain a favorite subject.

Another major work was the Greek Cycle, based on studies made during a visit to Greece in 1834–1835 and destined for the Neue Pinakothek in Munich. These were done in encaustic (a technique employing heated wax colors that fused after application), and Rottmann worked on them until his death. In these landscapes, the architectonic structure of rigorous, classical composition is combined with a dramatic treatment of color, expressed through light and other natural phenomena.

When Carl Rottmann came from Heidelberg to Munich in 1811, he saw Joseph Anton Koch's *Heroic Landscape with Rainbow* (ill. p. 12) and *Schmadribach Falls* (1821/22; Munich, Neue Pinakothek). It turned out to be a crucial experience. Beginning from such models, Rottmann developed a unique landscape style that made him one of the major German landscapists of the nineteenth century.

Intimations of this are already seen in his painting of the Eibsee. By means of sweeping horizontals, Rottmann evokes the majesty and sublimity of the mountains, emphasizing them all the more by contrast with the tiny figure on the outcrop in the left foreground. Otherwise the scene shows no trace of human presence or habitation. Water, rocks, and sky speak with their own voice, underscoring their wild, primeval character.

For all his precise observation of detail, Rottmann never loses himself in details but retains an eye for comprehensive form. In order to heighten the effect of the landscape almost to the point of pathos, he eschews topographic exactitude to include in the panorama view peaks that could never be seen simultaneously from a single vantage point – even adding a gigantic Mont Blanc that outsoars the Zugspitze. The result is a monumental background composition rising in pyramidal form, which appears detached from the remainder of the landscape by the intense, virtually supernatural illumination. The composition is given a solid visual base by the shadowy terrain sloping up from the lake.

The rocky outcrop in the foreground with the two figures marks the farthest point to which we as viewers can imaginatively enter the composition. The distant mountains, in contrast, are accessible only to the eye or to the flight of a bird – and perhaps only to one of the hikers depicted.

Rottmann set great store by this painting, and, as he instructed in a letter from Italy in 1816, definitely wished it to be shown at the Great Munich Art Exhibition, held only once every three years. This never came to pass, for reasons that remain unexplained.

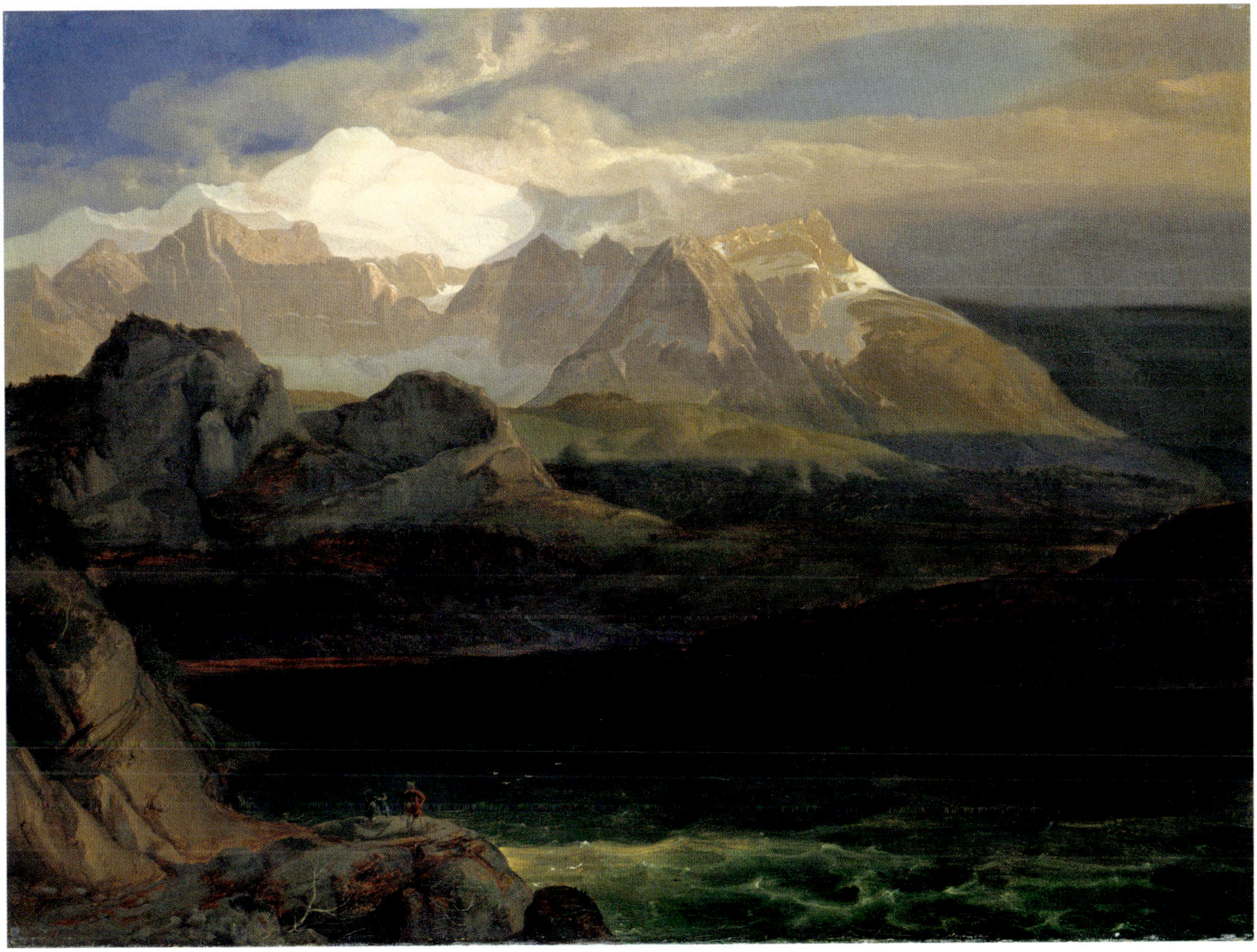

Mazeppa

Oil on canvas, 32.5 x 40.5 cm
Bremen, Kunsthalle Bremen

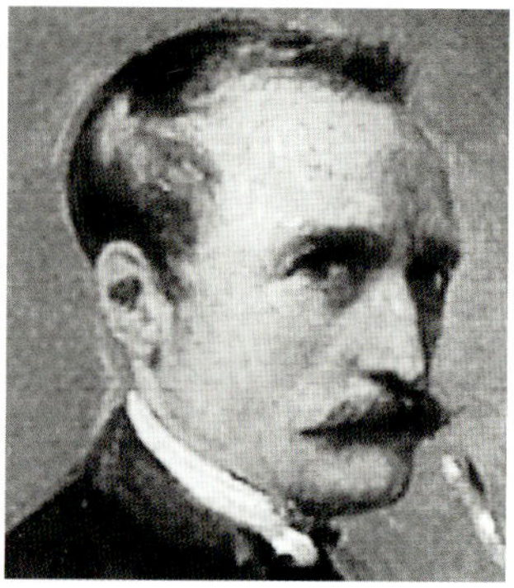

b. 1789 Paris
d. 1863 Paris

Horace Vernet was instructed in art by his father Carle, son of the renowned landscape and marine painter Claude-Joseph Vernet, and also studied with his maternal grandfather, Jean Michel Moreau, and with François André Vincent. After an Italian journey in 1820, he became an instructor of history painting in 1826 at the Académie des Beaux-Arts in Paris. From 1829 to 1835, he served as director of the French Academy in Rome.

In the years after 1830, he enjoyed the favor of the new Paris regime and became the most popular artist in France. In this phase, there emerged military and battle paintings – which brought him wide public acclaim under Louis Philippe, but which many critics rejected due to their hollow pathos – as well as portraits, oriental genre scenes, and satirical drawings. His illustrations to *Histoire de Napoléon* by Laurent l'Ardèches, published in 1839, became the model for Franz Kugler's *Geschichte Friedrichs des Grossen* of 1840, illustrated by Adolph Menzel.

His oil study *Mazeppa* of 1826, done in advance of the large painting in the Musée Calvet in Avignon, was based on a theme from Lord Byron's verse epic of the same name, which was translated into French soon after its publication in 1819. The story relates how Mazeppa, a Cossack chief, made illicit advances to the daughter of a Polish prince. As punishment, he was tied naked to the back of a wild horse, which galloped off with him. Exhausted to the point of death, he was finally saved by a Cossack girl.

Mazeppa not only represents a man whose animal instincts caused him to be subjected to an animal fate; he also embodies the outcast and pariah who is condemned by society. In this regard, Mazeppa could figure as a romantic symbol of artistic self-reliance and determination.

Théodore Géricault, Eugène Delacroix, and other painters treated the subject and in the year 1829 Victor Hugo wrote a poem on Mazeppa (*Les Orientales*, XXXIV), in which he interpreted the swift horse as the genius of the martyred man and merged the two into a single character.

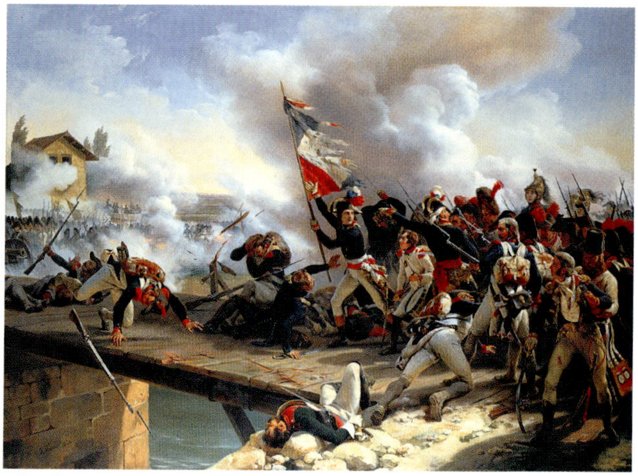

The Battle at the Bridge of Arcole, 1826

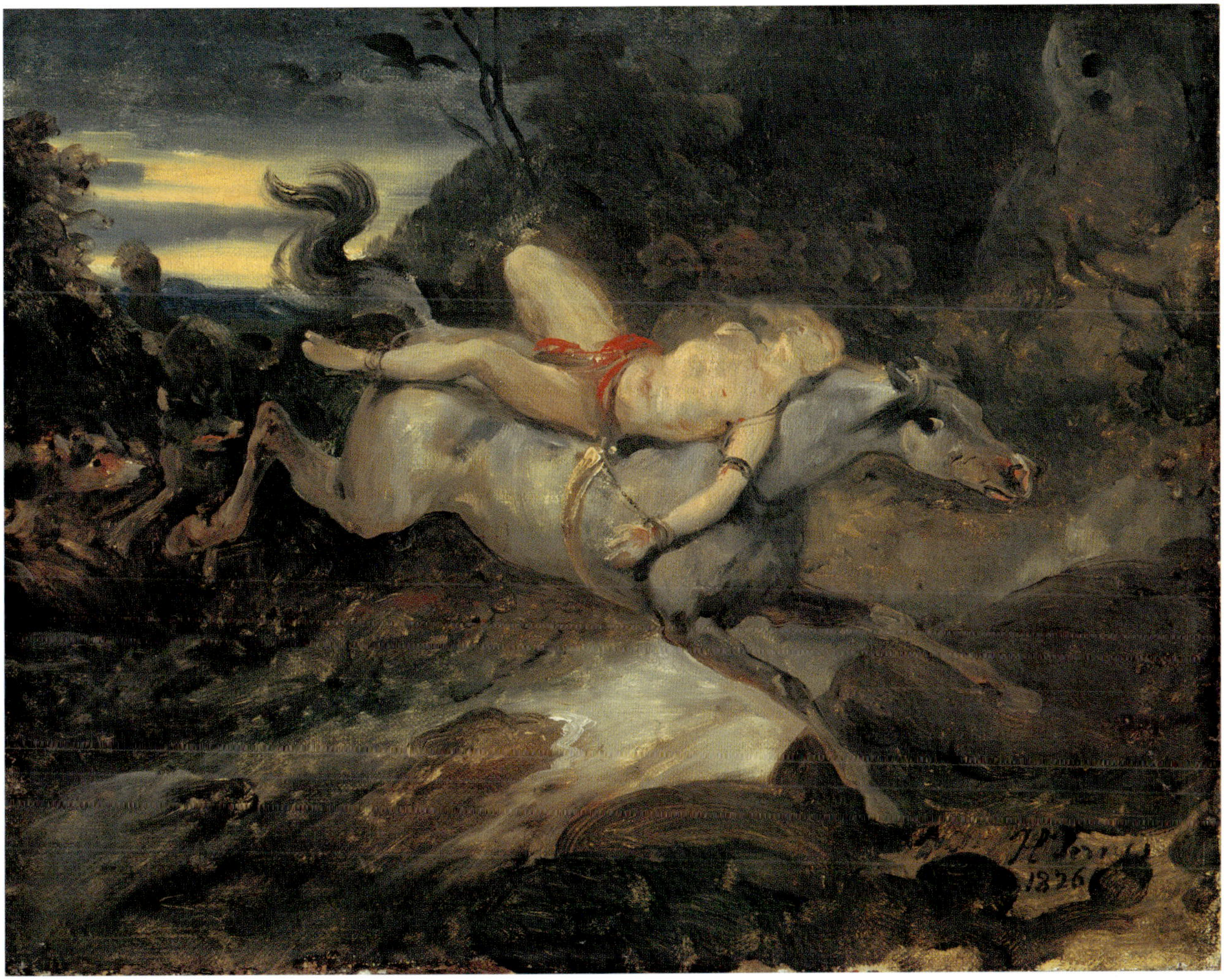

Italia and Germania (Shulamit and Mary)

Oil on canvas, 94.4 x 104.7 cm
Munich, Bayerische Staatsgemäldesammlungen, Neue Pinakothek

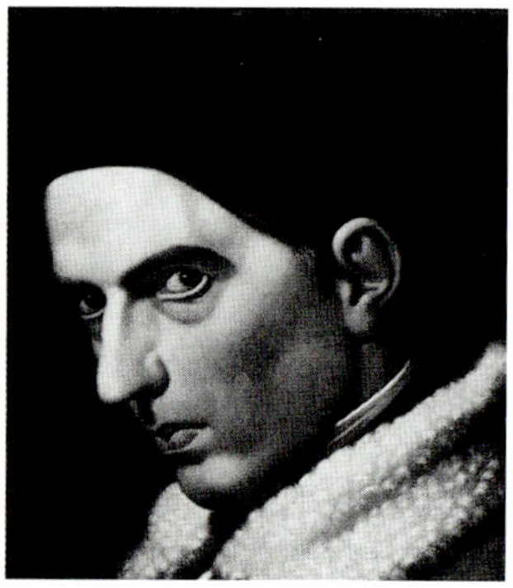

b. 1789 Lübeck
d. 1869 Rome

Overbeck, from an upper-class Lübeck family, is generally regarded as the founder of German Romantic art. Thanks to a study of Italian and German late medieval and Renaissance painting, he became disenchanted with instruction at the Vienna Academy, where he had enrolled in 1806.

In 1809, he and his like-minded friend, Franz Pforr, founded the "Lukasbund," or St. Luke's Brotherhood (named after the patron saint of painters), the first modern association of artists. Their goal was to revive the religious basis of art and the honest craftsmanship of the Middle Ages. The Protestant members of the group, including Overbeck, converted to Catholicism. Before the year was out, the young artists severed connections with the academy and went to Rome, where they found refuge at the monastery of S. Isidoro.

Their long hair prompted the Italians to make fun of them as "Nazarenes," a nickname that soon came to describe the movement they initiated. The group's first commission came from Prussian Consul General Bartholdy in Rome, to decorate the Palazzo Zuccaro with frescoes on the theme of the Old Testament story of Joseph. Decoration of the Casino Massimo with scenes from the Liberation of Jerusalem by Torquato Tasso was the next project, completed in 1827 Subsequently, the group dispersed, and Overbeck was the only one to remain in Rome.

This painting was begun in 1811 as a companion piece to Pforr's *Shulamit and Mary* (ill. p. 41), and remained unfinished after Pforr's death in 1812. Sixteen years later, Overbeck addressed the theme again, giving it a new emphasis of content and a new title. Now called *Italia and Germania*, the picture referred to a key point in the Nazarene agenda: an attempt to harmoniously unify features of Italian and German painting of the late Middle Ages and Renaissance, up to Raphael. Shulamit, on the left, appears as a dark-haired, laurel-wreathed Italian woman, idealized to a type that conformed to an ideal of feminine beauty harbored not only by German artists in Rome. Mary, on the right, embodies the Nordic, "Gretchen" type, with braids and a myrtle wreath in her blonde hair. Behind Shulamit extends the corresponding Italian ideal landscape, and behind Mary, the narrow lanes of a German town. The two women, facing each other with an expression of intimate trust, possess an inner monumentality that was completely lacking in Pforr's companion picture.

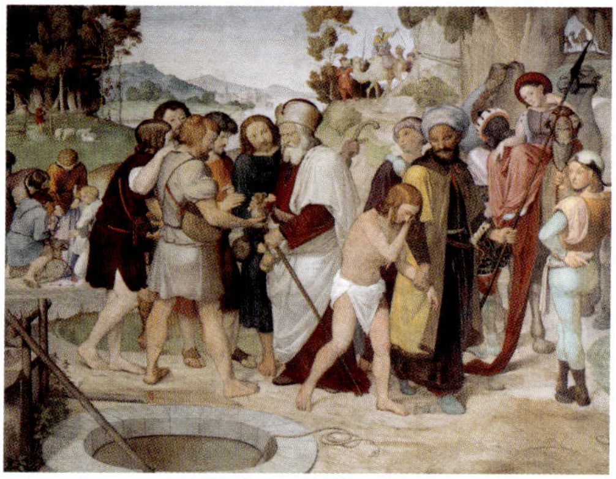

Joseph sold by his Brothers, 1817

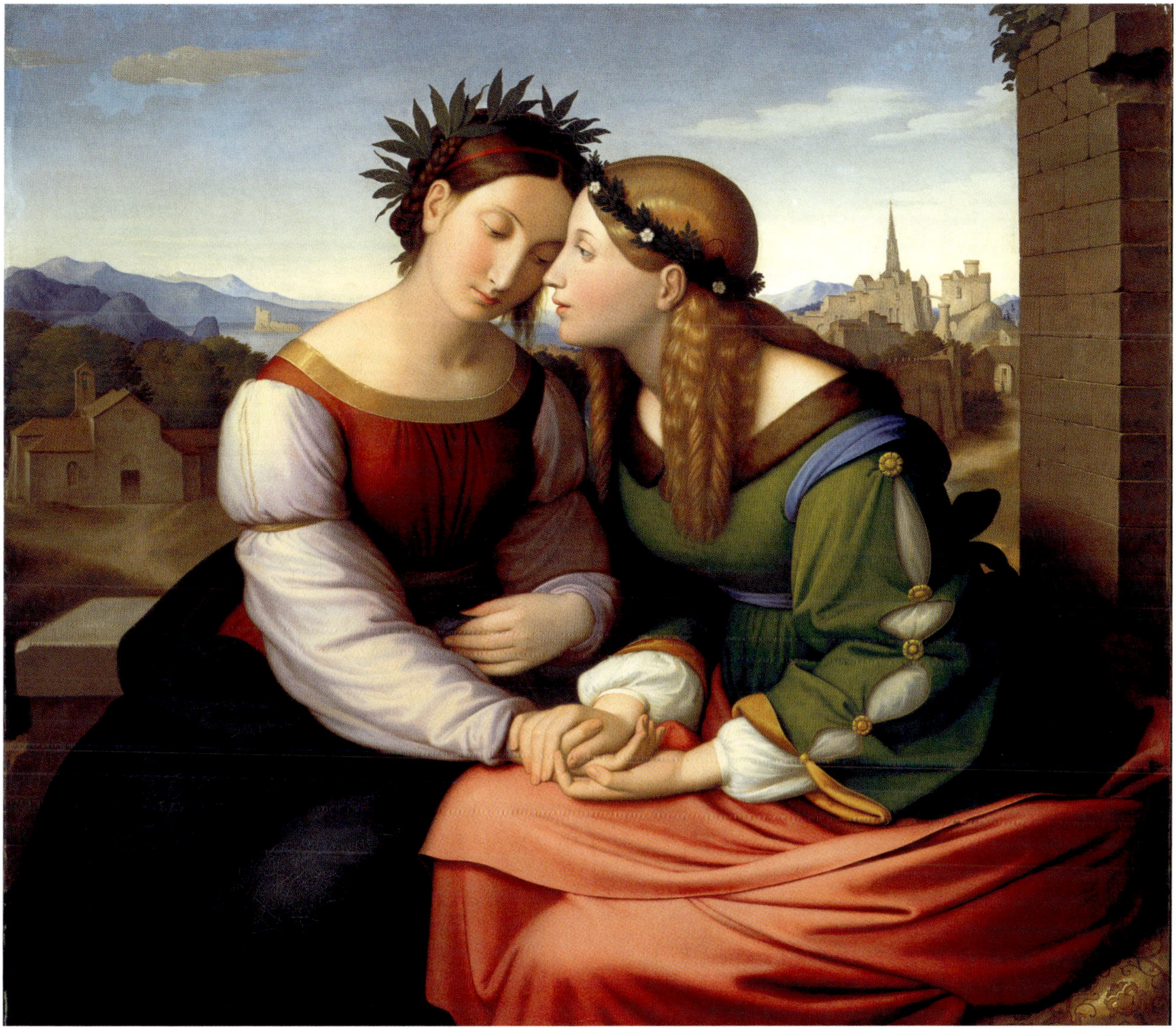

scene from the Apocalypse

Oil on canvas, 61 x 77 cm
New York, Collection Mr. and Mrs. Robert Rosenblum

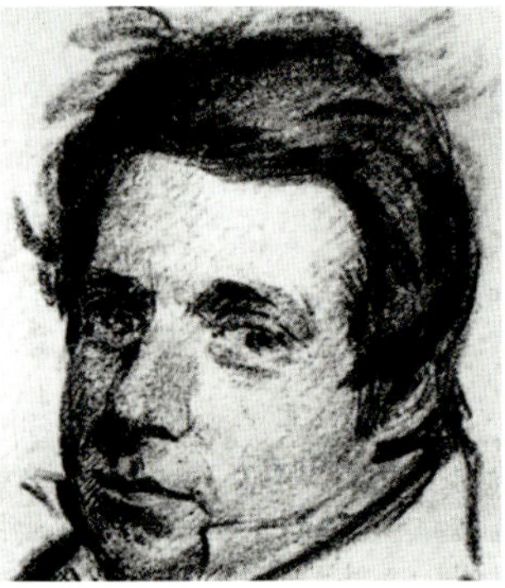

b. 1793 Killinick, County Wexford, Ireland
d. 1861 Exmouth, Devonshire

After attending the drawing school of the Royal Dublin Society and spending a brief period in London, Danby settled around 1813 for two decades in Bristol, in whose environs he painted the small, exquisite landscapes on which his fame today largely rests. In 1824, he moved to London, intending to challenge the reputation John Martin had achieved with large-format panoramas that sensationalistically appealed to the romance of horror and dread. William Turner and Richard Wilson now began to exert a profound influence on Danby's style. In 1825 he traveled to Norway, then in 1828 to Holland and Belgium. Forced to leave England in 1829 due to financial problems and a marital scandal, Danby established himself in Paris and Geneva, where he remained until 1840. Danby's oils, ink drawings, and watercolors, focussing on lyrically romantic landscapes, represents one of the most significant contributions made by any artist to nineteenth-century British landscape painting. He also concerned himself with religious themes, treated in a visionary manner.

The present painting is presumably one of four depicting scenes from the Apocalypse, which were ordered by the millionaire collector William Beckford as companion pieces to Danby's large-format work *The Opening of the Sixth Seal* (1828; Dublin, National Gallery of Ireland).

In a Romantic nocturnal landscape evoking the infinity of the cosmos appears a vision of the giant angel described in Chapter 10 of the Apocalypse, descending in a cloud from heaven with a rainbow over his head and legs like columns of fire. The natural scene in which the visionary apparition is set evinces a coloration and sophisticated painterly handling that explain Danby's rank as one of the finest British landscapists of the nineteenth century.

It is strange that despite the majesty and potential violence of the scene, which after all represents an omen of the end of the world, it has a quite serene, dreamlike effect. In this, it differs from the more sensationalist depictions of disasters by John Martin whom Danby, influenced at the onset of his career by his friend William Turner, considered his rival at the time this painting was done.

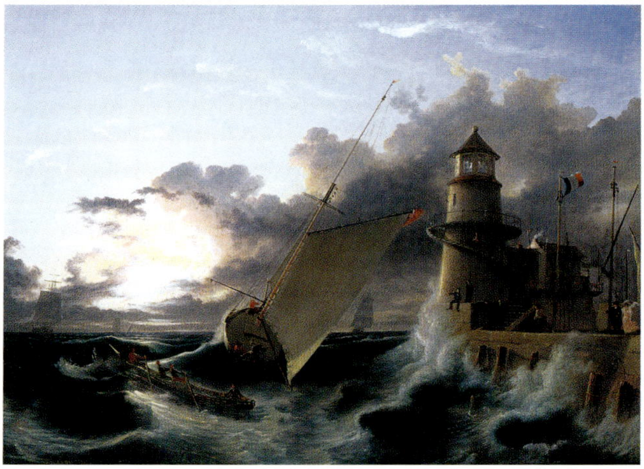

Boat by the Lighthouse, a Squall Going Off, undated

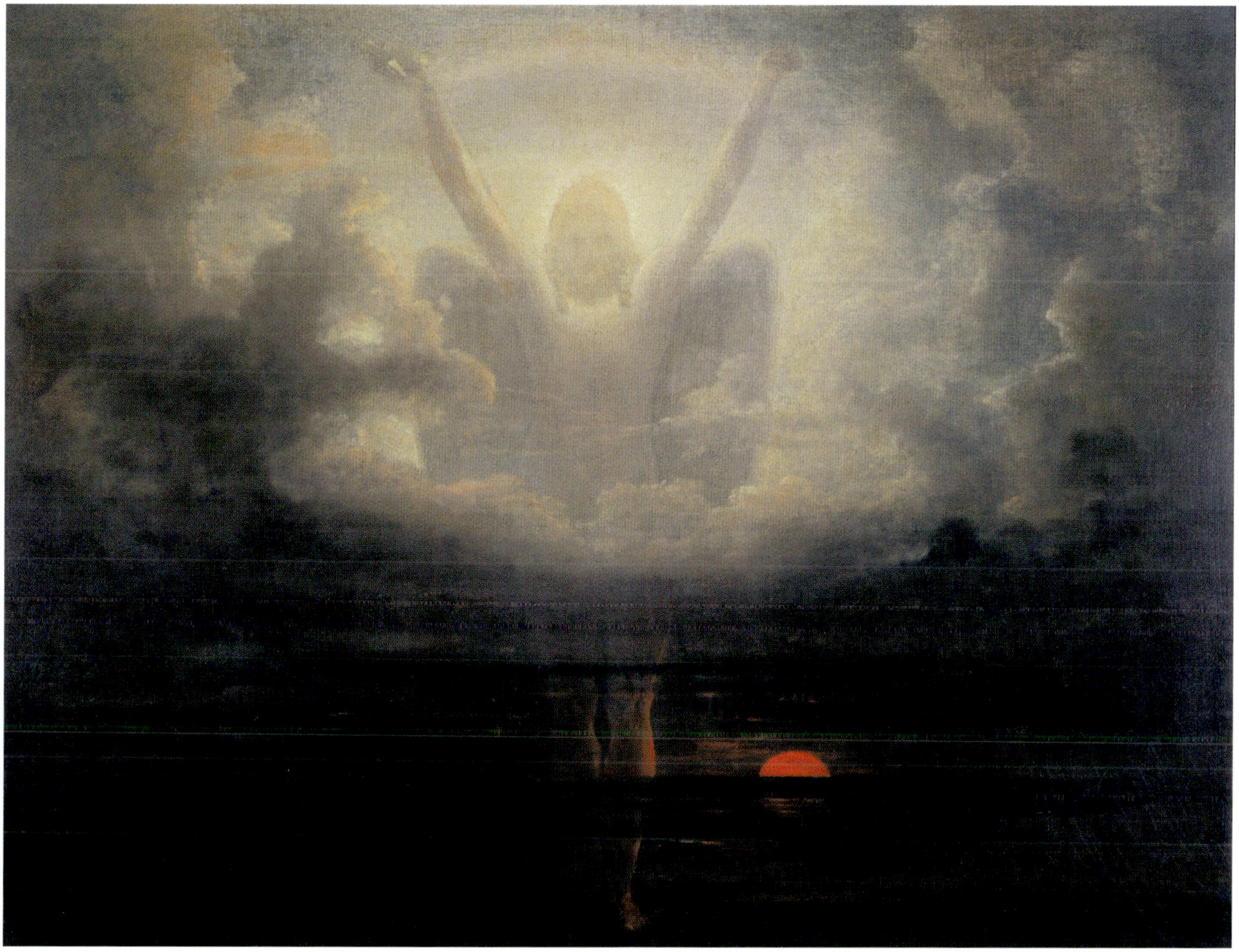

Devil's Bridge

Oil on canvas, 77.6 x 104.5 cm
Munich, Bayerische Staatsgemäldesammlungen, Neue Pinakothek

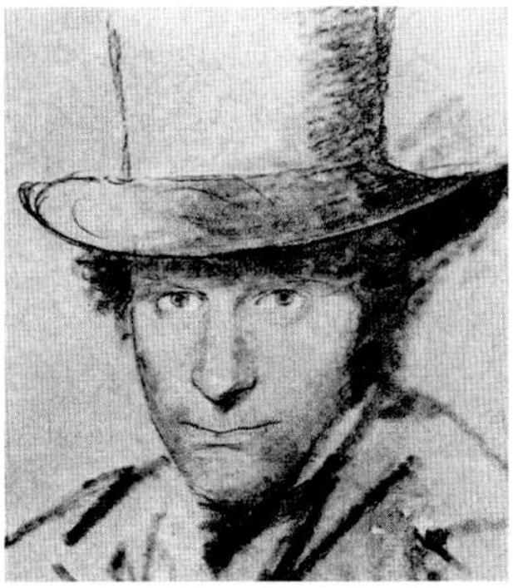

b. 1798 Cottbus
d. 1840 Berlin

Blechen was born in Cottbus as the son of a tax official, and was initially employed in a bank in Berlin. In 1822, he began art studies at the Berlin Academy. An important stimulus came from his acquaintance in Dresden with Caspar David Friedrich and Johan Christian Clausen Dahl, two artists who represented the poles that would characterize Blechen's own œuvre: Romanticism and Realism.

A journey to Italy in 1828–29 proved decisive to his development. The innumerable oil studies done there showed him to be a plein air painter with an affinity with William Turner, who was also active in Italy at the time, as well as with the French painter Jean-Baptiste Camille Corot, who had settled there. These studies made Blechen the major representative of early Realism in Germany.

In subsequent years, his Romantic strain again came to the fore. In pictures of an often somber mood, he depicted humans on the brink of disaster or just overtaken by it. Although he was given a professorship at the Berlin Academy in 1831, the public recognition he so coveted remained meager. The extreme subjectivity of Blechen's work was too much out of tune with contemporary German painting. He became deeply depressive in 1835, and four years later was diagnosed as mentally deranged. Like Carl Rottmann, Blechen was one of the finest colorists in nineteenth-century German painting. During his apprentice years in Dresden, his style was shaped by the work of Johan Christian Clausen Dahl, but above all by that of Caspar David Friedrich. Many paintings of the period have the character of variations on Friedrich, especially in terms of theme. The journey to Italy in the years 1828–1829 brought a decisive change in Blechen's art. His interest began to focus on visual phenomena, on the effects of light and color in landscape, rendered in a way that occasionally even seemed to anticipate Impressionism. Yet this did not preclude Blechen's propensity to place a Romantic emphasis on sentiments and sen-sations.

When Blechen returned from Italy, the *Teufelsbrücke*, or Devil's Bridge, at St. Gotthard Pass was still under construction. Its site in a valley enclosed by soaring mountains, the wild rapids of the Reuss River flowing beneath it, the uncanny lights and shadows in which the changing light of day plunged the scene – all of this conformed perfectly with the Romantic notion of the sublime, of a chilling, thrilling loneliness remote from the crowds and comforts of civilization. Three preparatory sketches were made for the composition. One, quite summarily executed in pencil, only suggests the topographical situation; the other two, in oil, show the final framing of the scene with its awesomely towering rocks and the arch structures of both old and new bridges.

Yet, the laborers resting by the path at the right, the scatter of building materials, the scaffolding and masonry of a new, higher bridge arch, announce that even in this mountain wilderness, technology is on the advance. Yet, is it really an optimistic belief in progress that speaks to us from this image? The bridge would seem too fragile, too exposed, to be able to lastingly defy the awesome forces of nature that reign in this Alpine realm. The new art of engineering is confronted here with the timeless sublimity of nature, as is a painterly emphasis that borders on the autonomy of color with a retention of the Romantic landscape motif as a conveyor of mood.

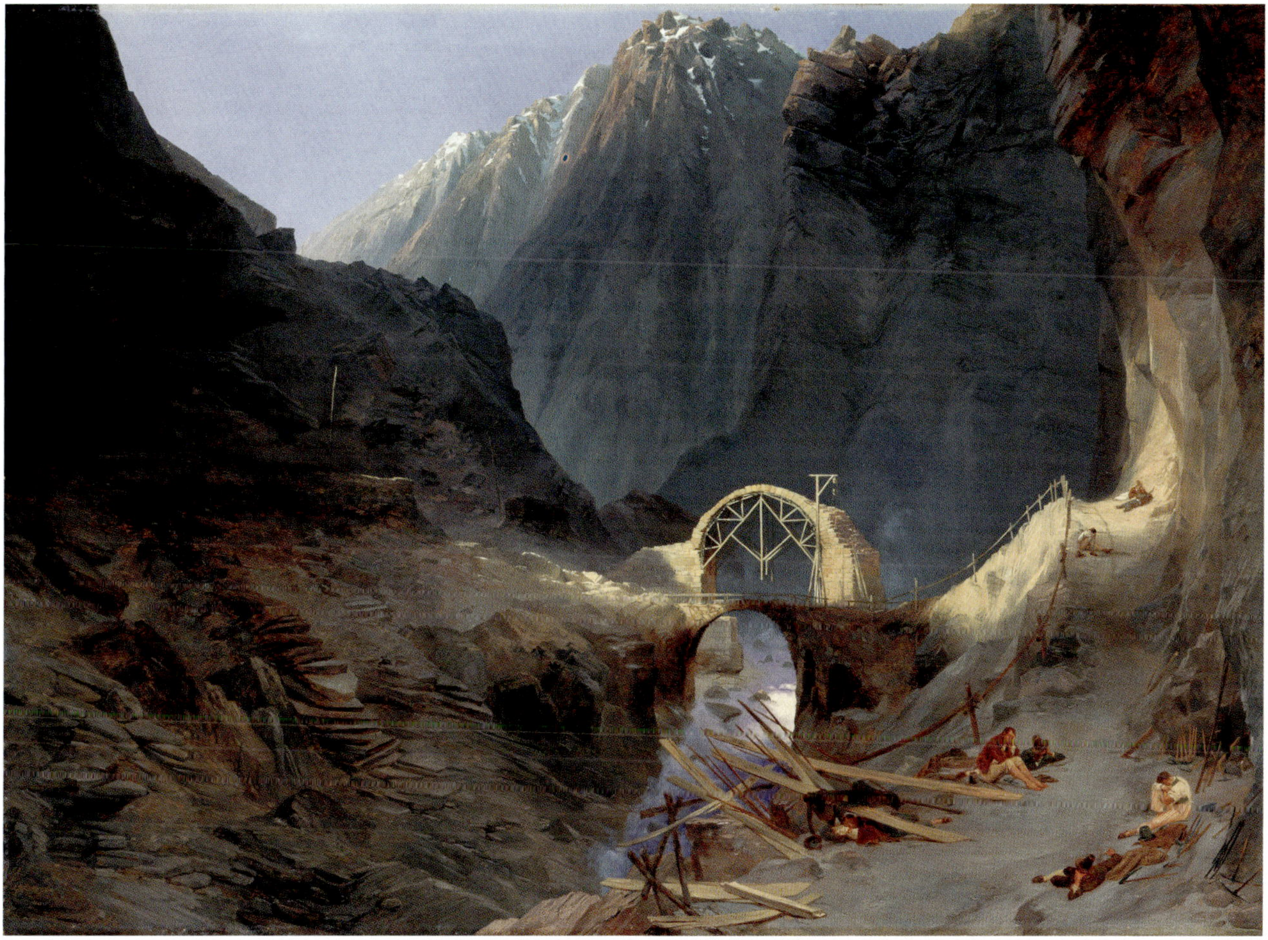

The Goethe Monument

Oil on canvas, 71.5 x 53.5 cm
Hamburg, Hamburger Kunsthalle

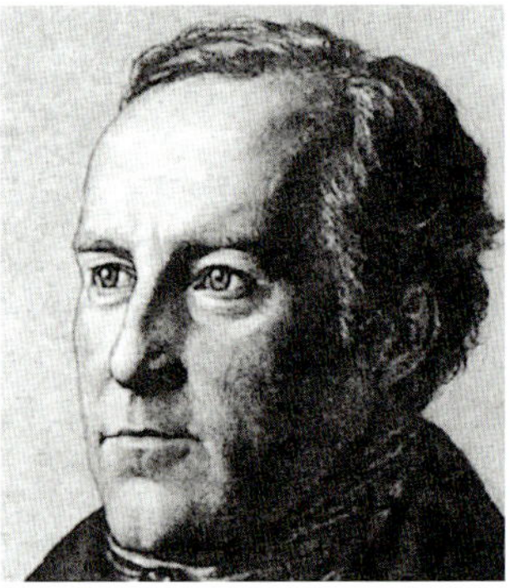

b. 1789 Leipzig
d. 1869 Dresden

After an initial training in drawing, from 1804 to 1810 Carus studied natural sciences, philosophy, and medicine at Leipzig University. Until 1814, he served as assistant doctor at the maternity clinic of the Triersche Stiftung in his home town, then received a professorship in obstetrics in Dresden. There, in 1817, he met Caspar David Friedrich, who would become a lifelong friend and lastingly influence Carus' landscape style.

After wide travels in many countries including Italy and England, from 1815 to 1824 Carus devoted himself to writing his *Neun Briefe über Landschaftsmalerei*, or *Nine Missives on Landscape Painting*, one of the most fundamental theoretical studies in the field of German Romantic art.

Carus was a great admirer of Goethe, who in turn highly appreciated both Carus' theoretical writings and his painting. His picture of 1832 is described thus in *Das Kunstblatt*, no. 18, 1836: "In a lonely rocky area stands Goethe's sarcophagus, and upon it a harp; moonlight falls through its strings, illuminating two angels who kneel reverently before it. Mists swirl around the base of the monument. It would seem that Goethe's manifold and magical contacts with Nature have inspired the ingenious artist to this Ossianic idea."

Goethe, who devoted himself so intensively to questions of the world and humanity, has been recast in Carus' picture into an unworldly and lonely Romantic figure. His imaginary grave evokes Romantic yearning in terms of an actual destination, an envisioned place of pilgrimage, an altar, a holy of holies.

"Just climb to the top of the mountains, look over the long ranks of hills... and what emotion grips you? There is a silent reverence within you, you lose yourself in unbounded spaces, your entire being experiences a silent purification, your ego vanishes, you are nothing, God is all."

Carl Gustav Carus

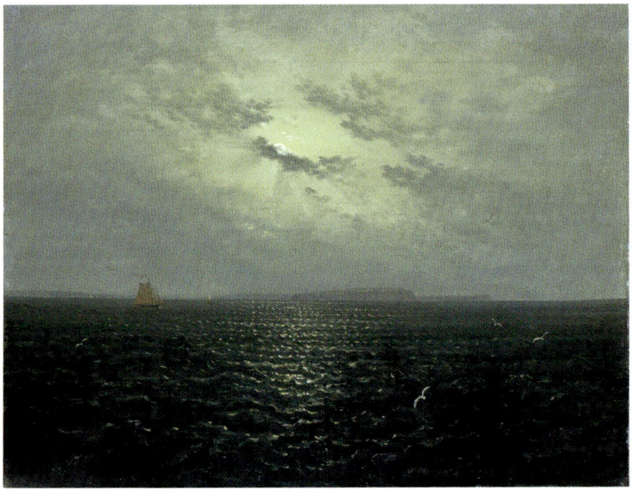

Moonlit Night near Rügen, c. 1819

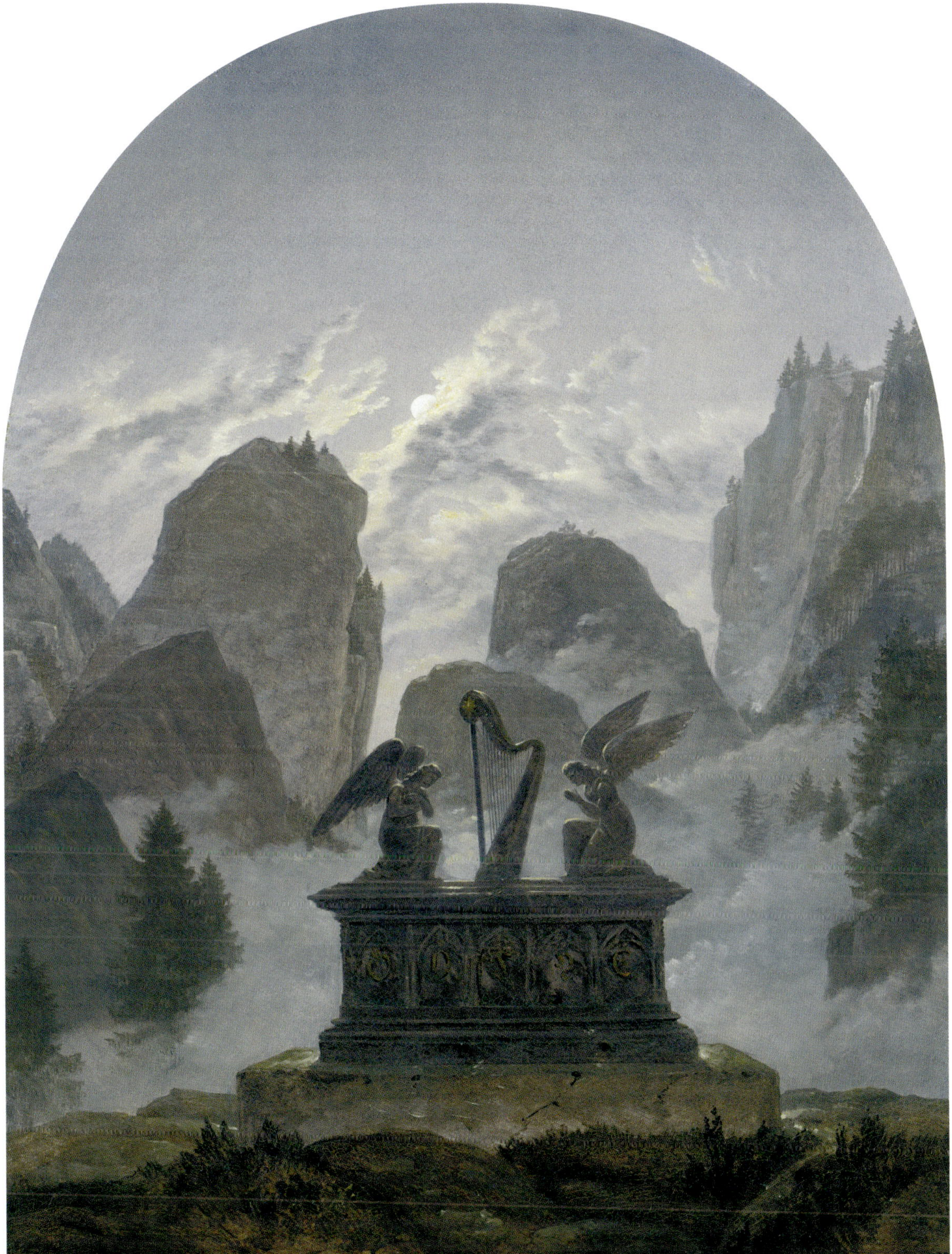

The Titan's Goblet

Oil on canvas, 49.2 x 41 cm
New York, The Metropolitan Museum of Art, Gift of Samuel P. Avery Jr., 1904 (04.29.2)

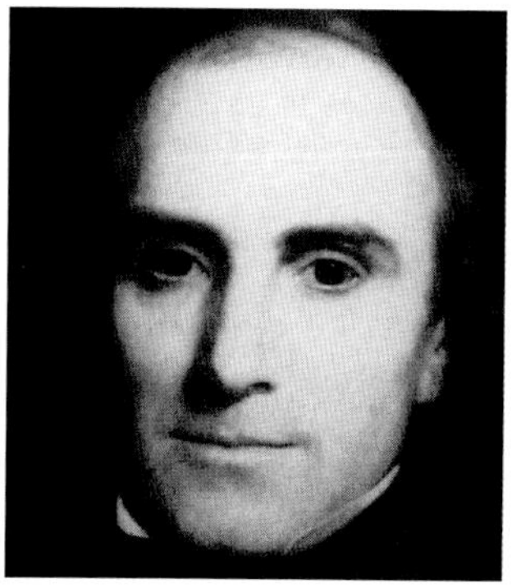

b. 1801 Bolton-le-Moor, Lancashire
d. 1848 Catskill, NY

Cole came from an Anglo-American family who left England in 1818 to return to the United States. With a training in drawing and woodblock engraving in England behind him, he entered the Philadelphia Academy of Art in 1823. Subsequently settling in Catskill on the Hudson, Cole became a co-founder and key representative of the Hudson River School, which established Romantic landscape painting in America. Direct, spontaneous landscapes painted in the wilderness of the Catskill Mountains brought rapid recognition and attracted New York buyers.

In 1829 and 1841–42, Cole went to Europe, traveling through England, Switzerland, and Italy and studying in particular the landscapes of Nicolas Poussin, Claude Lorrain, Salvator Rosa, and Jacob van Ruisdael. On his return, having also absorbed philosophical and literary ideas, Cole introduced a new type of painting to America: the symbolic, moral landscape, as represented by the series on the themes of *The Course of Empire* (1832; New York, Historical Society) and *The Voyage of Life* (1839/40; Utica, Munson William Proctor Institute). These are fantastic, symbolic scenes abounding in allegorical references. Rendered with a somewhat cloying colorfulness accentuated by theatrical lighting, they do not attain the fine quality of Cole's earlier atmospheric landscapes.

Founder of the Hudson River School, Cole in 1836 published an essay in the *American Monthly Magazine* in which he extolled the American wilderness as an expression of Divine Creation. To depict it, he recurred to the idealized composition and illumination of Claude Lorrain's seventeenth-century landscapes. In addition, Cole set great store by the cyclical arrangement of pictures, sequences in which a tragic light is cast on man's role in history.

Prompted by the picture's title, one might well imagine oneself gazing with a giant's eyes over an infinite expanse of mountains, high plateaus, and ocean bays that diminishes into the distance and virtually continues beyond the picture edges, with a seaside town lost, like a tiny anthill, in the grandiose wilderness panorama.

The compositional structure might recall earlier universal landscapes, were it not for a disturbing factor. On a rocky plateau projecting into the picture like a crossbar rises a huge stone goblet whose shaft consists of a gigantic primordial tree and whose base and rim are overgrown with forests interspersed with ancient settlements. The goblet is filled with water that serves tiny sailboats as a landlocked sea. It creates the impression of being a relic of the age of titans, who, according to Greek myth, populated the earth before men and gods.

The trick here is the employment of the Gulliver principle. What appears to tiny humans to be an entire boundless world is to the imaginary giant, the titan, merely an excerpt from it. Instead of Gulliver, one might think of the novella *Micromegas* by Voltaire. Published in 1752, it describes the journey of an inhabitant of Sirius through the universe and his experiencing of himself as alternately enormously huge and infinitesimally small, a total relativizing of dimensions, depending on what star he happens to be visiting. The fantastic quality of Cole's image, its play with levels of reality, would much later be appreciated by the Surrealists.

"None know how often the hand of God is seen in a wilderness but them that rove it for a man's life."

Thomas Cole

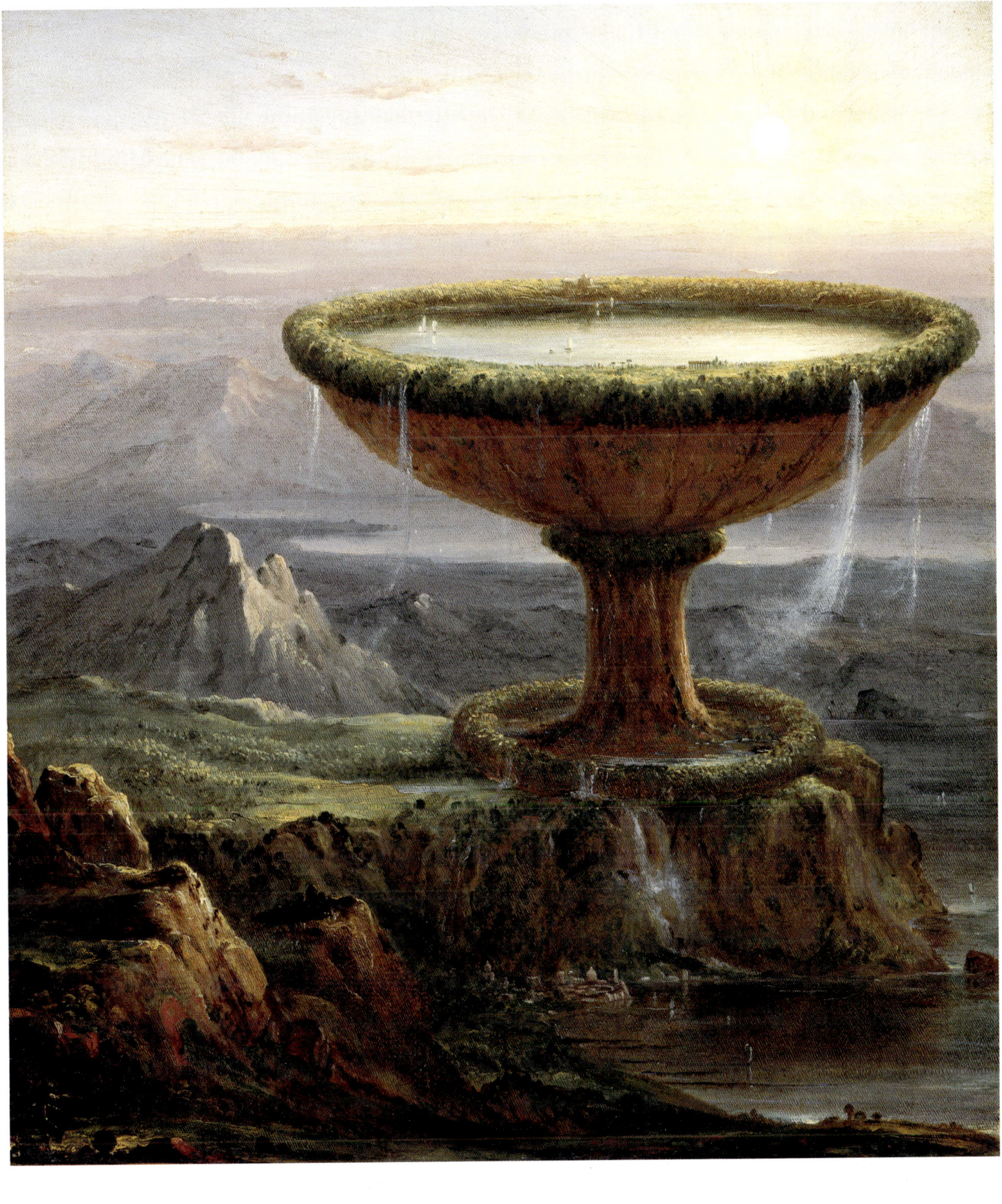

crossing at the schreckenstein

Oil on canvas, 116.5 x 156.5 cm

Dresden, Staatliche Kunstsammlungen Dresden, Gemäldegalerie Neue Meister

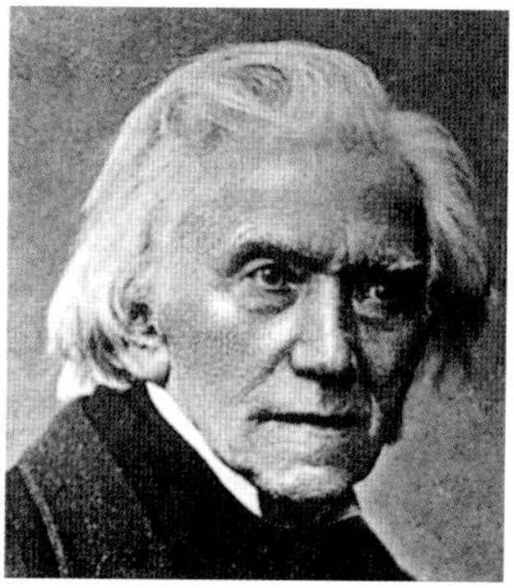

b. 1803 Dresden
d. 1884 Dresden

The son of a copper engraver, Richter made a name for himself with woodcut illustrations for books of fairy-tales, folklore, and traditional songs. He began to work in this field in 1838 and retained an interest in it until the end of his life. Initially wishing to become a landscape painter, he was granted a scholarship to Rome by Herr Arnold, a Dresden book dealer, in 1823. In Rome, he met Joseph Anton Koch and the Nazarene artists, and produced idyllic Italian landscapes. Back in Dresden, Richter was appointed professor of landscape painting at the Academy in 1836. Being unable to obtain funding for a second trip to Italy, however, he began to expand his repertoire of subjects beyond pure landscape. Richter took his students on walking tours through the Elbe Valley and through parts of Bohemia, making studies on which to base finished compositions. Here he evidently found what he had been searching for in his Italian landscapes: harmony between man and nature. Richter's last oil dates from 1847.

As a student at the Dresden Academy, Richter took his point of departure in that version of Romantic painting which had been shaped by Friedrich, Dahl, Oehme and others. During a trip to Rome in 1832–1836, despite close contacts with the Nazarenes, he then launched into idealized landscapes in the manner of Joseph Anton Koch. Yet Richter's attempts lacked the heroic pathos, the classical grandeur, and the inner monumentality that marked Koch's work. Even as his study period in Rome was drawing to a close, Richter was convinced he had to orient his efforts entirely towards the ideal Classical landscape, despite the risk of falling into an anemic mannerism of the kind to which many a Nazarene artist had succumbed. After his return to Germany in 1826, and especially after a hiking trip through the mountains of Bohemia, his intentions and with them his landscape style changed, in the direction of increased topographical accuracy. He also held fast to the notion of explaining the idea and content of a landscape through suitable accessory figures. These factors immediately came into play in a quick succession of depictions of the Schreckenstein in which Richter displays his closest stylistic and thematic affinities with Caspar David Friedrich.

The *Crossing at the Schreckenstein* was enthusastically received by Richter's contemporaries, and is still one of his best-known pictures in Germany today. The idea for it likely occurred to him during the hiking tour mentioned above.

In his memoirs, Richter recalled, "As I remained standing on the bank of the Elbe after sunset, watching the activities of the boatmen, I was particularly struck by an old ferryman who was responsible for the crossing. The boat, loaded with people and animals, cut through the quiet current, in which the evening sky was reflected. So eventually it happened that the ferry came over, filled with a colorful crowd among whom sat an old harpist who, instead of paying the penny for his passage, played a tune on his harp."

In his picture, Richter attempts to catch the simple, moving tone of a folksong, in order to lend resonance to the venerable idea of a "ship of life" in which all ages of man, from infancy to old age, are united. The young vagabond gazing up towards the castle ruins becomes a personification of Romantic yearning – depicted from behind to encourage us as viewers to identify with him – while the old singer invokes bygone times. The boat itself appears much too small to carry the people crowded into it, and seems immobilized in the middle of the river. The arch overspanning the composition is probably intended to give it a solemn, sacramental air.

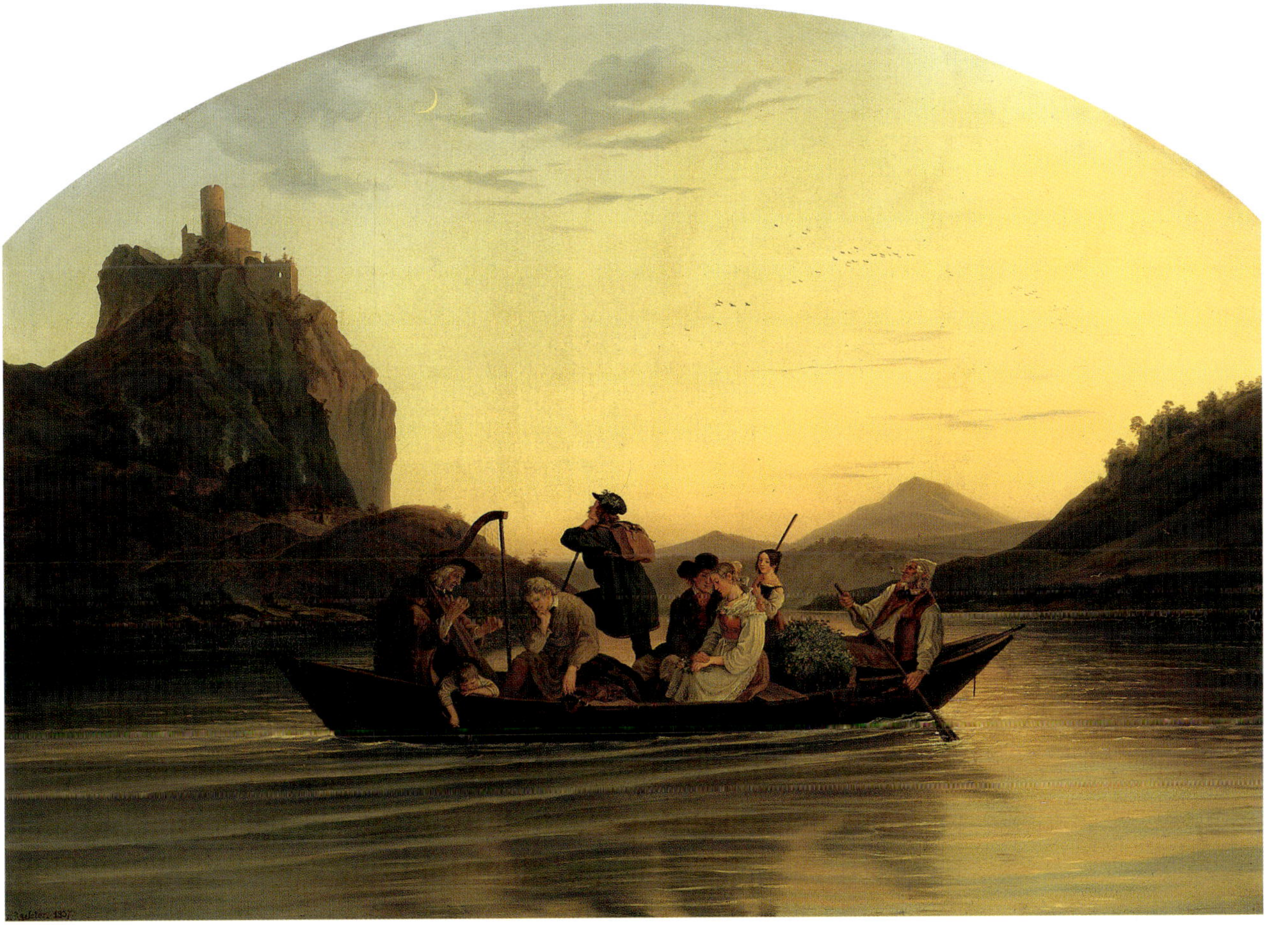

The Poor Poet

Oil on canvas, 36.3 x 44.7 cm

Berlin, Staatliche Museen zu Berlin – Preussischer Kulturbesitz, Nationalgalerie

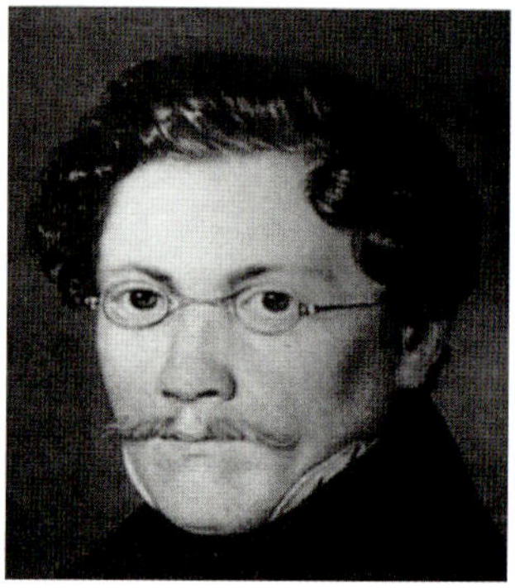

b. 1808 Munich
d. 1885 Munich

Spitzweg was and continues to be one of the most popular German artists of the nineteenth century. An apothecary by profession, he began to teach himself painting in the 1820s. Most of his pictures have a humorous side, evoking the yearnings for higher things of people with rather limited horizons, whether mental or financial. Thus Spitzweg's aspiring poet in his leaky garret, or the portly, elderly widower ogling a passing young girl. In 1851, Spitzweg traveled with his Munich artist friends to Paris and then London, where John Constable and the works of the Barbizon School left a lasting impression on him. He began increasingly to concentrate on landscapes, exploring the open brushwork technique developed in Barbizon. From then on, his figures tended to become incidental, mere witty asides rather than the main focus of the composition.

The Poor Poet of 1839, an early work, is surely the most famous of Spitzweg's, a painter of the Munich Biedermeier. It takes as its subject an eccentric representative of the brotherhood of poets – or perhaps philosophers – in his attic hovel, endeavoring to keep warm by burning his manuscripts in lieu of the firewood he cannot afford. But the stove has gone out, and, clad in nightgown and nightcap, the Biedermeier intellectual lies shivering in bed, an umbrella open above him to fend off the water dripping through the ceiling. Yet, he remains undaunted, his quill clamped between his teeth like a dagger, and he continues to compose, scanning a hexameter whose accents are marked on the wall over the bed.

At that period, the hexameter was the basic building block of epic poetry, considered its highest form. Correspondingly ambitious are the Latin titles of the folios stacked beside the bed, *Gradus ad Parnassum* (The Way to Parnassus). Yet one fears these, too, despite their claim to perpetuity, will soon merely find their way into the stove. Thus a strain of humor, indeed caricature, runs through this depiction of a bohemian life, which, when it was painted, was generally viewed in the Romantic light of the artist as an intrepid outsider.

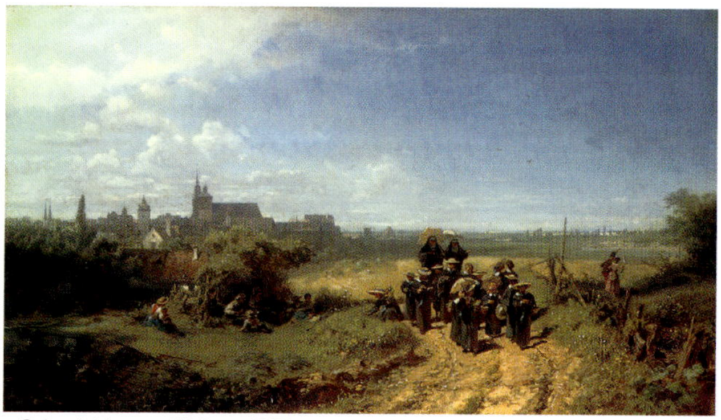

Schoolgirls on a Walk, c. 1860

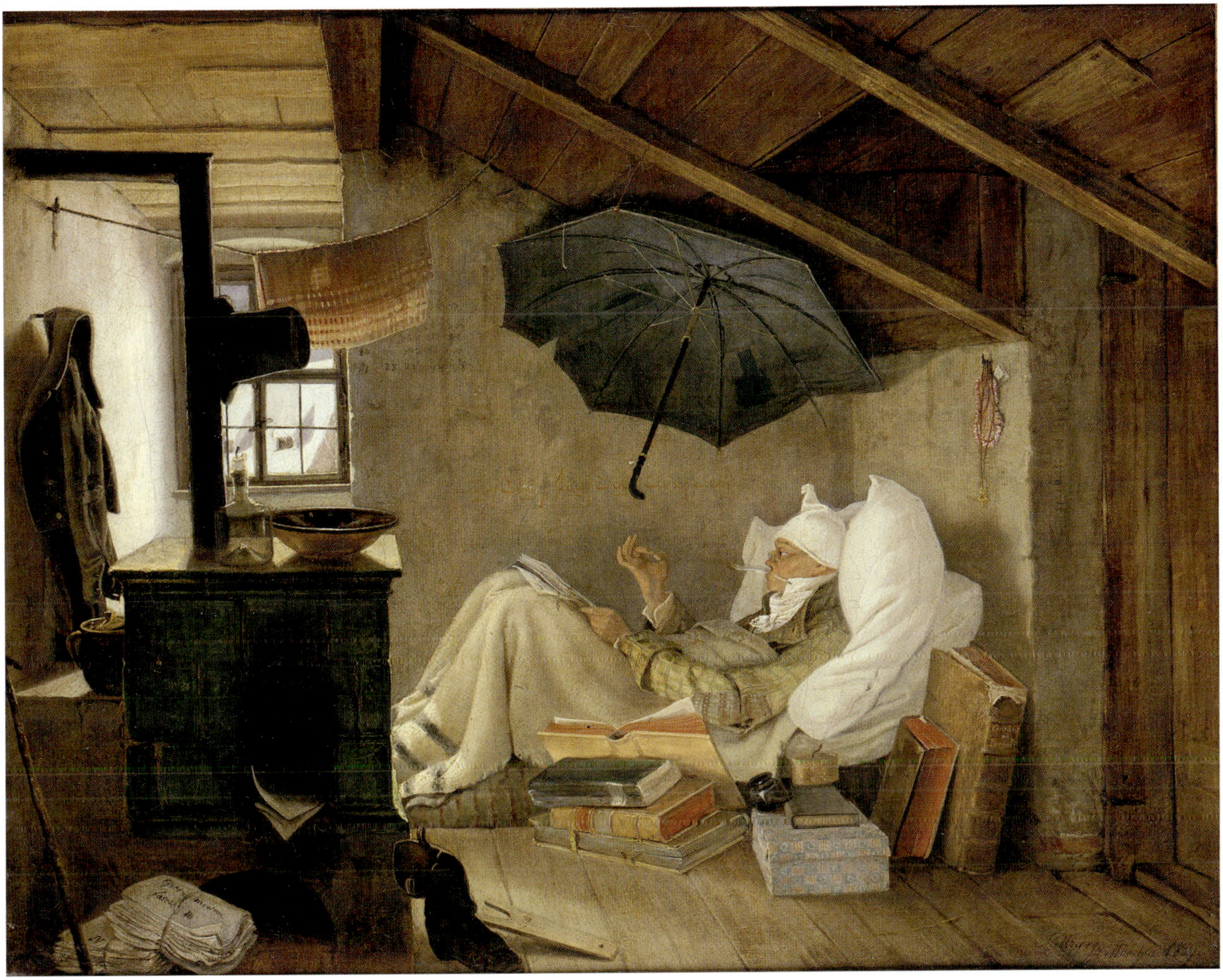

Pandemonium

Oil on canvas, 123.2 x 184.1 cm
New York, FORBES Magazine Collection

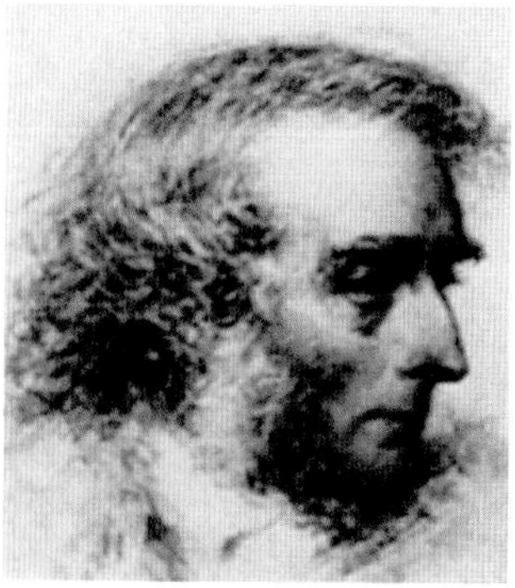

b. 1789 Haydon Bridge, near Newcastle
d. 1854 Isle of Man

Martin received his first artistic training in Newcastle, from the Italian painter Boniface Musso, then moved in 1806 to London, where for six years he earned his living as a glass painter. A confrontation with the works of William Turner proved crucial to his development. He was first represented at a Royal Academy exhibition in 1811. When, in 1814, his painting *Clythie* was ruined when varnish was accidentally spilled on it at the Academy, Martin became a sworn opponent of this institution. Still, he had his first great success there in 1816, with the canvas *Joshua Commands the Sun to Stop*. The 1820s brought forth a series of paintings depicting scenes of disaster, set in infinite, visionary spaces and full of theatrical, nightmarish lighting effects. Their basic mood largely derived from the artist's familiarity with John Milton's epic poem *Paradise Lost* and with the biblical Apocalypse. Despite huge public acclaim, the critics and the artist's colleagues remained unimpressed by these works, finding fault especially with their exaggerated and bombastic palette. Due not least to this criticism, Martin reproduced the paintings in large-format engravings, which found approval even among experts. His trilogy on *The Last Judgment*, for instance, was posthumously engraved (1854) and sent on a touring exhibition through Europe and the United States, which continued into the 1870s.

Pandemonium goes back to a passage in the first book of Milton's *Paradise Lost*, in which "Pandemonium, the palace of Satan, rises suddenly built out of the deep." In a diagonal perspective characteristic of Martin, a gigantic building complex extends along the waterfront. This recalls fantastic reconstructions of cities of antiquity as much as it does Martin's own designs for a walled road along the bank of the Thames in London. At any rate, despite the lightning-scored night sky and the eerie torchlight illumination, the structure makes one think of some hybrid administration building in a totalitarian state. Martin's Satan, whose invocatory figure stands on a rocky outcrop in the right foreground, has the look of an ancient Greek hero. Like Achilles outside Troy, he appears with shield and feathered helmet, but commanding an army not of besiegers but of demons and damned souls in their Cyclopean city.

But it would be wrong to classify Martin as merely a teller of trivial horror stories. Doubtless he loved to depict conflagrations, eruptions, or deluges in lurid illumination, never tired of rendering buildings from past ages that extended to infinity and dwarfed humans to insignificance, devoted himself to the rise and fall of civilizations as parables of inexorable transience. But these panoramas of catastrophe were the result of precise calculation and amazingly diligent historical and scientific investigation. Martin's imagination was fired by the prodigious and portentous, though at times it did not go beyond mere pomp and circumstance. His subject matter stemmed largely from the tradition of "black Romanticism," and he was also inspired by Turner's early depictions of awesome catastrophes. It was no coincidence that Victor Hugo lavishly praised Martin, and Heinrich Heine in 1844 compared him to Hector Berlioz. On the whole, though, his fantasy was admired both in Europe and in America; his palette, however was not. One commentator even said Martin's paintings were palatable only in the form of engraved reproductions.

At first Martin prepared his own mezzotint plates, but soon began to employ various professional engravers. The European market was flooded with prints of all sizes and prices based on Martin's compositions, including bootleg versions and copies. Martin became embroiled in copyright proceedings to an extent matched by no other artist of the period.

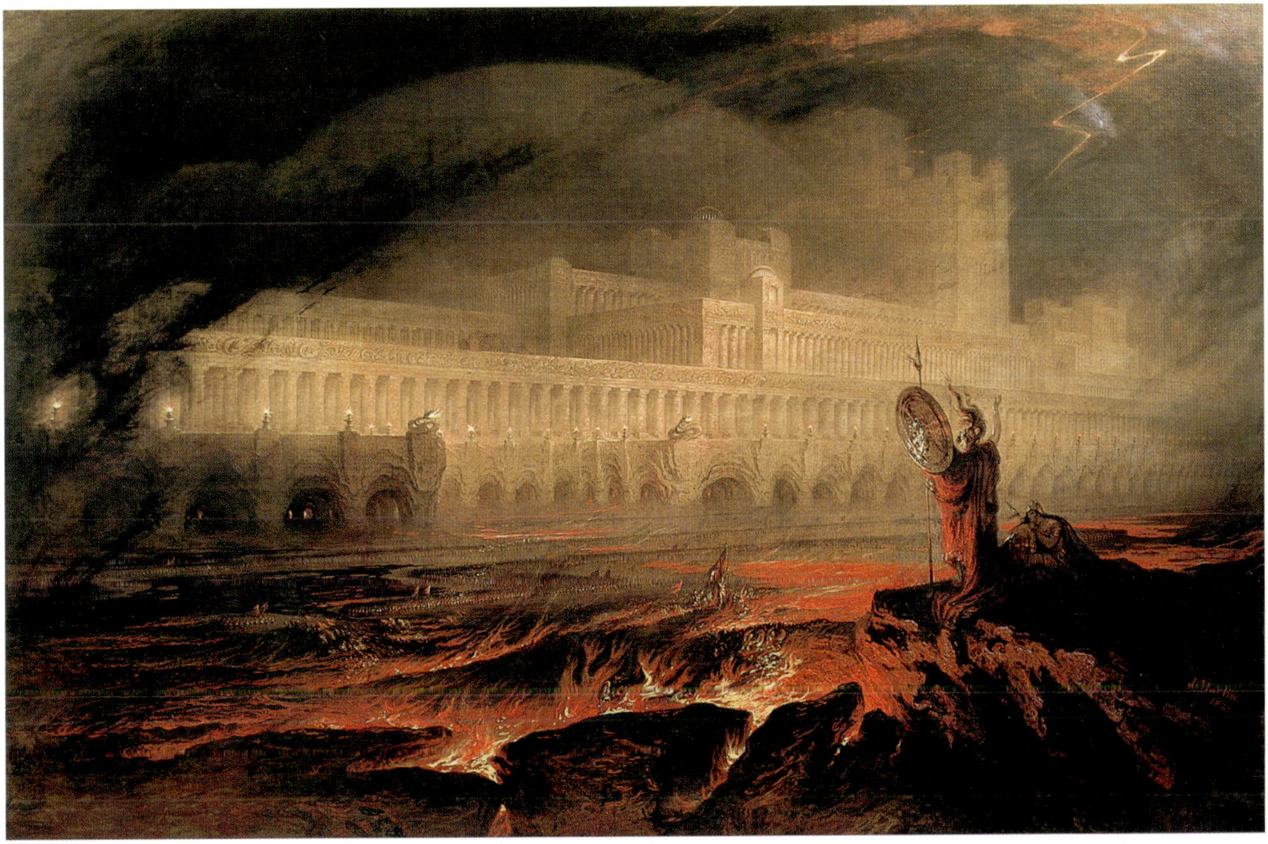

Peace – Burial at Sea

Oil on canvas, 87 x 86.7 cm
London, Tate Gallery

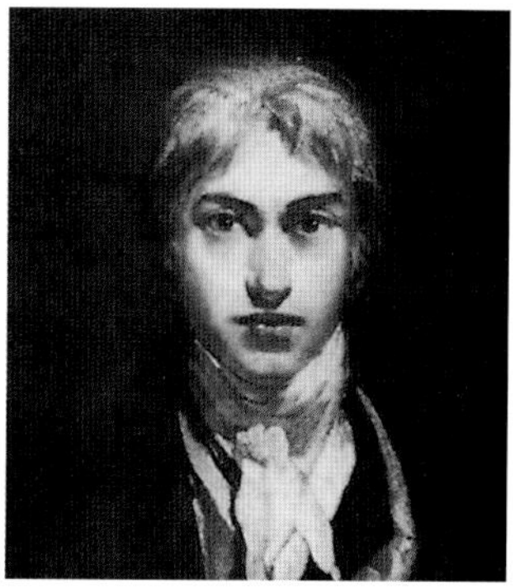

b. 1775 London
d. 1851 London

Turner was only fourteen years old when he was admitted to the Royal Academy Schools. He started his career by painting watercolors and producing mezzotints under the strong influence of John Robert Cozens' work. Then, in 1796, he launched into oil painting, working in the neoclassical manner of Richard Wilson and Nicolas Poussin, with results that found wide acclaim. One of the most prolific painters of his time, Turner traveled extensively in England, Scotland, and Ireland, and also on the Continent (France, Belgium, Holland, Germany, Italy). The year 1802 saw his first visit to Paris, where he studied the Old Masters in the Louvre, above all Dutch seascapes and Claude Lorrain's compositions, which lastingly influenced him. Turner's first private showing, at his own house, followed in 1804. During this period, thanks to an increasing concentration on the atmospheric effects of light, his original style began to evolve, a process that culminated during trips to Italy in 1819 and 1829. Like the works of Constable, Turner's seemingly effortless watercolors and oil sketches were based on impressions of nature, as for example the series of landscapes painted from a boat on the Thames in 1807. But his perception of the world differed vastly from Constable's.

Turner's pictures transcend ordinary appearances, conveying a visionary sense of the forces at work in the universe. In his atmospheric depictions of shipwrecks and natural disasters, perhaps inspired by such works as *The Battle of Trafalgar* by Philippe Jacques de Loutherbourg, who lived in Turner's neighborhood, reality and fantasy merge, and color is used to evoke the power of natural phenomena metaphorically. By abandoning form or merely adumbrating it, Turner lent color autonomy and endowed it with a puissance of its own. This achievement was to prove especially influential on twentieth-century art.

Peace – Burial at Sea was painted in memory of one of Turner's colleagues, the Scottish painter David Wilkie, who died on board a steamer returning from Palestine on 1 June 1841, near Gibraltar. Since the harbor had been closed out of fear of the plague raging in the Near East, Wilkie's body had to be given over to the sea that same night.

Turner translated this sad occasion into one of his most moving and impressive images, by contrasting a visionary rendering of light phenomena in the sky, in the reflections on the water, and on the distant coastline with the gloomy black solidity of the steamer under sail. When the painter Clarkson Stanfield told Turner he thought the sails unnaturally black, Turner is said to have replied that he only wished he had a color with which he could make them even blacker. Like an apocalyptic omen, the dark ship drifts over the water, its solid hull seemingly split in two by the golden glow of torches at the spot where Wilkie's body is being lowered into the sea. This vertical accent of light has the effect of some supernatural, heavenly apparition.

The most sublime cannot exist without mystery, said Ruskin, postulating Turner's compositions with their evocation of the infinite, their negation of objective description, and their ambiguous, "mystifying" themes as the adequate form in which to address the ineffability of this world. Turner exhibited the present canvas in 1842 alongside its companion piece, *War. The Exile and the Rock Limpet* (London, Tate Gallery), an allegory of Napoleon, suggesting that it, too, contained allusions to current political events.

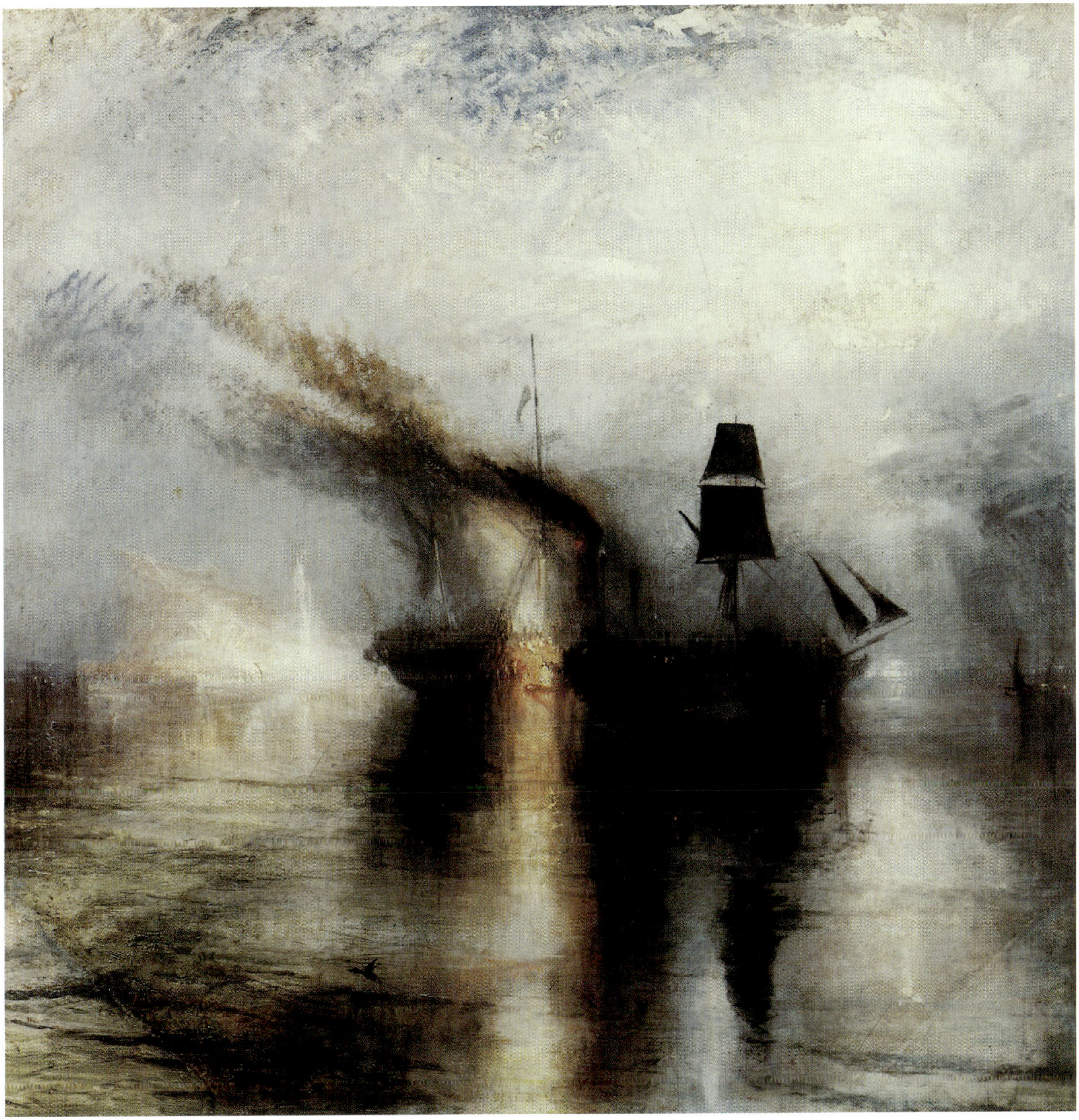

Fur Traders Descending the Missouri

Oil on canvas, 73.7 x 92.7 cm

New York, The Metropolitan Museum of Art, Morris K. Jesup Fund, 1933 (33.61)

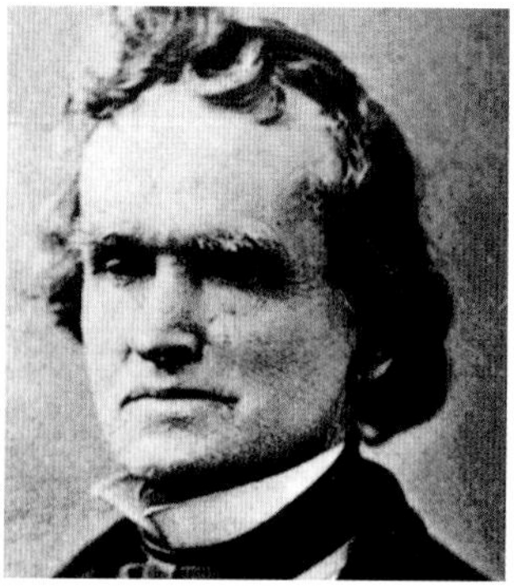

b. 1811 Augusta County, VA
d. 1879 Kansas City, MO

Bingham grew up on a tobacco farm in Franklin, Missouri on the Missouri River. After an apprenticeship as cabinetmaker and a brief study of theology and law, he attended the Philadelphia Academy of Arts in 1837–1838. Returning to Missouri in 1844, he began to paint scenes from the everyday lives of farmers, trappers, traders, and raftsmen, as well as genre pictures. Bingham's fame as a recorder of the domestic customs and traditions of the western states rapidly spread, especially as a result of the wide distribution of copper engravings made from his drawings.

On a visit to Europe from 1856 to 1859, Bingham spent most of his time in Paris and in Düsseldorf, where he had contacts with the German-American painter Emanuel Leutze and the Düsseldorf School. After returning to the United States, he held political posts that considerably restricted his artistic activity.

Bingham once described his aim as the depiction of "social and political characteristics." Yet his lyrical, delicately colored renderings of the Missouri River region seem more reminiscent of the early pioneer days as commemorated by Mark Twain.

At the same time as a number of American painters were exploring the still unspoiled wilderness of the western frontier, another group were devoting themselves to genrelike depictions of everyday life in the new nation's towns and countryside.

In his *Fur Traders Descending the Missouri*, Bingham depicts what was already a nostalgic memory of the world of hunters and trappers, as also described in James Fenimore Cooper's *Leatherstocking* novels from 1823 onwards. By the date of Bingham's painting, the fur trade had long been dominated by large companies that shipped their commodities by steamer and barge. Here, a father and son are still shown bringing pelts from animals they themselves have trapped to the nearest trading post in a primitive dugout canoe.

In a subtly balanced composition and with great sensitivity for atmospheric values, the boat lying in shadow – with a sharply silhouetted cat in the bow providing a marked accent – is set against a misty river landscape and a pastel-hued expanse of sky. The considered distribution of compositional emphases and the profound calm pervading the picture lend it a quality far surpassing conventional genre painting. At the same time, the natural scene is redolent of a melancholy mood that can justifiably be termed Romantic.

"To the beautiful belongs an endless variety. It is seen not only in symmetry and elegance of form, in youth and health, but is often quite as fully apparent in decrepit old age. It is found in the cottage of the peasant as well as the palace of kings."

George Caleb Bingham

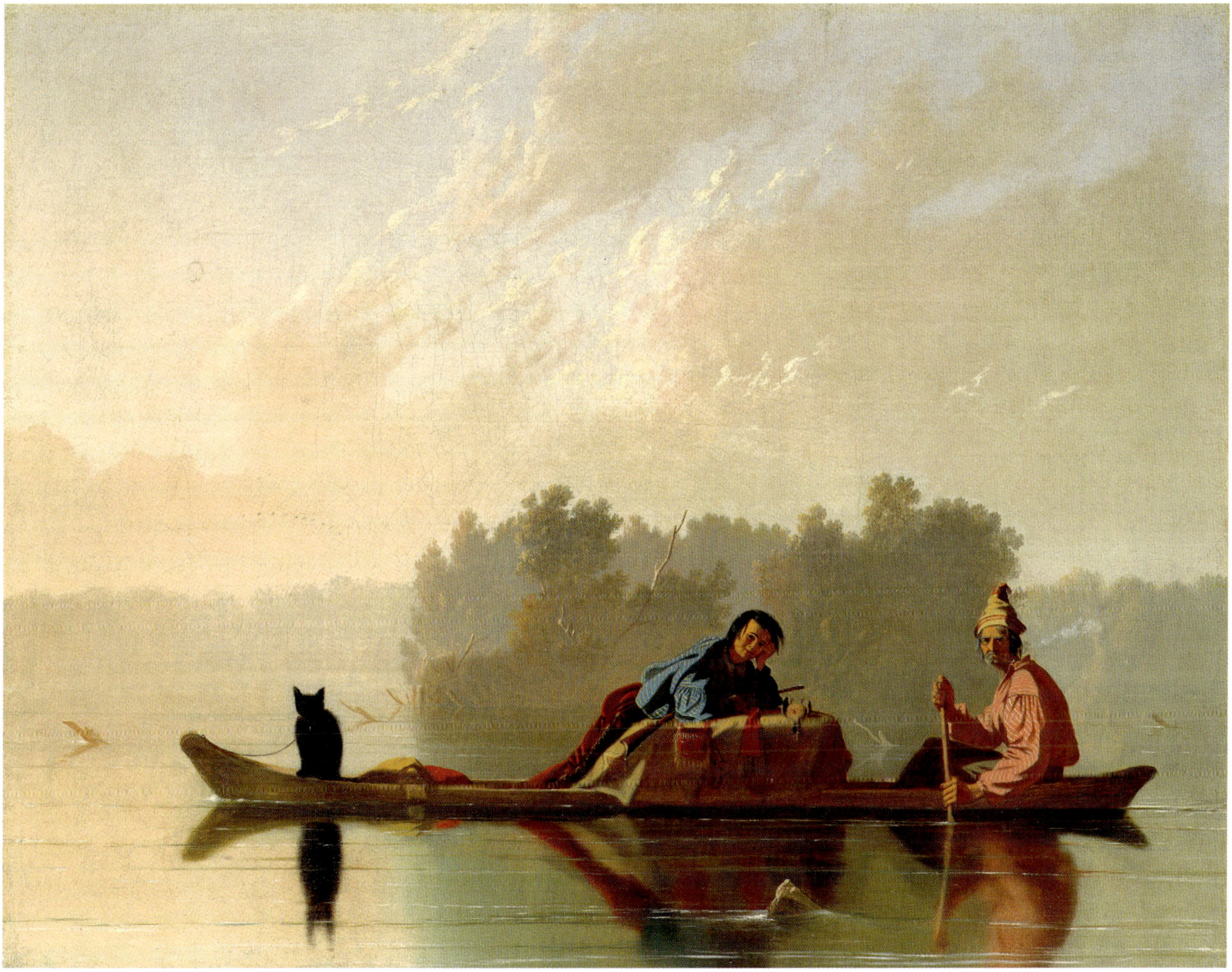

The Defense of Saragossa

Oil on canvas, 73 x 106 cm
Cologne, Wallraf-Richartz-Museum

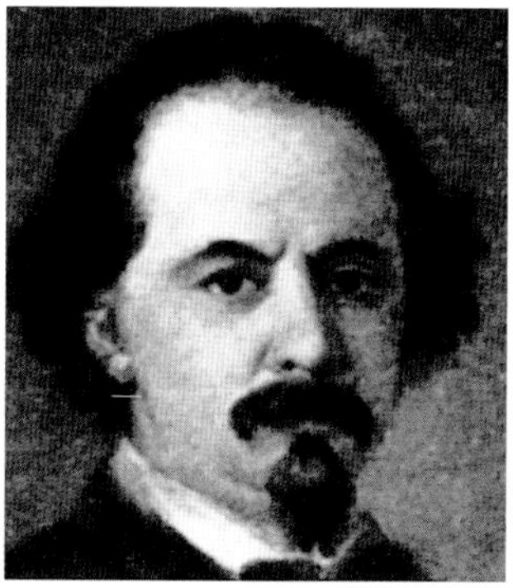

b. 1824 Alcalá de Henares
d. 1870 Madrid

Although he trained at the Madrid Academy with V. Camarón, José Madrazo y Agudo, and R. Tejeo, Lucas y Padilla was more or less self-taught and his work remained totally unacademic. Isolated from the general art scene, he concentrated in his early œuvre on impressions of Spanish life. Padilla attracted public attention with dramatically agitated figure paintings. Largely scenes drawn from the revolution, the Inquisition, and bullfighting, these were in part copies, in part free reinterpretations of works by Goya and Velázquez.

In 1852, he traveled to Paris, where he got to know Édouard Manet. 1856 and 1898 he spent in Italy and studied the work of Giovanni Battista Tiepolo, amog others. The fruits of a trip to North Africa in 1859 are Moroccan motifs reminiscent of Eugène Delacroix. Padilla also painted romantic landscapes and church interiors which betray the influence of his brother-in-law, Jenaro Pérez Villaamil, with whom he often competed in his works.

From June 1808 to 11 February 1809, the Spanish city of Saragossa under General José de Palafox y Melzi mounted heroic resistance to a siege by Napoleon's troops, surrendering only after over half of its inhabitants and defenders had fallen. Scenes from this bloody struggle were depicted in many pictures and leaflets of the day, as well as in countless works later in the nineteenth century.

Padilla shows an event taking place on the bastions in which only civilians, including many women, are involved. Darkly silhouetted in the foreground is a man gripping his rifle and preparing to attack, while a woman, turned away from us, tries desperately to stop him. Behind this pair, the composition culminates in a group of three figures, picked out as if by a harsh spotlight: a boy angrily brandishing his gun and two priests raising their crucifixes into a night sky ominously illuminated by distant conflagrations.

The important part played by women in Padilla's painting may seem surprising, but this circumstance reflects an attitude that was widespread in western and southern Europe around 1800. The terrors of the French Revolution and the Spanish War of Liberation had not only largely expunged the difference between soldiers and civilians, but had leveled that between the sexes as well. Goya in particular addressed this circumstance in many of his graphic works and showed the courage, and the occasional cruelty, of which women were capable in war.

The handling of lighting effects, the painterly treatment of details, and the background figures welded into an anonymous mass, all indicate the overwhelming influence of Goya, which extended to Padilla's entire œuvre. Yet, despite great efforts, Padilla never managed to achieve either Goya's skill or his well-nigh nihilistic transgression of thematic limitations, as seen for instance in *The Execution of the Rebels of 3 May 1808* (ill. p. 45).

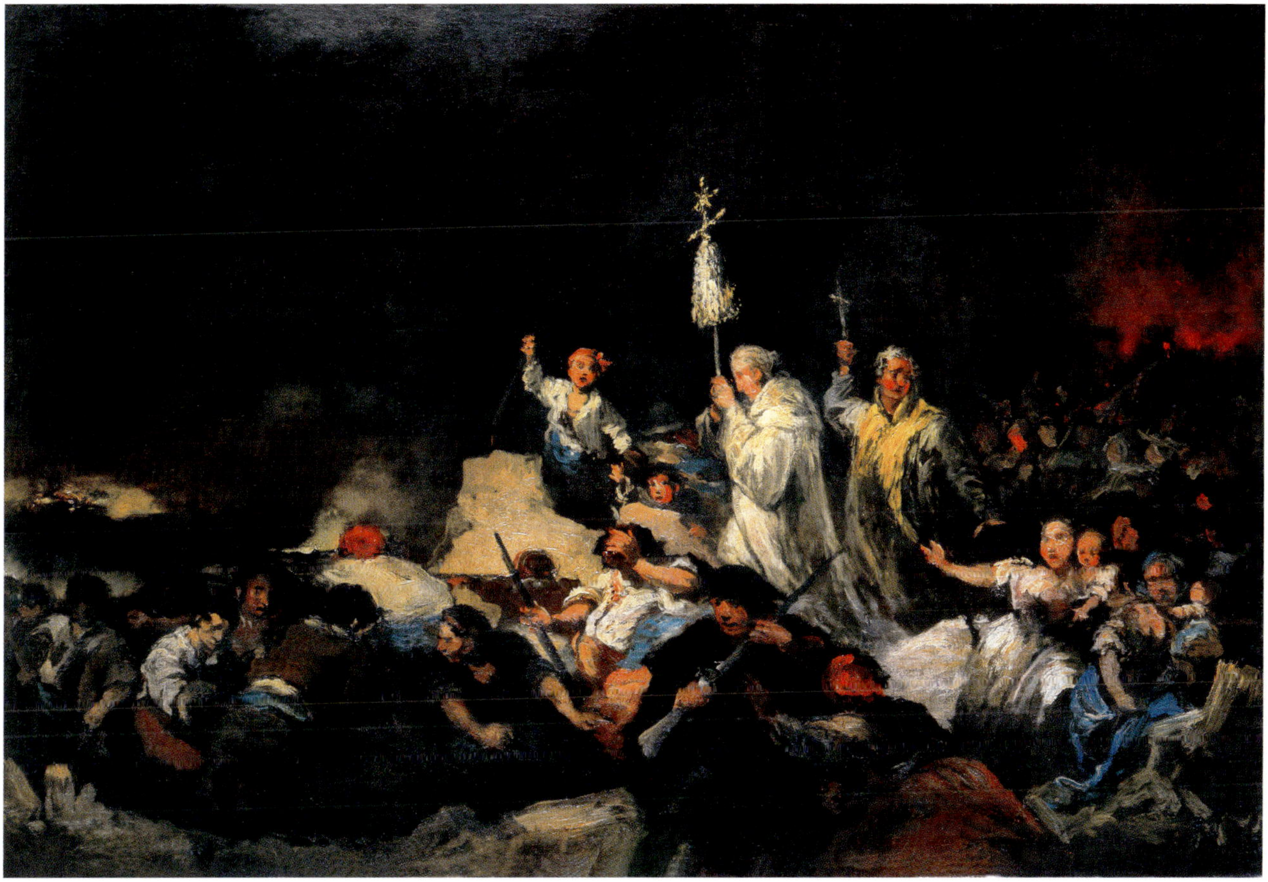

Niagara Falls

Oil on canvas, 108 x 229.9 cm
Washington, DC, The Corcoran Gallery of Art

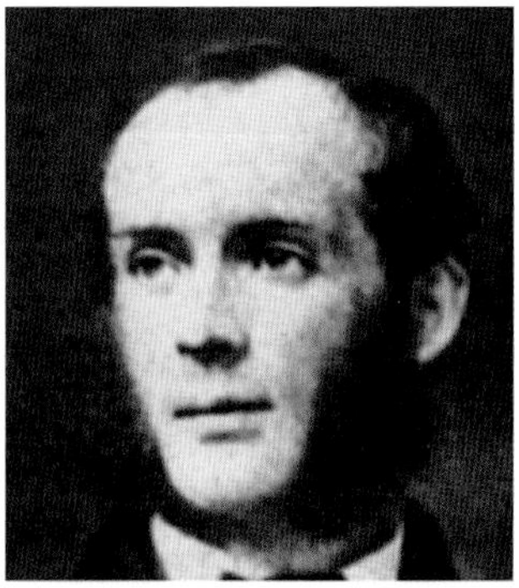

b. 1826 Hartford, CT
d. 1900 New York

After receiving instruction from two local artists at Hartford, Connecticut, Church studied under Thomas Cole at Catskill, New York from 1844 to 1848 and was soon seen as Cole's successor in the American school of landscape painting. His panoramic large-format landscapes differed from Cole's in their more objective and detailed representation of the environment, which reflected the artist's profound knowledge of the natural sciences. In 1853 and 1857, Church traveled through unexplored regions of South America. A European journey in 1868 took him by way of Greece to the Middle East; in 1869 he travelled through Labrador. His depictions of these places all showed a special interest in botany, geology, and meteorological phenomena, but rendered in a poetic, even Romantic manner, in the pale light of dawn or dusk. Like Fitz Hugh Lane, Church belonged to that generation of artists after Cole who did not think it essential to go to Paris or London for inspiration. Their aim was to paint nature in the state in which God created it before He created man. To Church, the "paradise" of America in its "virginal" charm embodied the elemental forces of nature. His evocation of these forces was an expression of his belief in the powers of the New World, in what he called "America's sacred destiny."

In both the painting and the literature of the period, the American landscape was frequently seen as being closer to the origins of Creation and as better embodying the symbolism of divine salvation than that of other countries. In view of the ensuing environmental destruction, compressed into the space of only a few decades, these notions soon had to be revised. Yet, such artists as Church and Albert Bierstadt, in landscape compositions of the 1850s and 1860s, obstinately continued to produce what M. Christadler has termed "heroically symbolic cosmogonies and operas in space." The American landscape was increasingly viewed in a nostalgic light, with a yearning look back to the days of the Pilgrim Fathers and pioneers; or ever more obvious attempts were made to salvage its sacred connotations for American viewers. This is the context in which Church's depiction of Niagara Falls should be seen.

With this painting, Church, a pupil of Thomas Cole, created one of the icons of American art, described by the critics as a symbol of the young nation. The extremely wide horizontal format, the horseshoe-shaped course of the masses of water roaring over the falls and confronting the viewer face on, and the horizontal strip of landscape running across the entire background of the picture, combine to produce the monumental effect of a gigantic panorama.

Remarkable are the delicate and, in many passages, diaphanous plays of color, which contribute to atmospheric transparency and stand in conscious contrast to the massive tectonics of the geological formations and the dynamic force of the element of water. One senses how intensively Church devoted himself to studies from nature and to understanding the laws of optics, an effort that enabled him to treat this daunting subject with such realism and immediacy.

The natural wonder in an unspoiled and awesome landscape, depicted from a high vantage point, takes on the aspect of a secular symbol of the political energy of a country and people who felt themselves called to redeem the world. The rainbow and the violet hue of the sky, shot through with astonishingly delicate gradations, seem to dissolve in the mist rising from the depths. The suggestion of the mysterious this conveys raises the image of nature, this "seat of God," to use the poet Thomas Moore's phrase of 1804, to a transcendent, symbolic level.

When it was exhibited in New York and London in 1857, the painting caused a great sensation and brought European recognition for the young art of the New World. The London Times, for instance, enthusiastically greeted the arrival of a "significant picture by an American landscape painter on an American theme."

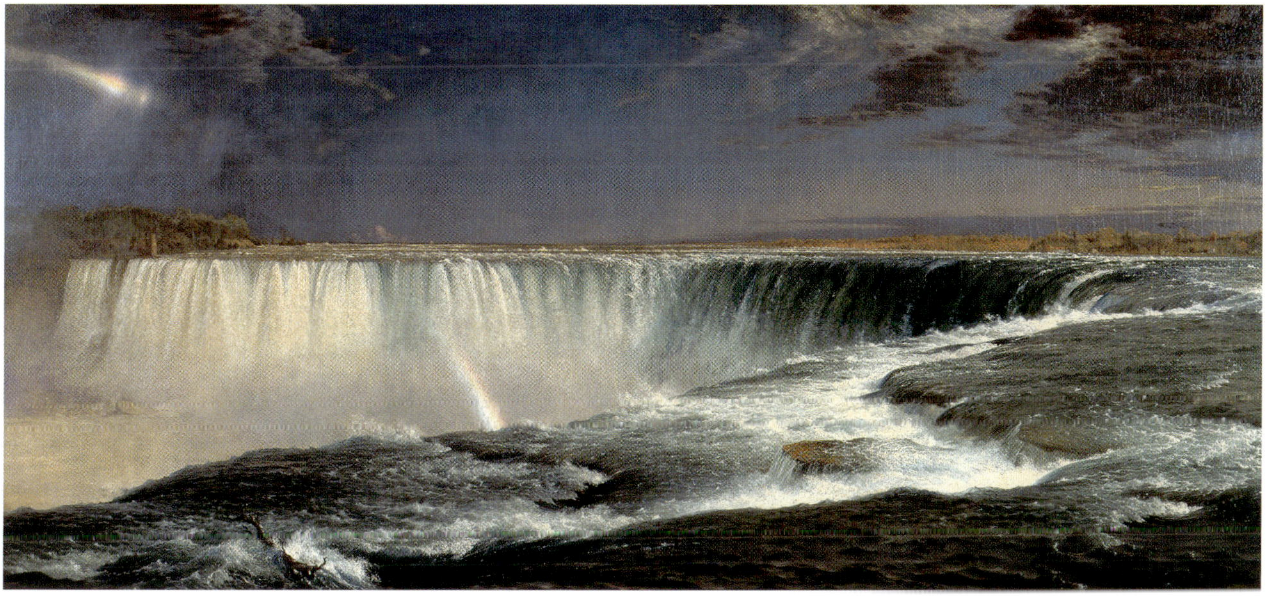

The Turkish Bath

Oil on canvas, diameter 108 cm
Paris, Musée National du Louvre

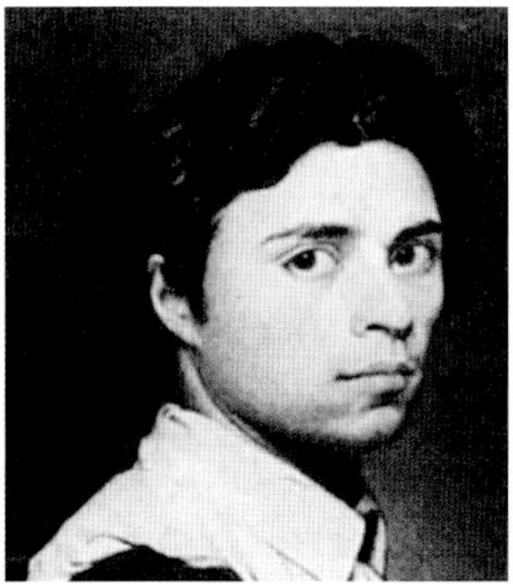

b. 1780 Montauban
d. 1867 Paris

Ingres's father, a sculptor and decorative stucco maker, instructed his son in drawing and sent him to the Toulouse Academy in 1791. In 1797, he became a pupil of David and in 1799 was accepted into the École des Beaux-Arts. In 1801, Ingres won the Grand Prix de Rome with *The Envoys of Agamemnon* (Paris, Musée de l'École Nationale Supérieure des Beaux-Arts). In 1806, he introduced himself as a portraitist at the Salon, but drew negative reviews, even for his great portraits of the Rivière family. That same year, an academy scholarship took him to Rome, where he stayed until 1819, producing much-admired portrait drawings of French society. He also immersed himself in Greco-Roman art and the works of Raphael, Holbein, and Titian, and, while in Florence that same year, was greatly influenced by Masaccio. Ingres's independence from the style of his mentor, David, already became apparent in early works such as the *Bather of Valpinçon* (1808; Paris, Musée du Louvre). He returned to Paris in 1824 and began to teach. In 1825, he was awarded the Order of the Legion of Honor by King Charles X and was elected a member of the Academy. By comparison to his many works in this mode, the precisely drawn and painted portraits were both freer and based more strongly on observation.

Ingres was also a master draftsman, perhaps the most significant of the nineteenth century, and left 4,000 sketches and drawings to his home town of Montauban. The Salon's disapproval of his *Martyrdom of St. Symphorian* (1834; Autun Cathedral) prompted Ingres to accept the directorship of the French Academy in Rome, a post he held from 1835 to 1841. On returning to Paris he finally met with enormous success and was awarded the Order of Merit in 1845. As president of the École des Beaux-Arts (from 1850), Ingres became the leader of the Classical school. At the World Fair of 1855, he was represented by forty-eight works. In opposition to Eugène Delacroix and the Romantics, and to the Realism of Gustave Courbet, Ingres upheld classical idealism, with its clarity of line as opposed to a sensuousness of color, though he also persued a close study of nature.

With this round painting, or tondo, Ingres went back at the age of eighty-two to a theme of his early period, bathers and odalisques. It was his last recurrence to a motif he had treated as early as 1859, in a work that was subsequently lost, of which only a photograph now exists. As regards details, the artist relied closely on travelers' descriptions of the Orient, for instance of the baths in the harem of Mahomet, or Lady Montagu's letters describing the Turkish women's baths. Such sources often mentioned beautiful women with milk-white skin and full, sensual figures. Yet, despite all their erotic magnetism, noted Lady Montagu in surprise, the naked harem women never behaved in a lascivious way, but rather appeared to her to exist in a state of innocent, natural beauty.

In this painting, whose round format was intended to recall ideal compositions of the Renaissance, such as those of Michelangelo or Raphael, Ingres attempts to emphasize this paradisal state through the soft and yet strongly modeled forms of the female nudes. Nevertheless, those in the right foreground in particular seem to exhibit their bodies, and perhaps a hint of lesbian love, in a direct appeal to the viewer's voyeuristic instincts. And the nudes next to them, due to their idealized forms and lack of individual characterization, legitimated by their exotic appearance and redolent of "Romantic charm," inadvertantly call up mental associations with the stylized bordello eroticism and pornographic photography of the period.

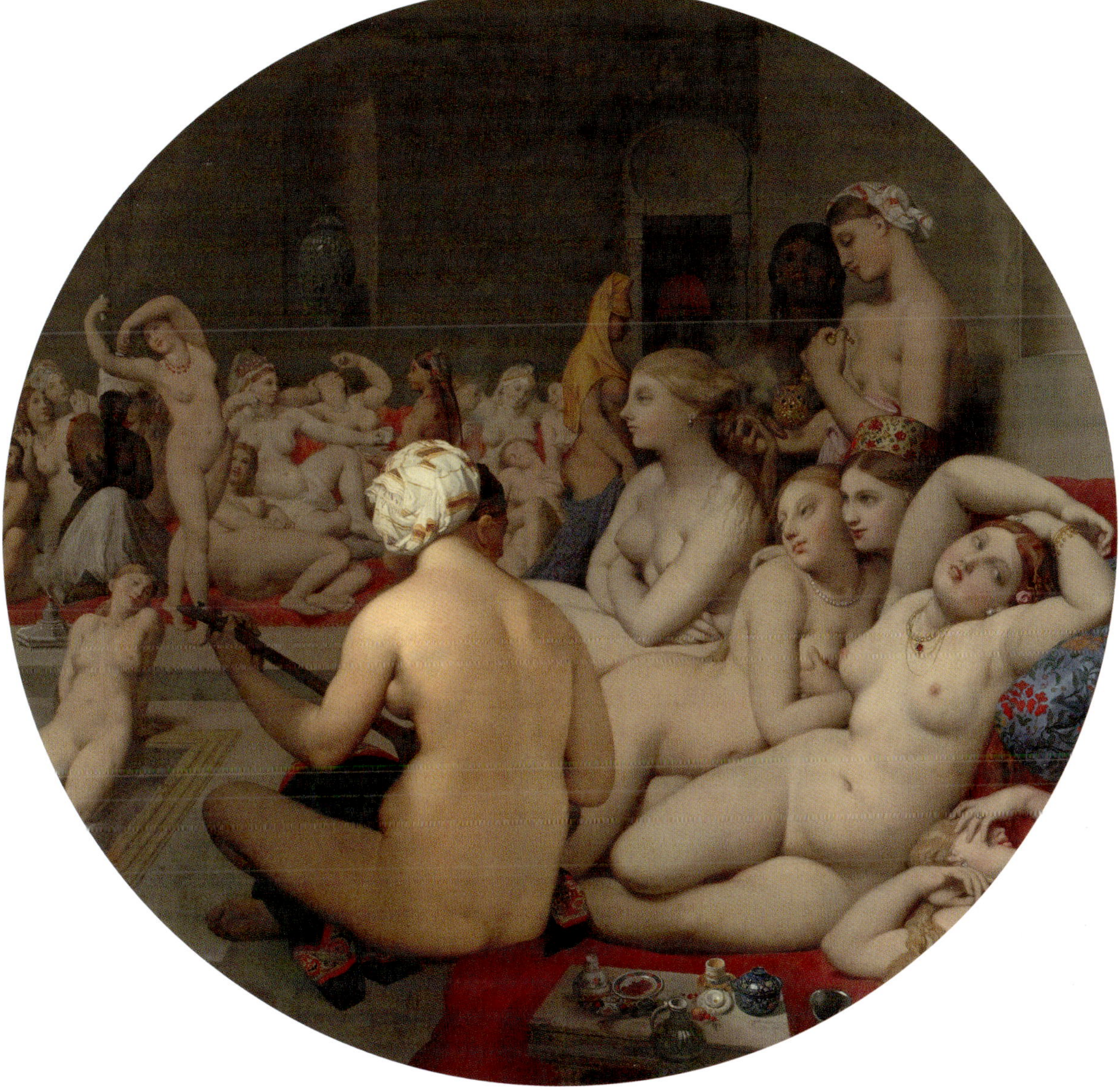

Half Dome, Yosemite

Oil on cardboard, 30 x 49 cm
Private collection

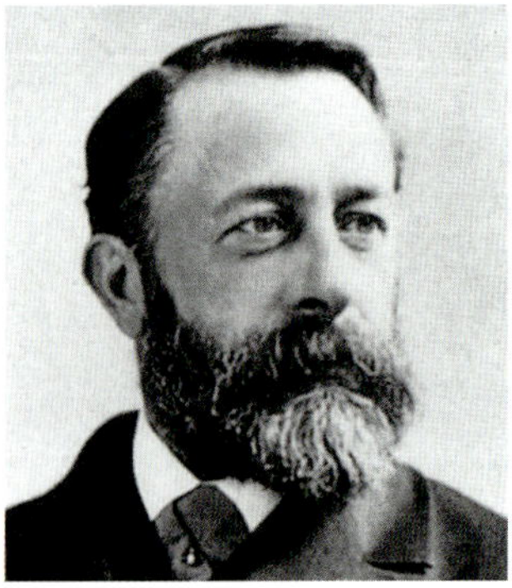

b. 1830 Solingen
d. 1902 New York

A year after Bierstadt's birth, his parents emigrated from Germany to New Bedford, Massachusetts. In 1853, he embarked on three years of study at the Düsseldorf Academy, where, like a number of other young American artists, he was influenced especially by the naturalistic landscapes of Karl Friedrich Lessing, Andreas Achenbach, and Johann Wilhelm Schirmer. After spending a winter in Italy, where he presumably first saw works by Claude Lorrain, Bierstadt returned to New Bedford in 1857. That same year, he joined an expedition to Wyoming und Utah, followed in 1863 by even more extensive travels through the American West. These experiences resulted over the next few years in large-format panorama views of regions previously undiscovered for art. Bierstadt became the founder of the Rocky Mountain School, a branch of American landscape painting that concentrated on romantically dramatized, sublime motifs rendered in heightened colors and striking illumination. After 1870, he lived for an extended period in San Francisco. Further Western travels followed, as well as, from 1867 to 1891, six sojourns in Europe, where Bierstadt devoted himself especially to depictions of Alpine landscapes.

The American painters known as "Luminists," in visions of landscapes transformed by light, aimed above all at suffusing natural scenery with the symbolism of Christian salvation. The mystical effects of light were to serve as a sign of divine transcendence. The expanses of sky over broad horizons in their works were rendered in a range of scorching reds, yellows, and violets of an intensity that, despite Turner, was unknown in European painting. Employing such means, the German-born Albert Bierstadt discovered the American West for art. Yet in spite of the sublime and romantically visionary character his prospects doubtless possess, the idealistic, religious connotations they were intended to convey remain no more than vague.

Half Dome, Yosemite was done as a preliminary study for a large-format work. As impressive as the area is in reality, Bierstadt exalts it to an almost mythical level and suffuses it with a visionary illumination that, admittedly, is not entirely free of a staginess that recalls the later technicolor productions of Hollywood. Still, Bierstadt's views, and the stereoscopic photographs of the Yosemite Mountains made by his two brothers, did contribute to the designation of the region as a national park. Apparently by this date, the only way to salvage the romantically sublime was in a nature preserve.

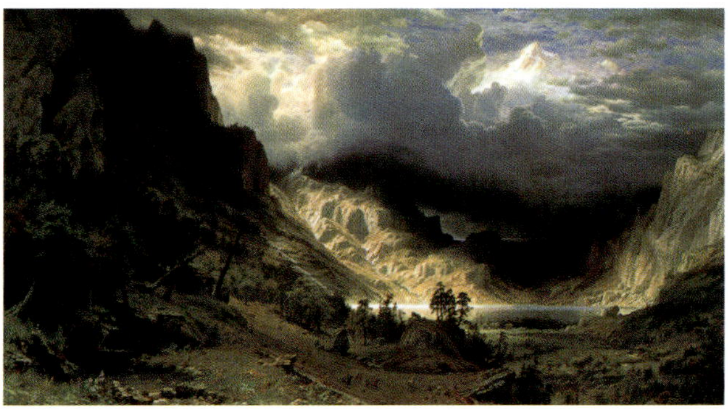

A Storm in the Rocky Mountains: Mount Rosalie, 1866

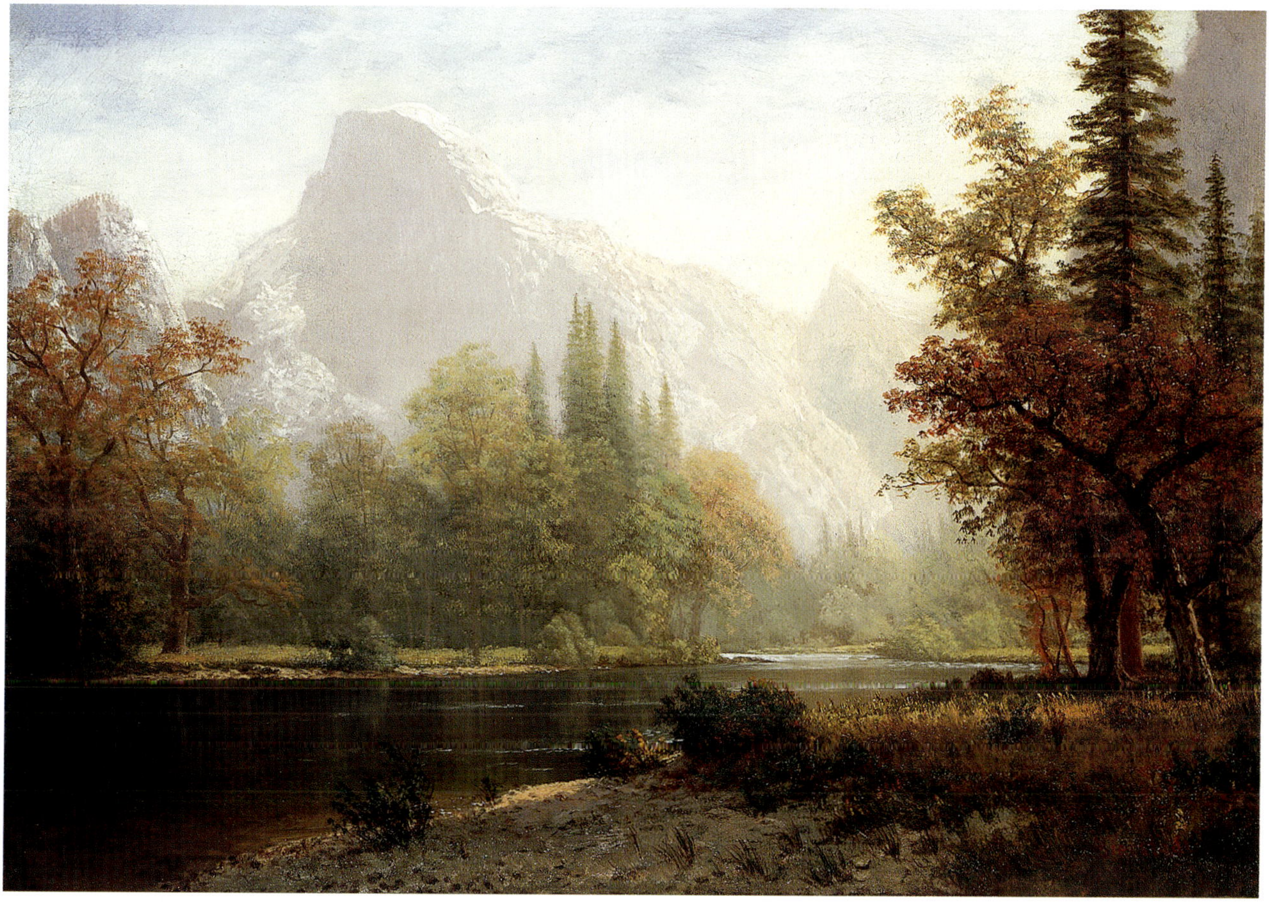

Agostina

Oil on canvas, 132.4 x 97.6 cm
Washington, DC, National Gallery of Art, Chester Dale Collection

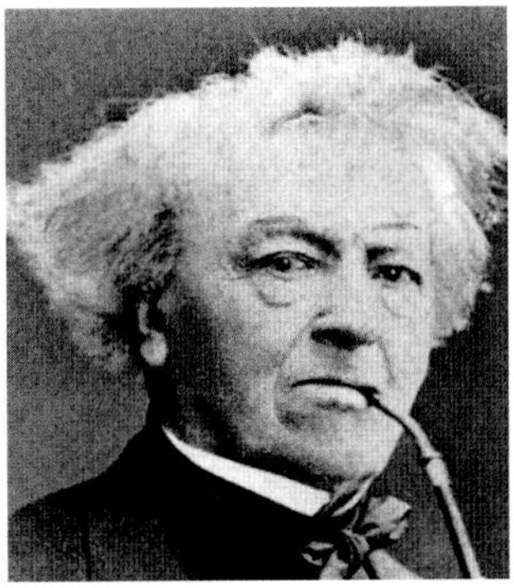

b. 1796 Paris
d. 1875 Paris

After a five-year apprenticeship in a drapery business, Corot studied painting from 1822 to 1825, first with Michallon, then with the neoclassical landscapist Victor Bertin. He also copied works by Claude-Joseph Vernet and others, including the seventeenth-century Dutch masters. Convinced that "a man can only be an artist when he has recognized in himself a strong passion for nature," Corot painted, or mostly sketched, outdoors, working in the forest of Fontainebleau, at Dieppe, Le Havre, Rouen, and Ville d'Avray, where his father owned a house. His first trip to Rome, from 1825 to 1828, would become decisive to Corot's development. He painted numbers of oil studies from nature, views of historical Roman monuments, and the scenery around Rome. These possess an unusual freshness, capturing the light and atmosphere of different times of day with delightfully subtle variations in tonal values. The paintings developed from these studies, such as *View of Nami* (1826; Ottawa, National Gallery of Canada), painted for the 1827 Paris Salon, are by comparison rather formal and neoclassical in manner. On returning from Italy, Corot worked in various parts of France. He made two further trips to Italy (in 1834 and 1843), and went to Holland (1854) and England (1862). His friendship in the late 1840s with the Barbizon artists Théodore Rousseau, Jean-François Millet, Constant Troyon, and Jules Dupré greatly influenced his art. Around this time, Corot's style changed. In romantically lyrical landscapes, or *paysages intimes*, he began to capture the fleeting moods of nature in silvery nuances of supreme delicacy. His landscapes inspired Impressionists, who wished to include him in their first exhibition.

Seen slightly from below as she leans on a stone balustrade, the figure of a young Italian woman rises monumentally and with well-nigh classical statuesqueness against an atmospherically diaphanous background, consisting of a rocky slope with farmhouses, a tree trunk cut off at the right edge of the canvas, and a predominant sky dotted with small, gold-tinged clouds. The dense blue and black hues of the woman's garments set the figure off markedly from the background ambience.

The dignified and serious basic mood of the picture is concentrated above all in the melancholy, shaded eye area of the face. The Italian costume, exquisite pearl necklace, and especially the noble facial features framed by wonderfully arranged black hair, exude a classical dignity, as if some figure of ancient legend had suddenly materialized before our eyes. She embodies the land of longing, Italy, and the charm of that intermingling of classical grandeur and subjective mood which every Romantic current in art again and again sought in the Mediterranean world.

"If painting is foolishness, then one must admit that it is a pleasant foolishness, which should not be shunned but instead sought out by people. One should love art, for it engenders quietude, inner peace and health."

Jean-Baptiste Camille Corot

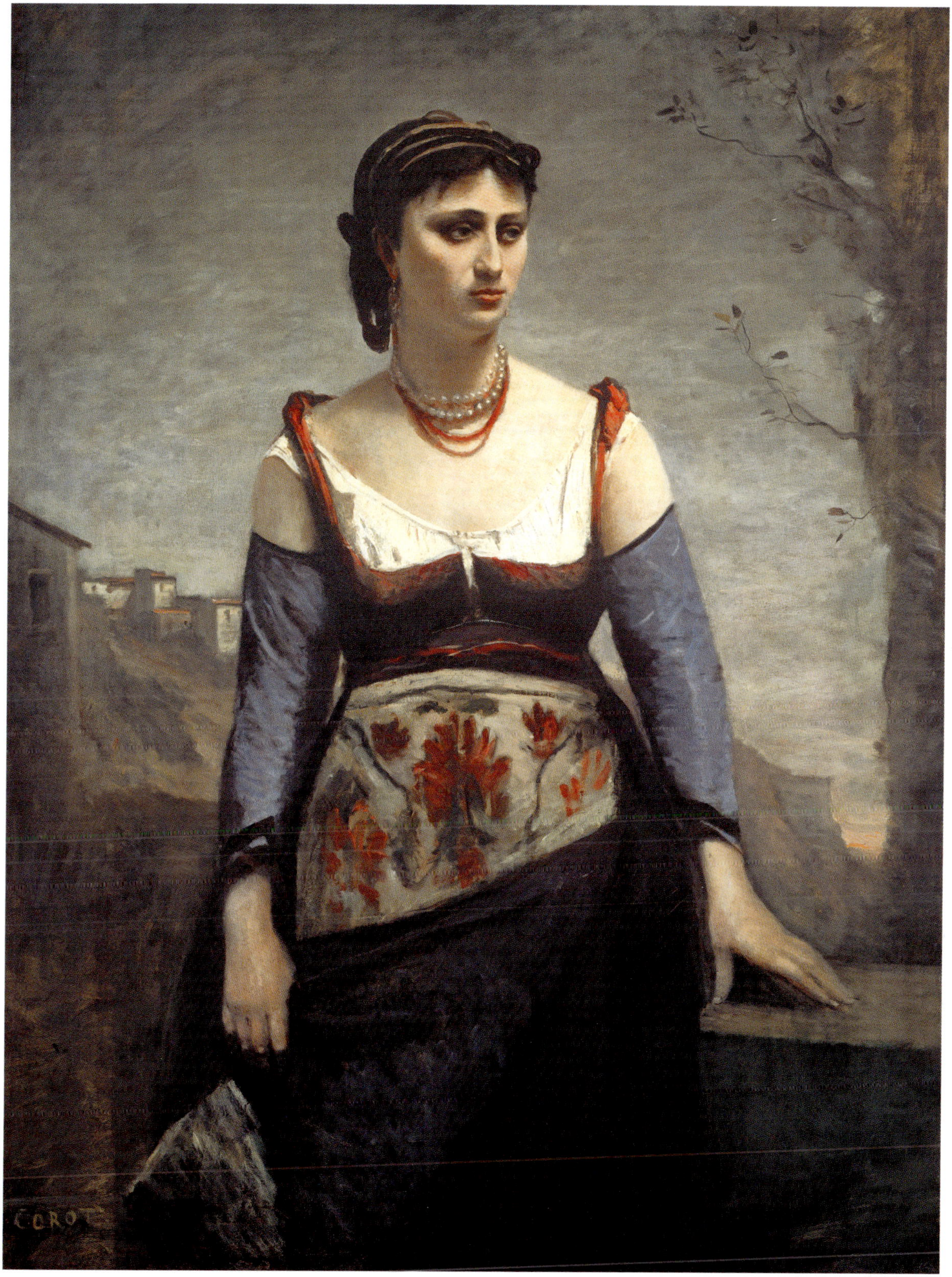
COROT

To stay informed about upcoming TASCHEN titles, please request our magazine at www.taschen.com/magazine or write to TASCHEN America, 6671 Sunset Boulevard, Suite 1508, USA-Los Angeles, CA 90028, contact-us@taschen.com, Fax: +1-323-463.4442. We will be happy to send you a free copy of our magazine which is filled with information about all of our books.

Hohenzollernring 53, D-50672 Köln
www.taschen.com

Project management: Juliane Steinbrecher, Cologne
Translation: John Gabriel, Worpswede
Design: Sense/Net, Andy Disl und Birgit Reber, Cologne
Cover design: Claudia Frey, Cologne
Production: Martina Ciborowius, Cologne

Printed in Germany
ISBN: 978-3-8228-5310-8

Photo credits:
The publisher wish to thank the museums, private collections, archives, galleries and photographers who granted permission to reproduce works and gave support in the making of the book. In addition to the collections and museums named in the picture captions, we wish to credit the following:

© Artothek, Weilheim: pp. 33, 40, 41, 63, 64, 67, 69, 71, 72, 78
© Bildarchiv Preussischer Kulturbesitz, Berlin 2006 – Jörg P. Anders: pp. 37, 49, 66, 73, 79
© Bildarchiv Preußischer Kulturbesitz, Berlin/Hamburger Kunsthalle. Photo: Elke Walford: Cover, p. 51
© Bridgeman Art Library, London: pp. 43, 68
© Museum Purchase, Gallery Fund, acc. no. 76.15, Corcoran Gallery of Art, Washington, DC : p. 89
© Hessische Hausstiftung, Schloss Wolfsgarten: p. 53
© Antonio Idini studio fotografoco, Rome: p. 32
© Kunsthalle Bremen, photo: Lars Lohrisch: p. 65
Photograph © 2006 Museum Associates/LACMA: p. 39
Photograph © 1999 The Metropolitan Museum of Art, New York: pp. 75, 85
© Board of Trustees, National Gallery of Art, Washington, DC: p. 95
© Rheinisches Bildarchiv, Cologne: p. 87
© 2006, Foto Scala, Florence: p. 31
© V&A Images/Victoria and Albert Museum, London: p. 61

Reference illustrations:
p. 30: François Gérard, *Ossian on the Bank of the Lora, Invoking the Gods to the Strains of a Harp,* undated. Oil on canvas, 184.5 x 194.5 cm. Hamburg, Hamburger Kunsthalle
p. 32: Tommaso Minardi, *Madonna of the Rosary*, 1841. Oil on canvas, 108 x 82 cm. Rome, Galleria nazionale d'arte moderna e contemporanea
p. 40: Franz Pforr, *Entry of Emperor Rudolf of Habsburg into Basel in 1273,* 1808–1810. Oil on canvas, 90.5 x 118.9 cm. Frankfurt am Main, Städelsches Kunstinstitut und Städtische Galerie
p. 42: Georg Friedrich Kersting, *Before the Mirror,* 1827. Oil on panel, 46 x 35 cm. Kiel, Kunsthalle zu Kiel
p. 46: Karl Friedrich Schinkel, *Gothic Cathedral by the Waterside,* c. 1813/14 Copy by Wilhelm Ahlborn, 1823. Oil on canvas, 80 x 106.5 cm. Berlin, Nationalgalerie, Staatliche Museen zu Berlin – Preussischer Kulturbesitz
p. 52: Carl Philipp Fohr, *Knights at the Charcoal Burner's Hut,* 1816. Oil on canvas, 54 x 66 cm. Berlin, Nationalgalerie, Staatliche Museen zu Berlin – Preussischer Kulturbesitz
p. 64: Horace Vernet, *The Battle at the Bridge of Arcole*, 1826. Oil on canvas, 194 x 260 cm. Christie's, London
p. 66: Friedrich Overbeck, *Joseph Sells his Brothers*, 1817. Fresco, 243 x 304 cm. Berlin, Nationalgalerie, Staatliche Museen zu Berlin – Preussischer Kulturbesitz
p. 68: Francis Danby, *Boat by the Lighthouse, a Squall Going Off*, undated. Oil on canvas. Private collection
p. 72: Carl Gustav Carus, *Moonlit Night near Rügen,* c. 1819. Oil on canvas, 38 x 47.5 cm. Dresden, Gemäldegalerie Neue Meister, Staatliche Kunstsammlungen Dresden
p. 78: Carl Spitzweg, *Schoolgirls on a Walk*, c. 1860. Oil on canvas, 32.1 x 54.1 cm. Munich, Bayerische Staatsgemäldesammlungen, Neue Pinakothek
p. 92: Albert Bierstadt, *A Storm in the Rocky Mountains: Mount Rosalie,* 1866. Oil on canvas, 210.8 x 361.3 cm. Brooklyn, NY, The Brooklyn Museum of Art

Page 1
JULIUS SCHNORR VON CAROLSFELD

Portrait of Clara Bianca von Quandt
c. 1820, Oil on panel, 37 x 26 cm
Berlin, Nationalgalerie, Staatliche Museen zu Berlin – Preussischer Kulturbesitz

Page 2
CASPAR DAVID FRIEDRICH

Chalk Cliffs on Rügen
1818, Oil on canvas, 90 x 70 cm
Winterthur, Oskar Reinhart Collection

Page 4
EUGÈNE DELACROIX

Orphan Girl at the Cemetery
1824, Oil on canvas, 66 x 54 cm
Paris, Musée du Louvre